Out of the Margins

A major new series from Falmer Press

Gender and Society:
Feminist Perspectives on the Past and Present

Series Editor: June Purvis,
School of Social and Historical Studies,
Portsmouth Polytechnic, Milldam Site,
Portsmouth PO1 3AS, UK

This major new series will consist of scholarly texts written in an accessible style which promote and advance feminist research, thinking and debate. The series will range across disciplines such as sociology, history, social policy and cultural studies. The series editor is interested in hearing from prospective authors. Before submitting proposals, a copy of the guidelines for contributors to *Gender and Society* should be obtained from June Purvis at the address above.

Out of the Margins:
Women's Studies in the Nineties

Edited by

Jane Aaron and Sylvia Walby

The Falmer Press

(A member of the Taylor & Francis Group)
London · New York · Philadelphia

UK   The Falmer Press, 4 John St., London WC1N 2ET
USA   The Falmer Press, Taylor & Francis Inc., 1900 Frost Road, Suite 101, Bristol, PA 19007

© Selection and editorial material copyright Jane Aaron and Sylvia Walby 1991

All rights reserved. No part of this publication may be reproduced, stored in a retrieval system, or transmitted, in any form or by any means, electronic, mechanical, photocopying, recording, or otherwise, without permission in writing from the Publisher.

First published 1991

British Library Cataloguing in Publication Data
Out of the margins: Women's studies in the nineties.
  I. Aaron, Jane   II. Walby, Sylvia
  305.4

  ISBN 1–85000–968–6
  ISBN 1–85000–969–4 pbk

Library of Congress Cataloguing-in-Publication Data are available on request

Typeset in 10/11.5pt Bembo
by Graphicraft Typesetters Ltd., Hong Kong

Printed in Great Britain by Burgess Science Press, Basingstoke on paper which has a specified pH value on final paper manufacture of not less than 7.5 and is therefore 'acid free'.

Contents

Contents

Introduction

Towards a Feminist Intellectual Space

Jane Aaron and Sylvia Walby

Building a world in which women are not subordinated requires the development of a world view in which this is possible. To do this, intellectual space is needed. Ideas are not simply produced from an individual's everyday experience but from discussion with others and the sharing and debating of personal histories, acts which give conceptual form to experience and reveal the personal as the political. And it is not enough, though it is necessary, for us to produce the best ideas, the ones which most accurately represent and interpret the world. To achieve recognition and influence as knowledge, our ideas need to be socially based as well as socially constructed. Unless they are rooted in institutionalized structures of knowledge, they will fade and disappear. We know this happened to the ideas of earlier waves of feminism. Feminists at the turn of the century in Britain and elsewhere produced complex, sophisticated accounts of the world from their own viewpoints (see Spender, 1983). Yet in the 1970s a new wave of feminists felt that they had to start from scratch in building a woman's view of the world (see Freeman, 1979; Morgan, 1970). Other radical traditions — Marxist socialism, for example — have always managed to maintain and build upon the work of their intellectuals: why not ours?

What have we done to build a feminist intellectual space this time? What have we managed to root in a permanent manner? What has worked, and what has gone wrong? During the 1970s and 1980s much feminist energy was devoted to the development of Women's Studies as a major growth area in higher education. Some would say that the attempt to establish within the academy a feminist intellectual space is in itself a problem, that in institutionalizing Women's Studies we are taming feminist knowledge: that it leads to its incorporation within essentially unchanged systems, and thus to our defeat. Although the force of this argument, and its timely warning, must be recognized, the question is — do we have a viable alternative? In a country such as Britain which, at the time of writing, finds it possible to accept a governing Cabinet without a single female member, the likelihood that the feminist movement could independently muster sufficient resources to fund permanent intellectual institutions of its own is remote. Market exigencies mean that the publishing trade, although it has done much to further the dissemination of our ideas in recent years, is dependent, like the media culture generally, on the fluctuating tastes of the consumer. Unless an appetite for feminist knowledge is continually developed in new generations of readers, our books will drop out of print and our journals will fold. Our ideas will be in danger of disappearing once again: the establishment of non-patriarchally biased knowledge will always require the building of an institutional space to let such ideas flower and be tested. At present, then, feminist formations within higher education do offer us a way ahead, although their usefulness will always remain contingent on the degree to which they resist incorporation.

Of course, the establishment and development of feminist research and teaching within our educational institutions has in itself never been, and never will be, an easy option. Other more conventional disciplines will always have more resources to offer their teaching staff and students than will feminism. This is inscribed in the relationship of the feminist enterprise to the patriarchal academy. It will never be otherwise, logically cannot be otherwise, since we are talking of a radical oppositional culture — no matter how much better, more accurate, more 'true' its knowledge — within a mainstream/malestream institution. The degree of our embattlement may change in individual instances, and there may be some exceptions, but the general relationship will not change. Sometimes, the fact that feminist knowledge is closer to empirical observations, more internally consistent in its concepts and theories, than malestream 'beliefs' may lead to 'legitimate' space being granted within the terms of the academy. But in general young, and not-so-young, researchers will always be subject not only to the seductions of the mainstream, with its authoritative stance and resources, but also to the lesser– or non–existence of resources to follow feminist questions. In every field, the academic community is structured as much to resist breakthroughs in knowledge as to further them: how much stronger will its resistance be to points of view and methods of analysis which cut directly across its ideological foundations. The establishment of feminist knowledge based on the notion of 'starting from where you are' — the only basis which (with its roots in the consciousness-raising techniques of 1970s feminism) can hope to resist incorporation — requires strategies of intervention before it can acquire even the tightest of academic breathing spaces.

We have several modes of intervention in academia. Firstly, we can be 'token women' in male schools and departments: here our role is to tell the men that we exist. In this role we can be feted or hated, though feting is more likely to be the lot of those who temper their outspokenness of feminist issues than those who do not. Secondly, we can caucus within the institution at large: feminist scholars typically survive in the academy by building intellectual networks beyond their departments. While men can often rely upon their department for intellectual nurturance, most feminists cannot. Such networking generally produces much-needed psychological solidarity, but whether it leads to more depends upon the degree of its success in evolving a further, third, mode of intervention, in which the informal support group establishes itself as a feminist research and discussion seminar.

Within such interdisciplinary forums, with a shared feminist point of view, our weakness within individual departments has been turned, paradoxically, into a strength, for it has brought about the fruitful development of new methods of feminist analysis drawing upon a number of differing fields of knowledge. It is of no surprise to find Women's Studies taking such an interdisciplinary form, since this is part of the day-to-day intellectual survival of feminist academics.

A fourth interventionist strategy now becomes a feasible possibility, to wit, the development of a Women's Studies teaching programme. It is at this point that the embryonic Women's Studies centre commonly encounters the full weight of institutional opposition. The financial straits which have circumscribed higher education in Britain during the last decade or so provide institutions with a plethora of ready rationalizations for the dismissal of Women's Studies course proposals, sparing them from having to confess to, or perhaps even to recognize, patriarchal bias. Full-time members of staff, they say, cannot be released from teaching obligations in already understaffed departments to teach Women's Studies, and no, part-time staff cannot be hired on an ad hoc basis for that purpose either, however well qualified they may be, for the institution cannot afford the financial risk. Caught in such Catch-22 situations, many academic feminists throughout the 1970s and 1980s put all the spare time, energy and commitment they could muster into the creation of aborted courses for which not one student was ever given the opportunity to enrol. And, given the nonexistence of Women's Studies Departments as such in Britain (unlike the USA), such courses as have managed to battle their way through to existence remain intensely vulnerable. Even if the post of the lone feminist sociologist, who has taken an admittedly rare opportunity to depart elsewhere, is filled, her department may not feel the least obligation to appoint another working in the same field, though the gap she leaves may scupper an MA in Women's Studies.

And yet, against all the odds, Women's Studies has flourished in Britain, through the involvement and commitment feminist ideas generate in teachers and students alike. We can now look back upon nearly two decades of the history of its growth within British educational institutions. In the early 1970s groups of women meeting informally across the country to discuss feminist issues set in train a series of developments which led to the establishment of the first Women's Studies courses in universities and in adult education. Significantly, given present-day fears as to Women's Studies's mooted disassociation from its grass-roots origins, these early formations were not limited to academic women, but were often made up of representatives from the local community at large as well as educational institutions. One of the first feminist university courses was started at Lancaster University in 1973 as a direct result of discussions between feminists at the university and feminist activists in the town. Similar groupings led to the formation of Women's Studies courses in university extra-mural departments and at various local branches of the Workers' Educational Association (WEA) from the early 1970s on. By 1977 the WEA was running such a large number of feminist courses throughout the country that it established a regular Women's Studies

Newsletter to keep its numerous participants in touch. In universities, polytechnics and colleges of higher education the mid-1970s saw the wide-spread setting up of individual Women's Studies courses within mainstream academic departments. This was closely followed by the introduction of taught postgraduate courses at the masters level in several universities and polytechnics in the early 1980s, which led in turn, by the middle years of the decade, to the establishment of a number of Women's Studies research centres within these institutions. Undergraduate degree programmes, typically beginning with first-year, minor, or joint degree programmes, began in the early to mid-1980s, taking off by the end of the decade.

As Women's Studies has developed an increased presence in the academy, its growth has accelerated. The success of the feminist enterprise elsewhere, and its proven capacity to attract students, frequently forms an effective culminating argument for feminists struggling to establish courses in their own, as yet unaffected, institutions. The increasing number of teaching and research bases have been matched by the growth of Women's Studies publishing, with the development of special journals and book series. Today in Britain Women's Studies exists at a majority of higher educational institutions, and at all educational and research levels. There are occasional backwaters, but these are — backwaters.

Beyond the perimeters of individual institutions, further levels of feminist intervention have been established in the form of national feminist networks within single disciplines, such as exist for almost all of the social sciences and humanities in Britain today. At an interdisciplinary level also, national, European, and international networks of Women's Studies have been set up. On a national level, the Women's Studies Research and Resources Centre, founded in the late 1970s, held listings of feminist research in progress, ran seminars and conferences on feminist theory and research and published papers in these areas. But in recent years the focus of this group has shifted away from academic research, and funding problems have led to a London rather than a national focus and to the end of its initial programme. During the second half of the 1980s the felt need for a new national association of Women's Studies in Britain led to the formal establishment of the Women's Studies Network (UK). Its aim is to assist in the further development of Women's Studies by acting, on the one hand, as a channel of communication and the facilitator of exchanges, and on the other, as a collective voice to ensure that institutional national resources are made available to enable the work to continue. That is, it aims to promote the development of both feminist intellectual ideas and the institutional framework necessary for them to survive and take root.

One way in which the Network seeks to further these aims is through the establishment of annual national and interdisciplinary Women's Studies conferences. This present volume consists of a selection of edited papers from two such conferences, held at Coventry Polytechnic in 1989 and 1990 respectively. The tone of both these conferences was largely positive: indeed, that Women's Studies has succeeded in becoming a major growth area in higher education in Thatcher's Britain, during years of unprecedentedly severe cutbacks in the funding of educational institutions, cannot but give us some cause for satisfaction. Nevertheless, any self-congratulatory tendencies were offset in both conferences by widespread concern about where the development of Women's Studies out of the margins of academic life might be taking us. In plenaries and workshops alike, speakers and participants discussed whether growth meant increased strength from new resources or a diluting of feminist ideas through integration and co-option. Questions were raised, for example, as to how far theoretical paradigms established outside the field of Women's Studies can aid in the development of feminist theory, and there was a call for the rematerialization of Women's Studies in women's experience. In particular, anxieties were expressed about the growing tendency to use the title 'Gender Studies' instead of 'Women's Studies' for purportedly feminist teaching programmes, and all that may imply in terms of a shift of attention away from the basic issue of women's subordination, as if we were in danger ourselves of succumbing to the self-betraying myth of 'postfeminism'. In the following pages of this book, papers such as Mary Evans's and Renate Klein's, Maggie Humm's, Jalna Hanmer's, Paulina Palmer's and Liz Stanley's, debate these problems.

The difficulty Women's Studies is seen as experiencing in maintaining an unequivocally feminist stance is not, of course, unrelated to the fragmentation which beset the Women's Movement itself during the 1980s. Faced with a proliferation of feminisms — radical, Black, lesbian, socialist, humanist — Women's Studies has been criticized for failing sufficiently to represent the cutting edge of radical feminism, and for marginalizing Black and lesbian issues within its own brand of anodyne 'academic feminism' (see, for example, Palmer, 1989, pp. 1 and 4; and Watt and Cook in this volume). The 1990 Network conference addressed this topic as a major concern within its 'out of the margins' theme: the development of Women's Studies out of a marginal position in the academy needs to go hand in hand with the parallel movement of previously marginal concerns within Women's Studies itself into central debates — 'needs to' because Women's Studies's validity as a discipline arising out of the politics of everyday female experience depends upon it. It cannot suffer any dominant discourse, particularly not one of its own making, to marginalize the reality of any lived experience.

Questions of difference within feminism feature as a pressing concern in the majority of the papers collected here, and a central section of the volume is devoted to the discussion of lesbian and Black women's experience, and their place — or displacement — within Women's Studies. Of the other three sections of the book, the first provides full accounts, much more detailed than the brief sketch outlined above, of the development of Women's Studies in Britain within all branches of further and higher education, including adult education and Access as well as degree courses, and compares the situation in Britain with that in Europe. Further chapters in this section discuss appropriate teaching methodologies and assessment procedures for Women's Studies courses, and outline its challenge to the institutional structures of education.

Jane Aaron and Sylvia Walby

The second section includes papers addressing the question of Women's Studies's relation to the feminist movement. A fourth, final section investigates the impact of Women's Studies upon mainstream disciplines, and demonstrates how the interdisciplinary nature of Women's Studies breaks down traditional subject barriers. Brief editorial commentaries introduce each separate section.

References

FREEMAN, JO (1979) *The Politics of Women's Liberation*, New York, Longman.
MORGAN, ROBIN (Ed.) (1970) *Sisterhood is Powerful: An Anthology of Writings from the Women's Liberation Movement*, New York, Vintage Books.
PALMER, PAULINA (1989) *Contemporary Women's Fiction: Narrative Practice and Feminist Theory*, London, Harvester Wheatsheaf.
SPENDER, DALE (Ed.) (1983) *Feminist Theorists: Three Centuries of Women's Intellectual Traditions*, London, Women's Press.

Section I

Women's Studies Today

Introduction

Women's Studies has expanded rapidly in Britain over the last two decades in a multiplicity of forms. The papers in this section address various aspects of this dynamic growth. They range from a comparison between Britain and the rest of the European Community, covering the diversity of Women's Studies in both higher education and adult education, to a consideration of the innovative teaching methods in Women's Studies.

Christine Zmroczek and Claire Duchen report on a survey of major programmes and centres of Women's Studies and feminist research in Britain, providing a useful listing and analysis of these. They compare British Women's Studies and feminist research with that in other EC countries, showing where Women's Studies has received considerable resourcing and where this is lacking, and asking under what circumstances Women's Studies receives this support and funding.

While the first paper focuses on higher education, Mary Kennedy and Brec'hed Piette examine adult education and Access courses. Adult education has always had a close relationship with grass-roots feminism, and has often provided an inspirational context for women to explore their ideas about the world. Access courses have provided women with non-traditional routes into higher education which they missed the first time around.

The papers by Cathy Lubelska and by Maggie Humm address the question of the transformation of teaching methods when women's experiences are placed at the centre of the curriculum. Cathy Lubelska argues that experiential concerns are significant to the development of the teaching of Women's Studies, not only its content, and require reassessments of the relationship between teacher and student, the individual and collective aspects of learning and research.

Maggie Humm also engages with the theme of the significance of women's experience for Women's Studies. The diversity of women's experiences is central to her paper, especially ethnic and 'racial' diversity. The importance of language and its reconstruction, of the place of personal history, and its reconstruction, are further themes.

Throughout, the papers deal with the question of the diversity of women's experiences and the form of Women's Studies. The field is dynamic and developing, not fixed or monolithic. Yet in a very few years Women's Studies has developed not only its own theories of the social world, but its own theories and debates about the construction of knowledge itself in both teaching and research contexts.

Chapter 1

What *are* those Women up to? Women's Studies and Feminist Research in the European Community*

Christine Zmroczek and Claire Duchen

Introduction

In this chapter, we have four aims: first, to describe and analyze the findings of the 1988–89 EC-sponsored survey of Women's Studies and feminist research (see pp. 12–20) as far as the UK is specifically concerned; second, to report on the changes that have occurred since completion of the survey; third, to compare the situation of Women's Studies and feminist research in the UK with the situation in other EC countries; and finally, to reflect on the European context and the implications it may have for Women's Studies in the 1990s.

In 1988–89, we participated in a survey of Women's Studies and feminist research in the UK,[1] as part of the study commissioned by the European Community (EC) about Women's Studies and feminist research in each of the twelve member countries.[2] This was the first project to try to gain a European perspective on the structures and concerns of Women's Studies and on the issues that are concerning students, researchers and teachers throughout the EC. The whole project was coordinated by *les cahiers du Grif*, the French-language feminist journal based in Brussels, Belgium. One important aim of the project was to collect data from each country which would form the basis of a European Women's Studies database.[3] With this end in mind, the coordinators supplied a questionnaire to be completed by each participant in the survey in each country and then translated into French before being entered into the database. One or two women from each country were asked to coordinate the questionnaire distribution and translation and to write a report summing up the current situation of Women's Studies and feminist

* Parts of this paper were published earlier in 'Women's Studies and Feminist research in the UK' by Christine Zmroczek and Claire Duchen in *Women's Studies International Forum*, Vol. 12, No. 6 (1989).

research in their country as it emerged from the questionnaire responses. The conclusion of the survey was marked in early 1989 by a conference held in Brussels which brought together over 300 women for three days of lively multilingual debate.

Although the survey was completed in 1989, developments in the UK since then appear to confirm our findings. Overall, we found that despite major obstacles such as lack of funding, generally inadequate resourcing and little institutional support, Women's Studies and feminist research were lively — and expanding. Our survey was not fully comprehensive due to the limitation of time and money available for it. Nonetheless, we believe that the results were representative of the range and nature of Women's Studies and feminist research in the UK in the late 1980s and indicate the way in which they are likely to develop in the 1990s. (See Appendix for a full listing of available courses.)

Women's Studies in Higher Education in the UK

Women's Studies now exists in one form or another in most institutions of higher education in the UK.[4] The structures of Women's Studies are determined and limited by several factors including institutional constraints, lack of funding and resources and the availability of feminist lecturers willing to take on the work without extra pay, time or other resources. The political climate is also important, as we will show.

Women's Studies courses are offered at both postgraduate and undergraduate level. A doctorate and master's degree can be taken in Women's Studies (despite the contradiction in terms of the latter!). Presently, students can only register for a doctorate in Women's Studies named as such at the University of York and at the Polytechnic of East London. In the summer of 1989, the first UK doctorate in Women's Studies was awarded by the University of York to a mature student whose research was on working-class women, domesticity and respectability. It is important to note that many doctorates are in fact feminist research, but are classified as part of a traditional academic discipline; for example, one woman's doctoral research on Women's Studies in Britain, the Federal Republic of Germany and the USA earned a PhD in sociology. This means that feminist research can sometimes be hidden within the academy, a situation which has serious implications for Women's Studies, and to which we will return.

There are several well-established master's degrees in Women's Studies; the first, at the University of Kent, began in 1980. In 1990, several new ones have been launched. For example, since the survey, at least five new postgraduate courses have been started, three in Women's Studies (Institute of Education, London; Polytechnic of Central London; University of Exeter), one in Women's History (Royal Holloway and New Bedford College, London) and one in Gender Analysis and Development (University of East Anglia). There are also degrees in gender studies, which is frequently regarded in the same light as Women's Studies, although there is a growing debate on the need to keep a clear distinction between these two rather different endeavours. (See Appendix for a full listing of available courses.)

Many Women's Studies courses are offered on a part-time basis, and sometimes through evening attendance (at postgraduate level in particular, but also for undergraduates at some polytechnics). Grants from funding bodies for postgraduate work in Women's Studies are now available (from the ESRC for example), but applying for a grant for a postgraduate degree is by no means a guarantee that one will be awarded.

It is now possible to obtain an undergraduate degree in Women's Studies at the Polytechnic of East London. Elsewhere, a handful of institutions such as the University of Lancaster and the Polytechnic of North London offer part of an undergraduate degree — one half or one third — in Women's Studies. As with postgraduate studies, most Women's Studies lecturers and students at undergraduate level are hidden within the traditional structures of higher education, with Women's Studies courses offered as options such as 'Feminism in History and Literature since 1800', 'Contemporary Feminist Thought' or 'Women in French Society since 1945'. Very, very few staff are hired specifically to teach Women's Studies.

Overall, then, the situation is that Women's Studies can be hard to find; staff, students and researchers are often isolated in their department, their institution and/or their geographical location. However, this has led to positive action, such as the establishment of Women's Studies Centres (see Appendix). At the time of our survey, there were nine of these, with others in various stages of planning, preparation and struggle with their institution for recognition and support. The role of these Centres in Women's Studies and feminist research will emerge more clearly in the next few years. However, it is already clear that they provide a much-needed institutional base for Women's Studies, support for staff and students and a valuable networking facility within and between institutions. The importance of networking has long been recognized and action has finally been taken. At the time of the survey, there was no national network for Women's Studies. In March 1989, the Women's Studies Network (UK) was formally established,[5] with a newsletter for members published three times a year.[6] At the time of writing (September 1990) two conferences and a day school have already been held and more are in the planning stages. Similarly, in 1988, there was not a comprehensive listing of UK Women's Studies courses and feminist researchers that we could consult. The Women's Studies Network is currently in the process of compiling a listing of this kind.[7]

Networking within different professional associations is also important; for example, the Women Teaching French group was formed in 1987 with overcoming isolation as one of its specific aims. Its first weekend conference will be held in November 1990. The Women's Caucus of the British Sociological Association (BSA) has been very active for over fifteen years and has seen to it that feminism is firmly placed on the agenda of sociology. Other women's caucuses are being formed, such as Women and Psychology begun in 1990. These networks provide both support and a place for women to debate issues of theory, pedagogy and ongoing research in their field, as well as being a way by which strategies for feminism within the field as a whole may be determined.

Networking at the European level is now recognized as important for Women's Studies and feminist research. Women's International Studies Europe (WISE) is soon to be formally constituted (November 1990)[8] and the ERASMUS programme allows both staff and students from all disciplines to be exchanged between European institutions of higher education.[9] There are many other transnational networks within a variety of disciplines or areas of study and activism, such as those concerned with peace and environmental issues or those involved in social policy research.

Students of Women's Studies

We have noted that many Women's Studies courses are course components, single elements of a degree in, for example, English Literature or Sociology. Students of Women's Studies may therefore have chosen the option without realizing the implications of their choice. A Women's Studies course will almost inevitably be significantly different from the student's general experience of higher education: some students respond favourably and are keen to reassess their own assumptions and to learn about sexual politics; others are quite disorientated and some are hostile. Students who specifically opt for Women's Studies or who are following a Women's Studies postgraduate course are often very different from the typical undergraduate or postgraduate. Many already have a commitment to feminism and are active in feminist endeavours outside the academy. Women's Studies students will frequently have to overcome various obstacles to get on the course, both financial and personal. Many are older women returning to education. Often women cannot register for degrees requiring full-time commitment and presence due to the demands of other responsibilities, such as family and household, and/or because they are self-supporting. They may opt for part-time courses but even this may be difficult. Many women may also lack the necessary qualifications for entry to degree courses. There are at least two ways in which these women can and do participate in courses: through the Open University, which has a longstanding Women's Studies course and a very well-attended summer school, or through adult education.

Women's Studies in Adult Education

Adult education is a very important and vibrant part of Women's Studies. As the courses are often not focused on an examination process, adult education can offer scope for innovation and is therefore ideal for Women's Studies. Participation in adult education is generally not dependent on entry qualifications; the low fees and even occasionally the provision of a creche all make it more accessible to women than other kinds of formal education. A wide range of Women's Studies courses are offered, usually based on local demand, from the more academic type such as women's history or sexual divisions at work, to the very practical, such as car maintenance for women. Women's writing courses are especially popular. Adult education courses often act as a stimulus for women to continue their education, sometimes through more formal channels. Many feminists are involved in teaching in adult education.

It needs to be stressed that women participate in adult education overall in far greater numbers than men, and that Women's Studies has a very high profile. However, adult education is often dependent on local government funding and has been subjected to major cuts, especially to non-vocational courses. Changes are noticeable in the types of courses on offer since the completion of the survey; the number, scope and variety of Women's Studies courses are diminishing and the focus is turning towards more general courses on literature (such as women writers or women and writing), courses on the self (massage, self-assertion, etc.) and practical business skills such as word processing, how to start your own company and so on.

Women's Studies at Large

There are several other areas of feminist activities which, although not formally designated as Women's Studies, contribute importantly to its vitality.

There are informal groups which arise from academic concerns, such as feminist history groups, thesis writers' support groups and other groups which meet to discuss ongoing research. Because they are informal, they are difficult to locate in a survey, but we had many responses from women involved in such activities.

There are groups not necessarily connected to the academy but whose work often results in publications or activities directly related to Women's Studies. For instance, Matrix is a group of feminist architects whose book *Making Space: Women and the Man-Made Environment* was one of the first to alert women to the importance of planning issues (Matrix, 1984) and who continue to publish widely on the subject. WHAM (Women, History and Museums) is a group started by women employed in museums who have organized several conferences, and produce a regular newsletter.

Other groups based on a common identity or experience have produced important publications, organized conferences, events and newsletters. For example, groups of Black women,[10] Irish women, working-class women and women with disabilities have all produced published collections in the last two years (see Grewal *et al.*, 1988; Lennon, 1988; Burnett *et al.*, 1989; Morris, 1989).

Resource centres, such as the feminist archives at the University of Bradford, the Fawcett Library and the Feminist Library in London, are essential to Women's Studies and feminist research. All such centres rely very heavily on volunteer workers and are desperately short of funds. The Feminist Library is a case in point: all its funding has been cut and it is now totally dependent on volunteer staffing, with significantly reduced opening hours.

Feminist publishers (some independent, some attached to traditional publishers) such as Onlywomen Press, Sheba, Pandora, Virago and the Women's Press are flourishing, and new ones appearing, such as the recently-launched Silver Moon Books. Many academic publishers have a Women's Studies list or include the work of feminists in their malestream lists. There is a great demand for feminist books from the general public as well as from academics. Feminist writers of all kinds are promoted nationally during the annual Feminist Book Fortnight, which was initiated during the first International Feminist Book Fair held in London in 1984.

Feminist journals are important. The main UK journals are *Feminist Review*, *Trouble and Strife*, and *Women's Studies International Forum*, which although international has a large readership and a substantial contribution from UK-based feminists. Special Women's Studies and feminist research issues of the more traditional academic journals are a regular event these days. Two new journals appeared in 1989, *Gender and Education* and *Gender and History*, and in 1990 the new *Women: A Cultural Review* has been launched; a new feminist magazine *Women Writing* now supplements the longstanding *Spare Rib* and *Everywoman*.

Feminist Research in the UK

There is an impressive range of feminist research in the UK, particularly in view of the fact that it is often done in addition to full-time work either in the academy or elsewhere. However, development across the disciplines is uneven. In 1990, the growth areas identified from the survey questionnaire still seem to be prominent: sociology leads the way with a concentration of work in health and social policy; literature and textual studies, with a particular interest in biography and autobiography; history, with emphasis on the history of women's employment, on the family, and on individual biographies; law and criminality; cultural studies, with emphasis on film. There is an increasing amount of work in the social sciences now being undertaken within a comparative or cross-national framework. This may be due in part to practical factors concerning research funding (funding bodies such as the Economic and Social Research Council are keen to support comparative research; the EC is a major source of research funding) and to political factors: there is a perceived need to learn and understand more about the ways in which different European societies function as 1992 approaches. There is also a growing body of work in what might broadly be defined as women and development studies. Feminist research in science, technology and economics in the UK still lags woefully behind most other subjects.

Significant and worrying in the response to the survey was the absence of information about Black Women's Studies and — as far as we have been able to find out — in 1990 there are still no formally named Black Women's Studies courses in the academy, and very few Black women in lecturing or research posts, although feminist research and publication is increasing. International and multicultural issues are on the agenda of Women's Studies at last, although not always very much in evidence.

Lesbian Studies, named as such, are virtually nonexistent within the academy, although lesbian perspectives are important to many Women's Studies courses and there is an increasing demand for lesbian publications. Lesbian Studies courses can occasionally be found in adult education but they are severely threatened by the Thatcher government's homophobic legislation and by the self-censorship in organizations and institutions to which it has given rise. For example, a well-attended long-running evening class in Lesbian Studies suddenly ran into difficulties as the following term's schedules were being planned. The problem, apparently, was over how the advertisement should be worded — should it be allowed to remain as Lesbian Studies — in case this was found to be against a law which at that time had not yet been enacted? This class does not appear as Lesbian Studies in the 1990 catalogue of adult education courses.

Overall, the uneven development of feminist research, its preponderance in the areas of intellectual endeavour traditionally allowed to women — the arts and humanities — and the significant lacunae that our survey has pointed to, would be a fruitful area for further investigation leading to development of Women's Studies curricula.

It is particularly impressive, in fact, extraordinary, that so much exciting, insightful feminist research IS being carried out, when there are so few paid full-time researchers in Britain, and of those even fewer are women and fewer still are involved in feminist projects. Feminist lecturers rarely have paid work time allocated to their research, and they manage to fit it in as and when their timetables and workloads permit, usually in their spare time, as do feminists in other full-time jobs. Women frequently make the decision to accept the limitations of part-time work and pay in order to find time for their research. Feminist research is often undertaken in the context of postgraduate studies, although, as noted earlier, there are few grants available, and many women can register only part-time and then fit their research around whatever other work they do to earn a living. These constraints and the problems they bring must be placed alongside a recognition that the majority of women still have responsibility for running a household and for childcare if they have children. In short, women engaged in feminist research frequently do so under enormous strain and with other commitments competing for our time.

To Be or Not To Be? Women's Studies in the Academy

Two sets of issues emerged from the survey as of particular importance: the place of Women's Studies in the academy, and the consequences of the current political climate for Women's Studies and feminist research. Within the academy, there is still debate over the very existence of Women's Studies, especially as a named and autonomous course or programme, and added to this more recently is the attempt to smother it by 'replacing' or 'superceding' it with 'gender studies'. In 1989 we noted the increasing popularity within the academy of the word 'gender' used to replace 'women'. Our speculations at the time on the reasons for this seem no less valid in 1990. Is it because it is seen by many men and by liberal women as less threatening? Is it because it allows the study of an abstract concept to replace the study of women and men? Is it because it depoliticizes the relationship between the sexes and assumes a false equality? Is it because it removes the focus from women, indeed because it allows women to be subsumed once more into the general (that is to say, into man)? Haven't we heard this somewhere before? Is it because it opens up a new area for men to work in (particularly sensitive NEW men who have not found Women's Studies welcoming to them)? In our view, it might well be all of these and probably more!

It is perhaps paradoxical that since the term 'gender' appears to be less threatening, and thus more academically acceptable, than *women*, some courses that are clearly Women's Studies — the content firmly about or focusing on women — have been called 'Gender Divisions' or 'Gender Issues in Contemporary Britain', and a number of Women's Studies centres have been called centres for the study of gender. So the use of 'gender' can be seen as a strategy used precisely to gain the necessary foothold for Women's Studies. We must, however, be alert to the problems of co-option by the institution, and to the dilution of the aims and activities of feminists through the involvement of men.

Let us state clearly that in our view the study of gender relations is valuable and necessary as in, for example, research on the gendered classroom or workplace, and indeed, has always been on the agenda of Women's Studies. But gender studies is by no means the same as Women's Studies and it should certainly not be seen as a replacement. The encroachment of gender studies on the hard-won and often none too secure place of Women's Studies in the academy is a danger now recognized by many UK feminists, as evidenced by the growing debate on the subject.[11]

The number one problem raised by our respondents was lack of institutional support. This was clear in terms of staffing levels, teaching hours, allocation of library funds, administrative assistance, etc. — in short the basic general requirements for tutors and students to organize and carry out stimulating and satisfying work in any field. Even where Women's Studies centres have been set up, the effort has come and continues to come from the women involved and not from the institution. Thus far there is very little evidence of any real institutional commitment to Women's Studies. As noted earlier, staff are rarely employed specifically to teach Women's Studies; they are attached to a traditional discipline in which they are expected to prove themselves, and at the same time take part in Women's Studies teaching and research, which then may be ignored in assessments of their workload and abilities. Most Women's Studies relies on the efforts and goodwill of a handful of staff, and if they leave or have to turn to other work, Women's Studies in that particular institution (or discipline, or department) may well disappear.

Women tend to be at the bottom of the hierarchical heap in the academy, low in status, frequently the first to be affected by cuts, often with only part-time and/or temporary contracts. It is virtually unavoidable to conclude that as far as the institutions go, decisions are made by men for men. Lip service is given to equal opportunities with no strategy for implementation to back up the words. Career structures do not account for disruption for parenting; promotion is difficult, and commitment to Women's Studies and feminist research can be an obstacle to promotion — or indeed to being employed in the first place.

Women as students in institutions are equally affected by the lack of resources for Women's Studies and by the lack of seriousness with which it is considered. The need to prove oneself in a traditional discipline, and the increasing difficulty of obtaining an academic post or funding for research, make it all the more discouraging for women wishing to pursue a career in Women's Studies and feminist research.

The Political Climate

The political climate of the 1980s has presented enormous problems for Women's Studies. The policies on education and research of the past decade have been a major factor in determining the contours of Women's Studies in the UK, with lack of adequate resourcing the overwhelming obstacle. It has been a time of retraction not expansion, a time of swingeing cuts, limited budgets which do not allow for innovation, few grants or sabbaticals, staff losses, deterioration of conditions and dropping morale. Recent changes which abolished tenure for new staff (and for staff who change status by promotion) are likely to have the effect of curbing academic freedom. In the case of Women's Studies, this could provide yet another opportunity for attempting to shut women up.

With the emphasis now on attracting outside funding for research, Women's Studies and feminist research are likely to suffer disproportionately, unless they are orientated towards social policy. Feminist research is rarely seen as a viable proposition by government or private funders in the UK, unlike for example Denmark, where Women's Studies has received substantial government support, or the USA, where feminists have been successful in attracting private funding for Women's Studies. A change of attitude to learning, based on utility and with an emphasis on business and management, is tirelessly encouraged by the Thatcher government through policy, legislation, and economic penalties and rewards. This has already had an effect on adult education and is also affecting feminist researchers, in terms of the kind of research receiving funding. The predominance of policy-orientated studies shown in our survey may be a reflection in part of the need to tailor one's research according to what will get funded. This is not to question the value of feminist social policy research; it is greatly needed, perhaps particularly so in view of the disastrous social consequences of Thatcherite government. The question, rather, is one of who will fund the work on feminist theory?

In 1990, we believe that both the positive and negative aspects of our reading of the situation at the end of our survey have been confirmed. That is, Women's Studies and feminist research in the UK continue to be characterized by dispersal of effort, with women simultaneously juggling many different involvements and interests in the field, very often unpaid and usually under-resourced. But there has nonetheless been an enormous growth of feminist research inside and outside the academy; a remarkable increase in courses and centres; and a thriving feminist book trade.

Across the Water: Women's Studies and Feminist Research in Continental Europe

As we have noted, comparative research is increasing; yet how much real contact is there between Women's Studies in the UK and in the rest of Europe? What can be gained from our counterparts across the water? Can we look to other European experiences for new ideas and ways of confronting the obstacles faced in the UK? In early 1989, Women's Studies and feminist research in the member states of the EC was reported and analyzed at the conference organized by the survey coordinators in Brussels referred to at the beginning of the chapter. Here, we discuss some of the main features described at that conference and subsequent developments in the EC, with the focus on the similarities with and differences from the situation in the UK. We will then turn to the possibilities for sharing ideas and resources transnationally, and for working with and learning from each other.

Main Features

Women's Studies and feminist research, as might be expected, have a very different shape in different countries. For instance, the Netherlands has two major feminist archives, about 200 feminist researchers, Women's Studies courses at most universities and Chairs for Women's Studies. In Italy, on the other hand, most Women's Studies takes place outside the university, with resistance to institutionalization a major factor in this. Danish feminists are in the enviable position of having Women's Research Centres in all of Denmark's five universities, an action programme for women voted by its parliament with major funding allocated to Women's Studies and feminist research. In Spain, Women's Studies and feminist research are only slowly becoming recognized as valid in and of themselves, but feminist perspectives are inserted by individual feminist teachers in disciplines such as sociology and history. The Belgian situation is complicated by the differential levels of resourcing of the French-speaking and Flemish-speaking communities. In spite of this, two of the most successful longstanding feminist projects (the University of Women and the *cahiers du Grif*) are based in Belgium. In France, the 1982 government-sponsored initiatives to encourage Women's

Studies ran out of money and were not refunded. There are, however, lively feminist research centres in four major cities. In Ireland, Women's Studies and feminist research is thriving, both inside and outside the academy. In the Federal Republic of Germany,[12] Women's Studies and feminist research is relatively well-established, with its vigorous activity demonstrated by the enormous number of women who completed the questionnaire (over 500), and by the healthy state of feminist publishing — the only country other than the UK where this was observed. Greek feminists, like the Spanish, are struggling to build a base for Women's Studies and feminist research in a country where women's rights constitute a relatively new issue and the educational system as a whole is under-resourced, with all research suffering as a consequence. Portugal does not yet have a women's liberation movement and consequently there has been little development of Women's Studies and feminist research. There is no university centre for research on women in Portugal, though there is a government department responsible for the 'condition of women'. Within the academic community, Women's Studies is low status and considered to be 'unscientific'. Luxembourg presents a different case, as students cannot complete a first degree in Luxembourg itself, but have to register for the second part of their degree in France, Belgium or Germany.

National Context

Women's Studies and feminist research in each country are very largely shaped by the socio-political context in which they exist and from which they grew. For instance, Greece, Spain and Portugal only emerged during the 1970s from long experiences of military dictatorships, during which the dominant view of 'women's place' concomitant with both right-wing politics and Mediterranean culture meant that the women's liberation movement in those countries (and therefore Women's Studies and feminist research) did not develop at the same time or at the same pace as movements in other EC countries. The issue of women's liberation tended to be subsumed into an opposition culture dominated by the labour movement and the Left rather than providing the impulse for an autonomous women's movement.

Other clear political factors influencing the shape of Women's Studies include: the existence of two linguistic communities in Belgium, which has been mentioned, and a split between a religious Catholic community and a non-religious community; the absence of rights in Ireland as basic as the right to divorce and access to contraception; close connections between feminism and Left political parties, where the women's liberation movement had been part of a resistance struggle, while other feminisms may refuse these connections; a wide variety of EC national policies on issues such as abortion, state-provided childcare facilities and laws affecting women's civil status and right to engage in paid employment. Each specific national context affects the questions asked and the problems confronted by feminists.

The economic situation of each European country plays its role: Greece, Ireland, Spain and Portugal are substantially less industrialized and less wealthy than their more northern neighbours and a North–South/rich–poor divide is apparent within the women's movement Europe-wide as well as in the broader relationships between EC countries.

Relationship to government affects the extent to which Women's Studies and feminist research is accepted, supported and integrated into national educational systems. Denmark, Holland and the FRG benefit from extensive central or local government support while in France, initial support from Mitterrand's socialist government has not been sustained. Always difficult, the relationship between an autonomous women's movement and government can be paradoxical: in Greece, the government claims to look after women's rights, declaring an autonomous women's liberation movement and consequently Women's Studies redundant, while in Spain, the government's claim is rather that as there are so many researchers who are feminists, state funding for Women's Studies and feminist research is not necessary.

Measuring state support by counting the number of teaching and research posts and the number of Women's Studies courses available in higher education may be one way of determining the level of institutional 'success' of Women's Studies and feminist research but it is not necessarily an accurate account. State support is not static: governments change, grants are awarded, withdrawn, allowed to lapse. Moreover, this quantitative evaluation may hide reality: in France, for instance, the six Women's Studies posts created in universities in the early 1980s were tied to traditional academic disciplines rather than being full Women's Studies posts; in the Netherlands, of the eight Chairs of Women's Studies apparently available in universities, several seem to be permanently vacant. Italy, on the other hand, only appears to have one Women's Studies course at university level — but this does not necessarily indicate lack of feminist teaching and research activities at that level or elsewhere. Denmark leads the field as far as funding is concerned and Women's Studies and feminist research seems to have the full support of the government. However, Danish women are concerned about the potential for deradicalisation contained within such a close government connection.

Women's Studies and Feminist Research and the Women's Liberation Movement

There is continued debate over the relationship between 'academic' feminism incarnated by Women's Studies, and a feminism that is outside the academy. This relationship varies tremendously from country to country. For instance, the situation described in Italy seems to be one where the vibrancy of the Women's Liberation Movement has no impact on academic feminism; in France the Women's Liberation Movement appears to be moribund whereas there is still some Women's Studies and feminist research in evidence; in Ireland, there are close links between university-based feminist researchers and teachers and non-academic feminists; in the FRG and the UK, the high profile of feminist publishing reflects public demand for both academic and non-academic feminist work. So, overall, the relationship between Women's Studies, feminist research and the Women's Liberation Movement is related to the particular political situation in which they operate, to the structures of the educational system and to the perceived goals of Women's Studies and feminist research.

What are Women's Studies and Feminist Research Anyway?

In fact, there seems to be little consensus over these goals amongst European feminists, or over the practice of Women's Studies, with the relationship between knowledge and politics at the heart of the debate. In a number of countries, women are seeking to establish their credibility in the eyes of the academy and do not seem to question the ways in which categories of knowledge have been defined. At the 1989 conference, we were struck by the number of times that women asserted the 'scientific' nature of their research, and we understood 'scientific' to mean 'objective'. Our own position was that knowledge itself is political and as such cannot be objective — hardly a revelation to Women's Studies practitioners in the UK, but assumptions of objectivity were not even questioned by some of the participants in the conference. In fact, it was clear that different women had fundamentally incompatible assumptions about a number of issues. For instance, one French researcher held that our role as teachers and researchers was to 'create and pass on knowledge', with no acknowledgement of debates over pedagogy in her words. Others simply accepted the right of men to be involved in Women's Studies and feminist research and seemed unaware of the furious debates over this issue. Questions of class and race were not so much skirted as simply absent, an absence unthinkable in the UK or USA.

Nor is there consensus about the nature of Women's Studies. The question, for some, is 'What are we talking about?' whereas for others it is rather 'What are we doing?'. This difference of approach seems to encapsulate the frequently-noted difference between a French orientation towards theory and an Anglo-Saxon problem-solving pragmatism. But this difference of approach reflects in part national differences and in part disciplinary differences: the failure of different academic disciplines to inform each other is a Europe-wide problem, despite the commitment of Women's Studies to interdisciplinarity.

The question of 'What are we talking about?', however, is of crucial importance in a very literal sense, whatever our cultural and intellectual tradition. Language and our ability or inability to understand each other was a major obstacle to communication at the Brussels conference and is a problem that must often prevent collaborative ventures. Beyond the purely linguistic difficulties, which are not negligible, there are the conceptual difficulties. Even where the words exist, do we understand them in the same way? We have mentioned the use of the word 'scientific' as one example. Another important example is the word 'gender'. There are many different ways to translate the word 'gender' into, for instance, French, where the most literal translation (*genre*) is the least appropriate. Greek women pointed out that in Greek, the word 'gender' is part of a nationalist vocabulary referring to the Greek gender/people, and so feminists use the expression 'social sex' instead. These cultural resonances have to be learned and shared; we cannot know them automatically, and translation is as much about culture as it is about 'simply' words. Other linguistic/cultural problems which impede our understanding of each other's work and our ability to work together concern the lack of equivalent social structures. One glaring example of this is the importance in the UK of 'caring' (as in 'women's work as carers') which simply does not exist as a concept in, for instance, France.

Working Together

From this account, it might appear that all we have in common are the differences between us: theory versus practice; North versus South; academic versus political; divided by national concerns and by language. This would be a partially but not totally true picture. Striking similarities also exist.

Women's Studies and feminist research have similar areas of strength, in particular sociology and the humanities; the same areas of weakness seem to be repeated across Europe, in particular, research in science and technology. Ironically, Danish women, who ARE researching into these areas, consider the UK to be on the cutting edge of science and technology, but as we have noted, there is very little evidence for such an assertion.

In spite of our differences, the desire to share information and to develop collaborative work seems strong among European feminists and a number of initiatives have been launched. We noted the increased interest in cross-national and comparative research work in the UK and this trend has been confirmed in all EC countries. Out of the 1989 conference, several suggestions were identified as valuable to pursue collectively:

- the regular updating of the *Grif* databank (deriving from the national surveys) of Women's Studies and feminist research in the member states

- the promotion of a feminist perspective in all teaching and research

- promotion of Women's Studies in higher education and creation of posts in Women's Studies in all establishments

- equal representation of women in education at every level of the hierarchy and in every discipline

- the establishment of a feminist lexicon, which would form the basis of a databank of terminology for feminist teaching

- the full use of existent EC structures and projects for Women's Studies and feminist research (for instance, the student and staff exchange programme ERASMUS should be used for Women's Studies; the language programme LINGUA should fund a specialized language-teaching programme catering to the linguistic needs of feminist researchers and teachers).

A further issue of great importance debated at the conference was that of the concept of 'Europe' itself. Concern was expressed about the effect on women's lives all over Europe of the tendency to use 'Europe' to refer only to the twelve member states of the EC. The upheaval in Eastern Europe since the conference entailing, effectively, the redrawing of the post-war political map, highlight the need to broaden the concept and to ensure that it is inclusive rather than exclusive, not only of the eastern parts of the continent but also of its southern neighbours. These countries (Turkey, Morocco, etc.) are very much involved in European concerns, economically and politically. The limitations inherent in a narrow view of Europe are highly pertinent for women. For example, women from the southern countries often migrate to the more affluent north in search of work, but are denied the rights accorded to EC nationals. The current debate over which women's rights will remain and which will be lost after the unification of Germany (abortion, childcare facilities) is another case in point.

It is, therefore, useful to reflect on Women's Studies and feminist research at the level of Europe rather than at the parochial levels with which we are most familiar. Feminist ideas from non-English language areas currently have little impact on feminist thinking in the UK, due in part, to lack of translation, in part to the large number of texts that English speakers already have at their disposal, and in part, to the typical British complacency shared by feminists about the need to learn other languages. An injection of ideas and approaches from other countries could add to the vitality of UK feminist thinking where the North American model for Women's Studies seems to predominate — for instance, there is a huge body of work in German which is virtually ignored in the UK. And why is work by Danish women but written in English specifically to reach a larger audience simply not known in the UK?

We have stated above how the political climate in each country affects the structures and the content of Women's Studies and feminist research; this is equally true of politics at the level of Europe, and will become increasingly so.[13] As 1992 approaches there are already some worrying signs of the likely impact on women of the revised social charter;[14] these signs — and other unforeseen side effects of European integration — must be monitored and analyzed. There is a very real need for Women's Studies to take these issues on board. Feminists have long recognized the artificial nature of man–made national boundaries: in the words of Virginia Woolf, 'as a woman, I have no country; as a woman, my country is the whole world'. We must remain vigilant about the shape that the concept and the reality of 'Europe' takes, so that women's voices are heard and so that the Europe emerging in the 1990s works for women and not against us.

Notes

1 In this chapter, we use the term UK intending to include women living in Northern Ireland. We are fully aware that many of them do not wish to be part of the UK, and our use of the term is descriptive only.

2　For the twelve national reports, see *Women's Studies, Concept and Reality* (les cahiers du Grif, 1989); for details of the UK survey, see Zmroczek, C. and Duchen, C. in *Women's Studies International Forum* Vol. 12, No. 6, 1989.

3　For further information about the database, contact Veronique Degraef, *les cahiers du Grif*, 20 rue Blanche, 1030 Bruxelles, Belgium.

4　The project as a whole was concerned with WS in higher and adult education and not in schools; as we had no responses from colleges of further education, the following discussion does not include their activities.

5　For details of the Network, contact the Secretary, Annette Lawson, 10 Holly Lodge Gardens, Highgate, London.

6　For information, contact the newsletter editor, Val Walsh, Communication/ Women's Studies, Edge Hill College of Higher Education, St Helen's Road, Ormskirk, Lancashire L39 4QP.

7　Contact Jackie Stacey and Lisa Adkins, Women's Studies Research Centre, University of Lancaster, Lancaster LA1 4YL (tel. 0524-65201).

8　For information about WISE, contact Jalna Hanmer, Dept of Applied Social Sciences, University of Bradford, Bradford, West Yorkshire BD7 1DP.

9　For information, contact the ERASMUS office at 15 rue Darlon, 1040 Bruxelles, Belgium.

10　In this paper we use the term *Black* as a political concept, that is, as we understand it, as a term used by women (and men) from various ethnic and cultural backgrounds to express a common purpose for political reasons in a racist and oppressive white-dominated society, whilst recognizing a great diversity of experiences and aims amongst them.

11　See Mary Evans, Renate D. Klein, etc. in this volume.

12　At the time of writing (September 1990), Germany is still divided into two nations. The unification of Germany is due to take effect on 3 October 1990. In the present East Germany, there is a growing feminist movement and WS at at least two universities, but these did not form part of the EC project.

13　For a discussion of the issues arising for women in Europe in the light of 1992, see *Women's Studies International Forum*, special issue on 'Women in Europe', forthcoming.

14　This was discussed at the recent (June 1990) conference on Women, Welfare and 1992, held as part of the series of cross-national research seminars on 'The implications of 1992 for social policy'. Papers from the conference are available from Professor Linda Hantrais, Department of Modern Languages, Aston University, Birmingham B4 7ET.

References

BURNETT, JUNE, COTTERILL, JULIE, KENNERLEY, ANNETTE, NATHAN, PHOEBE and WILDING, JEANNE (Eds) (1989) *The Common Thread: Writings by Working-Class Women*, London, Mandarin.

GREWAL, SHABNAM, KAY, JACKIE, LANDOR, LILIANE, LEWIS, GAIL and PARMAR, PRATHIBHA (Eds) (1988) *Charting the Journey: Writings by Black and Third World Women*, London, Sheba Feminist Publishers.

LENNON, MARY (Ed.) (1988) *Across the Water: Irish Women's Lives*, London, Virago.

MATRIX (1984) *Making Space: Women and the Man-Made Environment*, London, Pluto Press.

MORRIS, JENNY (1989) *Able Lives*, London, Women's Press.

Appendix

Women's Studies Centres in the UK

Women's Studies Centre
Darwin College
University of Kent
Canterbury
Kent CT2 7NX
contact: Clare Ungerson

Women's Studies Research Centre
University of Lancaster
Lancaster LA1 4YL
contact: Penny Summerfield

Centre for Women's Studies
University of York
Heslington, York Y01 5DD
contact: Mary Maynard

Women's Studies Unit
Polytechnic of North London
The Marlborough Building
383 Holloway Road
London N7 8DB
contact: Sue Lees

Women's Studies Unit
Coventry Polytechnic
Priory Street
Coventry CV1 5FB
contact: Susanne Haselgrove

Women's Studies Centre
The Polytechnic
Wolverhampton WV1 1SB
contact: Diana Holmes

Centre for Women's Studies
Sheffield City Polytechnic
36 Collegiate Crescent
Sheffield S10 2BP
contact: Eileen Green

Centre for Research and Education on Gender
Institute of Education
20 Bedford Way
London WC1H 0AL
contact: Diana Leonard

Hull Centre for Gender Studies
Hull University
Cottingham Road
Hull HU6 7RX
contact: Marion Shaw

West Yorkshire Centre for Research on Women (WYCROW)
University of Bradford
Bradford, West Yorkshire
BD1 1DP
contact: Hilary Rose

Postgraduate Degree Courses in Women's Studies

PhD at University of York, above address (contact: Nicole Ward Jouve).

MA: for information from the above institutions, contact the coordinator at the addresses given above.

MA in Women's Studies
University of Warwick
Coventry CV4 7AL
contact: Margaret Stacey

MA in Women's Studies
Polytechnic of East London
Livingstone House
Livingstone Road
Stratford
London E15 2LL
Contact: Maggie Humm (for BA in Women's Studies as well)

MA/Diploma in Women's Studies
University of Bradford
Bradford
West Yorkshire
BD1 1DP
contact: Jalna Hanmer

MA in Women's Studies
University of Exeter
Queen's Building
Queen's Drive
Exeter EX 4 404
contact: Lesley Sharpe (Dept of German)

MA in Women and Education
University of Sussex
Falmer
Brighton BN1 3RF
contact: Carol Dyhouse

MA in Women and Literature
Department of English
The University
Hull HU6 7RX
contact: Marion Shaw

MA in Women's History: Gender and Society in Britain and Europe 1500–
  1980
Royal Holloway and Bedford New College
Egham Hill
Egham
Surrey TW20 DEX
contact: Ruth White, Graduate Student Officer

Diploma in Women's Studies (two-year part-time course)
Polytechnic of Central London
309 Regent Street
London W1R 8AL
contact: Irene Brennan

MSc in Gender and Social Policy
Dept of Social Administration
University of Bristol
40 Berkeley Square
Bristol B58 1HY
contact: Liz Bird

MA in Gender Analysis and Development
School of Development Studies
University of East Anglia
Norwich NR4 7TJ
contacts: Ruth Pearson, Cecile Jackson

Chapter 2

From the Margins to the Mainstream: Issues around Women's Studies on Adult Education and Access Courses

Mary Kennedy and Brec'hed Piette

Introduction

The discussion of Women's Studies courses tends very largely to focus on the development of Women's Studies within higher education. While this is important, there is a danger that other areas of education may be left out. In many respects Women's Studies in adult education and Access courses is much closer to its roots in the Women's Liberation Movement where it has been possible to be far more radical. As Coulson and Bhavnani (1990, p. 67) observe:

> the often 'outsider' status of many of these initiatives combined with
> the direct involvement of feminists in some of them, has meant that,
> in varying degrees, they have been able to break out of some of the
> conventions and constraints of the racially structured malestream
> education and academia.

This chapter looks at the ways in which Women's Studies have been developed, and indeed changed, over the last two decades in two associated but distinct areas of education, namely, adult education and Access. (Access courses, in general, are aimed at preparing adults without standard entry qualifications for higher education.) While there are obvious similarities between the development of Women's Studies in these two areas and those in mainstream graduate and postgraduate provision, we would argue that there are also some issues and problems that are distinct. Women's Studies in adult education and Access can be seen as doubly marginalized: as provision for women — the majority of students and most of the part-time tutors; and also as being themselves marginal areas of education. However, they may have benefited from this situation, being freer to innovate than more publicly prestigious areas such as MA courses, so it has been possible for various radical forms of Women's Studies to flourish.

Perspectives on Adult Education

Looking back over nearly twenty years we can see that change has taken place in women's education in the adult education sector. Up to the close of the 1960s women's education generally meant cookery, dressmaking, body beautiful and general liberal studies. Women's Studies began first in the UK in the early 1970s in university extra-mural departments and in the Workers' Educational Association (WEA) where courses with such generalized titles as 'Women in Society' and 'Women in History' were offered. This development occurred only after many battles to resource and provide recognized space for such seemingly provocative and politically loaded classes for women only, which did not adhere to the 'balance-all-sides-of-the-question' liberal approach of traditional adult education. Women's Studies aimed at liberation and independence as the purpose of education, the subject of study being women-centred knowledge. The links with the Women's Liberation Movement were close; consciousness-raising was translated across into education through the recognition of experience and participatory methods of teaching which made us tutors feel on the cutting edge of new knowledge. Phrases like 're-make, re-source and re-vision' the world of education for women were inspirational.

Much of our innovatory work and theory as adult educators came out of the experience of being in Women's Liberation Movement groups, and was influenced by the writings of Figes (1970), Rich (1979), Rowbotham (1973), Millett (1971), Mitchell (1971), Firestone (1971) and by key articles such as Dorothy Smith's 'Women's Peculiar Exclusion from Culture' (1978). We were also quite clear that it was impossible to examine or mark Women's Studies and the knowledge that came out of oppression. We were the submerged, the subordinate half of the human race, fighting (later we would not use such military language) the dominant group, men, for our proper recognized place in the world (Baker-Miller, 1976). At this period the informal, open-ended, and non-examined classes provided by adult education were ideal seeding ground for Women's Studies.

The next stages were the development of Access classes for women in the Local Education Authorities, arising from the literacy campaign and the New Opportunities for Women/Fresh Start/New Horizon courses. Later, self-defence classes, which led to assertiveness training, and counselling courses opened up new areas of women's education. One much debated dilemma was how to extend 'traditional women's education' along more feminist lines without undermining the skills and achievement of women students. Meanwhile university adult education provision was offering more specialist and theoretical feminist courses in anthropology, autobiography, sociobiology, film studies, literary criticism, psychology, psychoanalysis, politics, theology and research-based history. And in 1981 Southampton University's adult education department set up the first women's education centre aimed specifically at second-chance working-class women (Thompson, 1983; Hughes and Kennedy, 1985; Taking Liberties Collective, 1989; Kennedy, 1987.) Lacking other openings for feminist studies, young women in particular filled these adult education classes, though they did not attract working–class and black women in any great numbers; here the LEAs were more successful through their Access provision. Many of these courses were taught by academic women lacking the opportunities to teach in higher education institutions, although by the early 1980s Women's Studies was beginning to be developed in higher education, and Kent University had established the first openly named Women's Studies MA by 1981.

The strategies of these adult education courses were to maintain a space for women to study together women's experience and knowledge with feminist tutors; and to extend feminist research and knowledge across the curriculum into all subject areas, which meant educating our colleagues and training part-time tutors. This latter strategy is now being more coherently targeted by equal opportunities policies which integrate issues of age, class, race, gender and sexual orientation into the teaching context. In the University of London extra-mural department, for example, Women's Studies classes grew from six in 1975 to twenty-nine in 1988, plus twenty-four interdisciplinary gender-based courses.

Politics of Evolution and Change

By the late 1980s there were new and different issues emerging which reflected the changing economic and feminist political climates in education. In brief these were: the welcomed expansion of Women's Studies into higher education institutions which attracted former students from adult education by providing them with the opportunities to study in depth for registered degree qualifications; government pressure on adult education providers which led to a decline in public subsidy, rising fees and difficulty in funding radical innovatory courses such as non-vocational Women's Studies; and the labour market need in the 1990s for more women workers. In the latter case Thatcherite utilitarianism has combined with economic enticements to push adult education towards expanding training courses for women entering upon or returning to work. The difficulty here is that, while the expanding possibilities are to be welcomed for women's independence through better work opportunities, education in a feminist understanding of the processes and power relations of employment is being pushed aside in favour of the quick 'hands-on' training approach, a situation reminiscent of the wartime mobilizations of women. In one sense women are no longer on the margins, as they are needed as the 'reserve army of labour' now, but can we hold to the centrality of women-centred education if we are not ourselves steering the boat into the mainstream of vocational education?

A more fundamental challenge for the long-term theoretical base and nature of feminism came from black women, lesbians and older women. These groups questioned, argued and demanded that feminism change, criticizing its existing premises as white, middle-class, young, heterosexual and Eurocentric. Such blinkered feminism could not claim to represent all women all of the time. Indeed feminists themselves were in danger of becoming the colonizers they accused men of being. Anger, criticism, struggles over the right to have separate groups, and over who could claim to speak for whom without first confronting and recognizing the differences between women, turned upside down and began to change the starting point of Women's Studies and women's education in new and diversely complex directions. In many respects more progress has been made so far around the issues of sexuality, and the provision of lesbian studies. We are still shying away from honestly debating our own racism, and fully integrating these much-needed new understandings into our feminism in theory and practice. However, these ideas and issues are slowly beginning to surface in the teaching and subject content of the curricula, particularly in Women's Studies, which has had to confront and begin to acknowledge 'difference' as a positive starting point in advance of other subject disciplines, pushed by its close connections with anti-racist teaching and multicultural studies, and women's work in equal opportunities policies (Minh-ha, 1987; Barrett, 1987; Brittain and Maynard, 1984).

Politics for Survival

Thus the situation in Women's Studies in adult education in the last decade of the twentieth century is complex in its specialisms and divisions as well as in its provision. Feminist ideas, research and practice have been a major factor in changing perspectives in adult as well as other areas of education and in broadening out the curricula in innovatory ways. The resistance to such radical changes is no longer overt, but it still continues under the surface; and women are still marginalized and their needs, as well as their knowledge, are still only partially recognized. The difficulty is to maintain the impetus, now that we are through the first stages of revolutionary vision, discovery, and solidarity — but we have survived and developed so far. As long as feminist theory continues in a state of permanent openness and questioning, accepting the painful but ultimately fruitful 'differences' between women, then we can avoid ossification and complacency. The problem is, can we maintain the ideals of being truly sisters under the skin, allowing for the diversity of experience and culture arising from age, class, disability, ethnicity, race and sexual orientation, without splitting into fragmented, quarrelling groups while we lack the 'tangible politics' of a broad-based women's movement to link into? In educational terms, how does Women's Studies maintain and reach out to mature women students, large numbers of whom are still frightened of being labelled as feminists? And how do we continue the 'perspective transformation' of all education and learning, with Women's Studies continuing to be the generator of feminist theory and practice?

We need to be realistic as well as visionary. The factors militating against our survival continue to be similar to those in the recent past. There is continuing male control of the structures of power and a temporarily silent misogyny. Not all women are feminists; many prefer the easier option of the status quo and fear the hassle of challenging the rules as defined by men.

There is the current political and economic climate in Britain which emphasizes training for work rather than education into understanding or 'really useful knowledge' for women. The reluctance to acknowledge women's disadvantaged, secondary role persists in citizenship, income, work, family responsibilities, their safety needs — the list of wrongs not righted is endless.

On the positive side, the factors for survival are strong. Women have analyzed the politics and structures of power and now have a better understanding of how it operates. In education the participatory methods of teaching and learning have influenced, and continue to influence, the ways in which women can share knowledge and work together. Feminist research and theory has breached some exclusive disciplinary barriers leading to more open-ended ways of interdisciplinary study, which is particularly appropriate to mature students' learning needs and experience. Women's Studies, by forefronting women, has helped to raise the status and achievement of women's traditional skills, arts and crafts. Finally we have learned to network together in education among ourselves and with our students, as well as in other interest areas. In other words, we are visible now. But however mainstream we may become, women's studies will still be needed as a 'subversive space' (Aird and Lown, 1989; NIACE, 1989; WEA, 1989) for women to study in together because without the dynamo of question and challenge based on honest feminist research and open debate, we could slip back into a token, if unwilling, conformism.

Women's Studies and Access Courses

Like Women's Studies, Access courses have been a notable growth area in education during the last decade. In 1986 it was estimated (Mason, 1987) that there were at least 150 Access courses in England, and by the end of the decade the numbers had grown considerably beyond this. Access courses are the most recent development in attempts to attract adult students without standard entry qualifications into higher education. They have their origins in work pioneered by the City Lit in the 1960s (Hutchinson and Hutchinson, 1986), and by the Open College of the North West in the late 1970s. Tutors working with adults on literacy courses and other forms of basic education soon realized that many of their students had both the capacity and the desire to carry on with their education beyond this. The Access movement, however, really got under way and was given Government approval when a Department of Education and Science circular was sent around to a number of Local Education Authorities in 1978 encouraging them to set up Access courses for members of ethnic minorities (Mason, 1987). There have been two main reasons for this development. Firstly, the desire to improve access to higher education for those who are under-represented there, in particular working-class students, women and members of ethnic minorities. This is essentially a radical perspective and as far as women are concerned also a feminist one. The second reason was a fear that demographic trends would lead to a downturn in the number of 18-year-olds available for higher education, and a consequent dearth of graduates available for employment. It is probably fair to say that those involved in teaching Access courses have been particularly interested in the first of these reasons, but that in so far as they have been supported by institutions of higher education and, to a certain extent, by government, this has been mainly for demographic and market reasons (Wilson, 1990).

While the term 'Access' is applied to a wide range of courses, most of them are courses designed to prepare adults for higher and professional education. Frequently there is a close link between the Access provider (usually a college of further education) and a local provider of higher education (usually a local polytechnic) (Evans and McCulloch, 1989). In some cases students who are successful on the Access course are guaranteed a place on a particular course in higher education. In other cases there is no such direct link and students are prepared for a wide range of potential courses. On some courses all the students have very clear plans to continue into a particular, perhaps vocational, course, whereas, in others, many of the students who embark upon the course are still undecided about what they want to do on its completion. Working-class women, in particular, may well be very uncertain about their future direction and lack confidence in their ability to continue with their education. The large cities, and London in particular, now have a huge range of Access courses with links into many courses, both vocational and non-vocational (104 Access courses in 1990–91 in Inner London are listed by the London Open College Federation, 1990).

The philosophy behind Access courses has meant that they are frequently taught within local communities, and, to a large extent, on the users'/students' own terms (Kearney and Diamond, 1990). There is often some scope for student negotiation of areas that will be covered and students are encouraged to follow their own interests (Diamond and Kearney, 1987). Students have far more control over the content of what is taught and over methods of assessment than with 'A' level or degree courses. In this respect Access courses have followed the feminist approach taken by Women's Studies in adult education and applied it to this wider group. Feminist concerns have also informed the care that is usually taken in ensuring that the practical barriers to attending courses are minimized. Creches are generally provided, teaching hours will fit into the school day or take place in the evening, fees will be negligible and, perhaps most importantly, students will be able to carry on receiving benefits while attending the course (Diamond and Kearney, 1987). This effort and sensitivity on the part of the tutors, and the (by adult education standards) not inconsiderable resources that have been put at the disposal of the courses, has meant that they have very largely succeeded in reaching women of all social classes, ethnic minorities and a wide range of ages.

The content of Access courses varies, but most are in the humanities, social sciences and computing, with areas such as women's history and women's health being popular topics. Study skills and confidence building are vital elements in all Access courses as it is recognized that adult students need particular help in these areas. Other distinguishing features are small group work and a lot of tutorial support, particularly in the most well-resourced courses. Assessment will vary but is usually non-traditional, such as continuous assessment of a wide variety of study projects, and examinations, where included, are likely to be for practice only or constitute a small amount of the total assessment. Access courses have very specific teaching philosophies, drawing upon students' own experience and knowledge as a valid base for learning. Tutors aim to build on these by working outwards from personal experience towards academic and theoretical analyses rather than supplanting them with academic 'knowledge'.

Many of the tutors as well as the students on Access courses are women and feminism has played a major part in the development both of content and the participatory method of teaching adopted. These courses should be seen as a significant part of women's education. As Coulson and Bhavnani (1990, p. 67) point out:

> we would argue, [that] such developments [i.e. Access courses] are a central reference point for 'academic' women's studies while, of course, often being a route on to such women's studies courses. In this way, they are also a source of organic links between studying for degrees and an overall political project, part of whose aim is to empower women.

Issues and Problems

In general Access courses have succeeded in what they set out to do. Their students have gone from them onto degree courses which they successfully complete in the vast majority of cases. Having completed degrees most go on to gain employment. Access courses have also achieved their aim of reaching out to working-class and black women. And, most importantly perhaps, they have exerted some influence on teaching methods in higher education through presenting to the system students who are mature and articulate, and who have radical ideas about what higher education should be about. Women who have gone into Access courses will often have been politicized, and are likely to be aware of feminist issues and how these relate to their own experiences. Such recognition, although at times uncomfortable, seems very positive. Niggling questions remain: 'access to what?' and 'what is it that higher education in the current climate offers to mature women students who have been given confidence and high expectations by their Access experience?' These are vital questions as, while Access courses may constitute valuable experiences in their own right, their *raison d'être* is to get people into higher education.

As students enter the 'mainstream' they are confronted by a system which is still by and large dominated by male teachers and traditional methods of assessment. Despite the rhetoric that is heard about the need to encourage and provide for mature students, universities and polytechnics are still very largely geared to the needs of 18-to-21-year-olds. Very few courses indeed at undergraduate level use the feminist and adult-oriented approaches that students have got used to on their Access courses. As far as content is concerned, first degrees in Women's Studies are conspicuous by their absence, and many degrees even in the humanities and social sciences have very little feminist or other type of radical content.

Many of the changes currently taking place in higher education are not particularly helpful to mature students. For instance, there is a strong emphasis on technological/vocational education whereas most Access students are interested in the humanities and social sciences. Some developments that could potentially be appealing to mature students, such as the development of open learning packages, the flexibility of Credit Accumulation and Transfer Schemes (CATS) and part-time modes of study, are available, but more importantly, mature women are not faced with a particularly supportive or feminist atmosphere in higher education, despite great efforts by the still very few feminist tutors. Most women students arriving in higher education from good Access courses are disappointed with many aspects of what they find. It is to their credit that most of them continue for three years and often gain very good degrees.

What can be done about this mismatch between Access courses and higher education by feminist tutors in both areas? Access tutors need both to carry on with the excellent practices they have developed within a climate of diminishing resources while still preparing students for higher education as it really is. It is tempting but unrealistic to expect the changes to come mainly from higher education. It is vital that tutors in both areas communicate with each other about their methods and expectations. Higher education tutors need to make their institutions aware that rhetoric about equal opportunities (now perhaps heard more often than some years ago) must be matched by action that takes into account the needs of mature women students. Some of the policy moves towards 'market-type efficiency' being seen in many institutions of higher education may be unhelpful in this context. Teaching mature students who have had relatively little previous educational experience is more consuming of resources than the traditional methods that have been developed for teaching 18-year-olds, but also more rewarding.

The Future

Fielder (1990) and Wilson (1990) both suggest that the type of Access courses that are described here may be on the wane. This is partly because the cut back in resources, and the effect of government training initiatives, make it harder for students to attend Access courses while claiming benefit. Also, general open Access courses which were particularly attractive to women, and led primarily into degrees in social science, the humanities and education, may be giving way to more specialized and targeted developments. These are likely to be vocational courses, particularly technology and business, and courses aimed at particular groups, still under-represented in education, for instance, members of ethnic minorities.

While some of these developments are to be welcomed, particularly for the opportunities they offer women to follow well-paid careers, and in giving new opportunities to black women, the feminism of the more general Access courses may be becoming diluted. There seems to be a feeling that women need opportunities to study 'vocationally relevant' courses rather than their own position as women.

As mentioned earlier, Access courses derived from two main impetuses: the first being the radical and feminist one of increasing opportunities; and the second being the fear expressed by various authorities that the downturn in the number of 18-year-olds meant an increasing need for educating or, in particular, training adults. These two influences no longer seem to be moving in the same direction. There is a real danger that the kinds of Access courses that seemed to be part of the feminist enterprise, and that produced a new breed of student — mature, working-class, articulate, demanding, politicized and more often than not female — is quickly disappearing.

The development of Access has been very important for many women, particularly working-class and black women who have gained entry through it into higher education. They have been given an opportunity they almost certainly would otherwise never have had. It has also been an arena where Women's Studies has been experienced by a more diverse group of students than those at undergraduate or postgraduate level. Courses have often been able to be very radical with fewer institutional constraints than in higher education. What remains to be seen is whether Access courses of a feminist and radical kind are to remain a permanent feature of the education scene or whether they were merely a staging post from the old liberal courses to the new vocational training courses for adults.

Conclusion

Women's Studies in both adult education and Access now seems to be at a crossroads. One positive way of understanding the complexities of its continuing development is to think in terms of concepts of change rather than just notions of disadvantage. This is not to accept that disadvantage where women are concerned has disappeared. Indeed, the label is too freely bandied around as an excuse to provide more market-led utilitarian education and training for women by policy-makers and employers, with the implication that women somehow are responsible for their own second-class position, and must therefore be guided into suitable educational channels. This paper has briefly tried to show that there has been change over time through the development of participatory teaching and learning methods; the use of innovatory assessment; and the recognition of the practical obstructions women face in attempting to gain an education through support such as creches, sensitive timetabling, low fees and disabled access. It is these radical, innovatory and flexible practices, backed by feminist theory, which have to be maintained in the future.

However, despite these achievements, this is not a time for complacency. There is a very real danger of a dilution of the feminist component in Women's Studies or education courses. This can happen, for instance, on courses where there is a strong emphasis on the technical and vocational. While welcoming new opportunities for women in these areas we hope that such developments will not be at the expense of feminist analyses; these must continue to be explicitly developed.

There is also a danger in the possible slippage effect of the newly evolving gender studies on the identity/ies of Women's Studies. The evolution of gender studies out of the revolutionary impact of feminism is important because men too have begun to study the construction of masculinities: femininity and masculinity are no longer an invention of feminists. But, as Mary Evans has suggested in her essay (in this volume) the politics of power relations between women and men in gender studies may mean that women disappear (again) within the generality of humanity. Thus the study of gender can have a more neutralizing effect — i.e. be more acceptable and respectable — in educational terms, and this opens the door once again to a blurring of the differences between women and men. We are still uncertain whether feminist ideas and Women's Studies are strongly enough rooted — let alone women being economically, educationally and emotionally equal to men — to be able yet to risk losing any of their identity.

We have argued that, in the past, Women's Studies in adult education and Access have been crucial in the wider development of Women's Studies. In particular they have been, in part, responsible for maintaining the radical edge of women's education. Moving forward from this base we have to develop the 'subversive space' for inspiration and innovation in collaborative networks with other women; recognize and act upon the creative tensions of difference and diversity between women; maintain the pressure for curriculum change by propagating feminist ideas and research; and continue to open out educational access for women who are, after all, over half the human race. We may be changing gear, but we are not changing ideals. The policies and strategies we need now to further develop in these areas are more complex and subtle than they were ten or twenty years ago, and we will continue to need allies as well as to rely on our own efforts. Women's Studies has, to an extent, become part of the mainstream now; we must ensure that in this movement from the margins we do not lose the inspiration or the histories of what we have done — or what we are going to do.

References

AIRD, E. and LOWN, J. (1989) Conference on *Women Educating Women: Exploring the Potential of Open Learning*, 23 September, City University, London.

BARRETT, M. (1987) 'The Concept of "Difference"', in *Feminist Review*, No. 26, pp. 29–41.

BRAH, A. and HOY, J. (1987) 'Politics of Urban Experience: Teaching Extra-Mural Courses', in *Multicultural Teaching*, Vol. 6, No. 1.

BRAH, A. and HOY, J. (1989) 'Experiential Learning: a new orthodoxy?', in WEIL, S.W. and McGILL, I. (Eds) *Making Sense of Experiential Learning: Diversity in Theory and Practice*, Open University/SHRE.

BRITTAIN, A. and MAYNARD, M. (1984) *Sexism, Racism and Oppression*, London.

COULSON, M. and BHAVNANI, K. (1990) 'Making a Difference — Questioning Women's Studies', in BURMAN, E. (Ed.) *Feminists and Psychological Practice*, London, Sage, pp. 62–75.

DIAMOND, J. and KEARNEY, A. (1987) 'Access Course Development: A Case Study', in *Journal of Further and Higher Education*, 11, 2, pp. 51–57.

EVANS, B. and McCULLOCH, A. (1989) 'Access Courses: the First Decade', in *Journal of Further and Higher Education*, 13, 3, pp. 15–29.

FIELDER, R. (1990) 'The Access Course is Dead ...?', paper delivered to South Yorkshire Open College Access Forum, Sheffield City Polytechnic.

FIGES, E. (1970) *Patriarchal Attitudes*, London, Faber and Faber.

FIRESTONE, S. (1971) *The Dialectic of Sex*, London, Jonathon Cape.

HUGHES, M. and KENNEDY, M. (1985) *New Futures: Changing Women's Education*, London, Routledge and Kegan Paul.

HUTCHINSON, E. and HUTCHINSON, E. (1986) *Women Returning to Learning*, Cambridge, National Extension College.

KEARNEY, A. and DIAMOND, J. (1990) 'Access Courses: A New Orthodoxy?', in *Journal of Further and Higher Education*, 14, 1, pp. 128–138.

KENNEDY, M. (1987) 'Labouring to Learn: Women in Adult Education', in McNEIL, M. *Gender and Expertise*, London, Free Association Books, pp. 103–123.

LONDON OPEN COLLEGE FEDERATION (1990) *Inner London Access Courses 1990–91*, London, Grosvenor Press.

MASON, R. (1987) 'The Logic of Non Standard Entry: Mature Students and Higher Education', in *Journal of Further and Higher Education*, 11, 3, pp. 51–59.

MILLER, J. BAKER (1976) *Towards a New Psychology of Women*, Harmondsworth, Penguin.

MILLETT, K. (1971) *Sexual Politics*, London, Hart Davis.

MINH-HA, T. (1987) 'Difference: A Special Third World Women Issue', in *Feminist Review*, 25, pp. 5–22.

MITCHELL, J. (1971) *Woman's Estate*, London, Penguin.

NATIONAL INSTITUTE OF ADULT AND CONTINUING EDUCATION (1989) *Adults Learning*, 1, 4, December, Leicester.

RICH, A. (1979) *On Lies, Secrets and Silence*, London, Virago.

ROWBOTHAM, S. (1973) *Woman's Consciousness, Man's World*, London, Penguin.

SMITH, D. (1978) 'A Peculiar Eclipsing: Women's Exclusion from Men's Culture', in *Women's Studies International Quarterly*, 1, 4.

TAKING LIBERTIES COLLECTIVE (1989) *Learning the Hard Way*, London, Macmillan.

THOMPSON, J. (1983) *Learning Liberation*, London, Croom Helm.

WEA (1989) *Women's Education Past, Present and Future*, London, WEA.

WILSON, P. (1990) 'Looking beyond the "Consensus": Access to Higher Education', in *National Association of Teachers in Further and Higher Education Journal*, March/April, pp. 18–20.

Chapter 3

Teaching Methods in Women's Studies: Challenging the Mainstream

Cathy Lubelska

Given the enormous growth of Women's Studies over the last two decades the methods by which it is taught in higher education have received scant attention.[1] Considering the challenge which feminist research and theory constitutes to mainstream academic practice it is incongruous not to alter our methodological approaches as teachers to the acquisition and understanding of 'knowledge'. Through its theories and research feminism continues to elaborate methodologies which harmonize with its fundamental aims and objectives, especially the validation of women's experiences. Yet the methods which we employ in our teaching remain, by and large, traditional, mainstream and oddly incongruous with our goals. Innovative methodology, in its widest and most dynamic sense, should encompass the ways we teach and the environment in which we do this. The consequences of neglect are serious. How we teach is as, if not more, important than what we teach. The content and weighting — theoretical, thematic, disciplinary — of Women's Studies courses vary enormously, and serve broadly similar aims. Yet the ways in which we acquire and disseminate our chosen 'body of knowledge' are crucial if we are to practice what we preach and most fully meet the objectives which we commonly attach to our courses. Although the failure to critically re-evaluate approaches to teaching Women's Studies jeopardizes our aims, much current teaching practice continues to be inappropriate. An important factor here is undoubtedly the challenge which a radical change in our ways poses not only to the mainstream but also to now established traditions within academic feminism. A positive way forward is to make this challenge explicit through our methods of teaching.

Many of the observations in this paper are gleaned from my own experience of developing interdisciplinary courses for a major honours scheme in Women's Studies. They are not definitive, but indicate ideas and strategies which our course team found helpful and effective in our teaching.

A focus on women's experiences and their validation distinguishes Women's Studies as a distinct subject of study within higher education. As core philosophies and aims tend, quite rightly, to be pervaded by a pre-occupation with women's experience it is essential to ensure that the methods of delivery employed really do meet our objectives. The question of what constitutes a meaningful and relevant learning experience for students needs to be addressed within this context. This paper argues that a comprehensive appreciation of the importance of experience to Women's Studies provides a framework within which both to devise and to evaluate the effectiveness of our methods.

The Aims of Women's Studies

There is no one definitive philosophy or list of aims for Women's Studies. Indeed, one of its most exciting features is the enormous variety of courses which have been developed. Nevertheless, where experiential concerns are paramount they indicate some of the priorities. In no particular order, these would usually include the following. We need to examine the experience of women, in particular their experience of oppression, as comprehensively as possible and to try and explain the differences and similarities which are revealed. In doing so we utilize not only a range of disciplinary and inter-disciplinary perspectives but also, in particular, alternative perspectives based on women's experience and feminist theory. Methodologies which reflect the distinctiveness of Women's Studies, and its impact as a subject of study, centre upon experience as the context of everyday life, and upon the inter-relationship between the emotional and the intellectual in the validation of women's experiences. Here the knowledge gained from experience is the distinguishing feature of an integrated approach to the study of women by women. This is the key resource against which both the traditional academic disciplines and alternative feminist modes of thought, creativity, analysis and research are appraised. Explicit here are the challenges posed both to the mainstream and to feminism by a truly woman-centred experiential approach to study. This is given substance and practical application through approaches to teaching which stress a cooperative environment of learning, where women's experiences are treated as shared resources which are collectively analyzed. Within this context the relationship and tensions between the emotional, subjective and experiential knowledge of women and the intellectual, objective, expertise of mainstream knowledge are highlighted (see de Wolfe, 1980).

Experience and Women's Studies

If Women's Studies is to fulfil its potentially productive role within both education and the women's movement then its relevance to all women needs to be clearly demonstrated. Regardless of their other differences all women have experience which is unique to them. Within a context of learning which demonstrates the value of both individual and collective experiences in the creation and exploration of shared resources for Women's Studies, the diversities and commonalities amongst women are more readily appreciated.

Making clear the value of each student's experiential contribution provides a common point of access and a means of enabling everyone, in particular those who might feel themselves disadvantaged judged by conventional academic criteria, to participate.

In recognizing experience as the context of everyday life, students start rather than finish with an interdisciplinary perspective. Lived realities do not fall into neat disciplinary categories, nor do the ideas and sources through which we attempt to make sense of them. The sheer breadth and variety of women's experiences, and the myriad of ways and situations in which they are felt, range across and go beyond the concerns of other disciplines. Here students begin with a context within which the distinctive, interdisciplinary concerns of Women's Studies are identifiable. Students can then learn to evaluate both mainstream and feminist perspectives insofar as they reflect and explain women's experiences.

Where the comparative and shared experiences of women are treated as the shared resource of all women, the interconnectedness of the personal, intellectual and political, and thus of Women's Studies with the women's movement, is more easily appreciated. In turn, students are empowered by approaches to learning which demonstrate the potential of the skills, knowledge, and ability to change which experience generates. The extent to which the 'expertise' and perspectives of the academic disciplines represent and comprehend the realities of women's lives, and the contributions of feminist analysis here, are more readily appreciated where women are encouraged to positively re-evaluate their own experiences. Discussion of women's social roles, for example, as housewives, mothers, carers and workers, can be reassessed using women's experiences to identify and affirm the skills, labour, knowledge and values which women really do, and can, contribute to society. Recognition of the incongruities between the representations and status of women and their lived realities empowers students to question their own and others' assumptions, and to explore women's real social worth and potential, both personally and politically. Comparisons of the experiences and perceptions of domesticity amongst different generations of women can draw explicitly on the shared resources of students. The significance of factors such as socialization, economic trends and opportunities, mother-daughter relationships and changing images of femininity is considered within a context where the relevance of issues of difference clearly extends beyond, and enriches, the more usual concern with race, class and sexuality.

In working from experience Women's Studies starts with its own woman-centred perspective, which clearly distinguishes it from the other disciplines upon which it explicitly draws. The exploration and affirmation of women's experiences starkly contrasts with the absence, suppression or distortion of experiential factors evident in mainstream approaches. An environment of learning where students are actively engaged in the development and application of methodologies appropriate to the retrieval and understanding of women's experiences generates its own resources. These are the sources, methods and frameworks of explanation from which to develop a new and growing alternative body of knowledge on which students can increasingly draw. This enables students to come to, rather than from, orthodox disciplines with a healthy scepticism about their potential contribution. The interdisciplinary, intertextual experience of women is a touchstone against which the value of all methods and perspectives, mainstream and feminist, can be appraised.

In stressing its centrality to Women's Studies experience is seen both as the context of everyday life and as primary evidence about women's lives. The accessibility of our methodology is revealed. Through starting by asking our students what they know of their own experiences and those of other women, we are consciously stressing the value of resources which they all possess. This provides an introduction and framework for the methodologies and concerns of the rest of their studies. By continually asking, throughout our teaching, what is our evidence, how do we acquire and make sense of it, we are directing students to the sources, methods and explanations, the key components of both our own experiential knowledge and that of the academic disciplines upon which we draw. Through starting from, rather than moving to, experience in addressing these questions, students can learn to use the resources which it provides in uncovering the distinctiveness of Women's Studies in relation to the other disciplines and perspectives which are introduced to them. What also becomes clear is the hierarchy of experience whereby some women's experiences appear to be accorded more visibility and importance than others; this then informs the varied contexts in which students consider issues of inequality and difference.

Methodologically, the priorities are to explore ways of gaining access to this evidence and of making sense of it. In doing so, as the omissions and distortions in non-experiential and disciplinary approaches to the study of women become clear, so, more provocatively, do the reasons for these exclusions. Where our methodologies explore experience as both a source and explanation, a new body of knowledge exposes not simply the inadequacies of the mainstream but the role which it plays in the academic and political oppression of women. In retrieving women's experiences, the consensus of the disciplines about what constitutes acceptable academic practice and knowledge is revealed as an obstacle to the validation of those experiences, and as part of the apparatus of our oppression.

Our starting point, then, is the recovery of women's experiences; only from that basis can we move on. Without at least some aquaintance with the distinctiveness of women's experiential knowledge and the ways in which this might be unearthed and explored, neither we nor our students can begin to evaluate its validity. Nor can we appraise the methods and critiques, from both the mainstream and feminism, regarding the so-called subjective knowledge which is generated, until students at least have some idea of what this is. By implication, we cannot start to explore how, why and to what extent women's experiences have been omitted, obscured or mangled by disciplinary analyses until we have some inkling of what these experiences are. Any exploration of the strengths and weaknesses of the disciplinary and theoretical positions which we ourselves utilize and, critically, of the incongruities between these and our experiential concerns, cannot be undertaken by students until these concerns become tangible to them.

Recognition of this final point is crucial if we are to make Women's Studies accessible and comprehensible to students. In introducing them to the bodies of knowledge and, in particular, to the theoretical perspectives in our possession, there are real dangers that these will appear abstract and remote, as indeed some of them do, unless we convey them within a context where the substantive importance of experience is already established and consistently focused. Our failure to do this can all too easily give rise to feelings of inadequacy amongst students, an indefensible consequence given our aim of empowering women.

The Challenge of Teaching Women's Studies

Women's Studies demands a learning environment in which its core distinctive experiential concerns are constantly focused. This is vital if our intellectual and political aims are to be achieved. Those teaching Women's Studies need to be aware of the extent of the personal challenge that can be involved. The resources which we ourselves bring to Women's Studies are conditioned by our experiences both as women and as professional or would-be academics. The challenges to the mainstream which become explicit through our preoccupation with experience can be the source of painful tensions. Whilst the growth of feminist studies is testimony to the desire to confront these difficulties, it is itself compromised by its own relationship to the mainstream. The exploration of methodologies which aim, practically, to validate women's experiences helps expose those approaches and explanations, within and outside feminism, which are obstructive or unhelpful to the pursuit of this goal. It is only through the appreciation of these tensions, and the willingness, explicitly, to work through them, that Women's Studies can realize its full potential.

Approaches to Teaching: Some Suggestions

What follows is by no means comprehensive but provides some indication of appropriate practices in our approaches to teaching.

Firstly, Women's Studies requires a supportive and cooperative environment of learning if it is to productively generate and explore its key experiential resources. Wherever possible this should involve small groups of students, more than one — preferably several — tutors, a minimum of lectures, and as many workshop and project-based activities as possible. Although we can be considerably constrained by resources, and by both institutional and student expectations, we should at least strive to move as far as we can in these directions.

Secondly, in exploring women's experiences we need to utilize all the evidence available to us. This does not mean an uncritical acceptance of all sources as valid evidence, but neither should we dismiss sources simply because they have been discarded as irrelevant, subjective or trivial by the mainstream. In fact, quite the contrary: by re-evaluating these sources in the light of our concern with women's experiences we can explore how such a dismissal has effectively excluded this evidence 'from the record', as well as recognizing what has been excluded. As these missing ingredients contain evidence of women's subordination, students can then begin to see why they are absent from the mainstream and thus the part which it plays in women's oppression. Experiential accounts of pregnancy and childbirth help reveal patriarchal structures of knowledge and authority, and the ways in which these can operate to silence women; to control their bodies — and their lives. Wider consideration can then be given to the different meanings and experiences surrounding maternity, birth control and reproductive technology according to race and class. Both the evidence yielded by the experiences of, for example, black or working-class women, and the neglect of these by mainstream and feminist studies, highlights other oppressions and differences amongst women (see Higginbotham, 1989). The study of conventionally disregarded sources is a way in for students to what can otherwise often be presented as complex, inaccessible and all too abstract theoretical issues. We also need to re-examine conventional sources from a woman-centred perspective to see if we can yield our own conclusions about their significance. Where interdisciplinary analysis of government social policies, of the law and of the media — concerning, for example, sexual harrassment, equal opportunities, the regulation of womens' sexuality, mental health, physical and sexual abuse or pornography — is informed by women's experiences and feminist theory, this can provide insights into those structures, processes and ideologies which oppress women, as well as indicating strategies through which these may be challenged.

Thirdly, we need to be adventurous in our search for appropriate methodologies to use with our students (see Klein, 1983). These should be selected, appraised and refined according to what they can reveal about women's experiences so that, again, students question motives for their exclusion. By far the most effective way for students to assess research methodologies is to experiment with them and apply them. Through casting the student as researcher her findings can become an original contribution, an addition to our resources, which other students and we ourselves can share, evaluate and learn from. The divison of teacher and taught, of expert and novice, characteristic of most teaching situations, is diminished and questioned in this context. There are a number of approaches, more or less experiential, which would be appropriate here, for example, oral histories and life histories, conversational analysis and variants on the theme of experiential analysis. Those methods in particular where the normal relationship between researcher and object-of-research is jettisoned for one where both the researcher and subject participate in framing, interpreting and, possibly, in being changed by the research, can be most instructive. Small-scale and straightforward projects can be undertaken by students as a means of exploring the potential of such approaches, for instance, a discussion of experiences of education involving three women from different generations, one of whom is the 'researcher'. Many central issues can be raised in this way: the exploitative nature of much conventional research, the role and legitimacy of the expert, the importance of women's own interpretation of their experiences as part of our resources, the nature and value of subjectivity, etc.

Fourthly, in drawing upon other disciplines and extending the boundaries of our own knowledge as teachers we need to be receptive to what other disciplines may have to offer us. Most of us who work in Women's Studies have come from other specialisms and probably still teach within these. Our involvement in Women's Studies is quite rightly influenced by our disciplinary origins, to a greater or lesser extent. We are concerned to apply and adapt these disciplinary perspectives to our work in Women's Studies. Yet the interdisciplinary nature of Women's Studies demands more. We need to work with women from other disciplines not just in the design of our courses but through joint teaching, to familiarize ourselves with other disciplines and to engage in theme-based workshops and symposia where women from several disciplines reflect together upon how they would tackle an inherently interdisciplinary issue, for example, reproductive technologies. Too often it is left to the students to attempt to synthesize the separate disciplinary elements with which they are fed. We can actively demonstrate how this can be done, as well as the problems encountered, through our approaches to teaching.

Fifthly, our methods of assessment should reflect the learning situations which our students encounter. If we stress shared resources, cooperative projects, student research and the value of each student's skills and experiences, we need to explore appropriate methods of evaluating these. Joint assignments and dissertations, peer-group, oral and continuous assessment can be more appropriate and subtle means of testing the achievement of our objectives than traditional examinations and individual essays. We also need to be clear about what we are assessing. Much of what is 'learnt' on Women's Studies courses is part of a process which may never end; it can also be deeply personal for the students concerned. We need to allow them as much scope as we can reasonably give to design their own projects and assignments, and to encourage them to articulate their own intellectual understanding and self-development by being flexible about the form those assignments should take. For some students a piece of creative writing or role play can reveal far more of their appreciation of feminist issues and ideas than any number of carefully researched, conventional essays.

Finally, we should regard ourselves as participants in the learning process alongside our students. In recognizing the experiential resources and interdisciplinarity of Women's Studies we acknowledge that we do not know everything, that our own expertise is limited and, quite possibly, flawed. If we are willing to experiment with new methodologies we must be prepared to revise or change our views in the light of what we discover. If our students, too, are encouraged to experiment and to offer their experiential

47

resources, then we must also be prepared to learn from them, indeed, we should relish the prospect. Our role as teachers and as expert definers and givers of knowledge is therefore legitimately questioned. If we are not receptive to such a consequence then we are in danger of perpetuating the 'tyranny of the expert' which has been so instrumental in the oppression of women. But if we can accommodate this then we are helping to empower our students and extending the boundaries of our own experiential knowledge. The risk is that we will compromise our professional status within the mainstream, but to teach Women's Studies is a radical, and risky, vocation.

Note

1   But, for one important exception to this neglect, see Thompson and Wilcox, 1989.

References

DE WOLFE, PATRICIA (1980) 'Women's Studies: The Contradictions for Students', in SPENDER, DALE and SARAH, ELIZABETH (Eds) *Learing to Lose: Sexism in Education*, London, The Women's Press.
HIGGINBOTHAM, EVELYN BROOKS (1989) 'Beyond the Sound of Silence: Afro-American Women's History', in *Gender and History*, i.
KLEIN, RENATE DUELLI (1983) 'How to do what we want to do: Thoughts about Feminist Methodology', in BOWLES, GLORIA and KLEIN, RENATE DUELLI (Eds) *Theories of Women's Studies*, London, Routledge and Kegan Paul.
THOMPSON, ANNE and WILCOX, HELEN (Eds) (1989) *Teaching Women: Feminism and English Studies*, Manchester, Manchester University Press.

Chapter 4

'Thinking of things in themselves': Theory, Experience, Women's Studies[1]

Maggie Humm

It is very clear that current Thatcherism is producing a great deal of surplus value in the form of academic texts which define and redefine theory and some exchange value in the courses machine which recuperates Samizdat dissidents and turns them into marketable men. Between these two poles the representation of women's experience is short-circuited. Gayatri Spivak calls academics the 'disc jockeys' of an advanced capitalist technocracy (Spivak, 1987). It is not surprising that the broadcasting of feminism by traditional 'disc jockeys' acknowledges the sexism of curricular content but refuses any parallel reorganization of pedagogic or institutional frames.

Transforming institutional structures with the insights of feminism is a particularly difficult task at this moment. Cuts in budgets, staff redundancies and the marketing of higher education courses as cost-effective units constitute a crisis scenario that imperils progressive change. To avoid the abstraction of gender studies or the conservatism of integration, Women's Studies has always had a strong urge to praise marginality for the critical stance it proves.[2] Yet this creates a paradox for teachers trying to fight the *institutional* marginalization of women's experience.

The key issue for me in Women's Studies is the relation of feminist teaching (and what that would be) to women's experience, minority representation and women's social needs such as confidence gaining.

The issue is shot through with tensions:

- The *rigid* politics of the academy.

- What role personal experience can play in the classroom, and in assessment.

- The difficult work of showing how theory can give support to women's experiences.

The idea that women students in Women's Studies can enjoy the authority of their own experience is not new. But the placing of experience into a non-libertarian institution with formal assessment reduces student authority and is self (and feminist) defeating.

This is the central dilemma for any educator trying to produce a genuinely democratic pedagogy in a restrictive institutional and political context. What kinds of enquiries illuminate this educational firmament? From the early 1970s the development of a feminist sociology of education has given us a cutting edge against the patriarchal power relations which are our classroom and institutional structures. Anne Marie Wolpe in *Feminism and Materialism* argues that where the focus of attention is on the individual in the educational system, rather than on the complex of structures which give rise to the experiences of individuals, such a focus lacks explanatory power (Wolpe, 1978). We need, in other words, to have a theory of education which recognizes patriarchal relationships as a central organizing principle in the processes of educational reproduction as well as within the labour process of an institution itself. For example, Jenny Shaw, among others, has shown that the social advantages of mixed schooling (and these are, in any case, only advantages in learning gender-appropriate behaviour) are far outweighed by the academic disadvantages for girls (Shaw, 1976). Eileen Byrne in *Women and Education* revealed that mixed schools actually reduced the chances of women teachers holding senior and powerful positions (Byrne, 1978). Feminist research has enabled us to see that, at all levels, education merely preaches a philosophy of change for the individual while maintaining a highly prescriptive, exam-conscious and sometimes sexist, ethnocentric and homophobic structure.[3]

State education is also based on a systematizing impulse of language control. In schools, the marginalization of genuine bilingual education, and the tensions throughout education between non-standard and standard 'dialects', all work to reinforce institutionalization and to minimalize ethnic and experiential linguistic diversity. Many basic questions remain to be asked before we can begin to construct a coherent argument about gender and communication. We need to know much more about how communicative relations provide a basis for gender definitions, in particular contexts. (The context I am using is therefore deliberately specific to my institution.)

The precise nature of these institutional restrictions and the structure and logic of British higher education is explicit in any institution's language, pedagogy and assessment procedures. For example, typical Polytechnic modes of address read:

- Is the applicant's attendance at this course relevant to *his* work in your department?

- Is it in *his* own personal interest to attend?

- Is *he* the member of your staff most likely to derive the greatest benefit from it?

Gender inequalities characterize the institutional structure of my Polytechnic, as of any other, as well as its discourse. At present, the distribution

Table 1   *Gender distribution of management posts, Polytechnic of East London*

Post	M	F
Rector	1	
Deputy Rector Academic	1	
Deputy Rector Validation	1	
Deputy Rector Policy	1	
Heads of Department	24	2

of management posts between male and female staff members is as shown in table 1.[4]

Women are very under-represented within the domains of governance and authority. Added to this there is often a total absence of women altogether in many subject areas, for example engineering, land surveying and technology. Replicating social categories, educationists operate a sexual division of labour and a discursive justification for their power operations in pedagogic practices.

Put more simply, an education system controls its students through a pedagogy whose 'content' is completely arbitrary and whose power is dependent on a glorious discursivity. So that even if women's experience is voiced in every syllabus, the plot of education would remain tightly scripted.

Women in education, like women in fiction, often lose their identity when assessment becomes the closure for women students that marriage in fiction is so often for women heroines. The working over of personal experience has little place in dissertations and examinations. The tendency of bourgeois language to formalism and abstraction has often been described (see Bernstein, 1977). It also might be described as a masculine mode of address. Dissertational rhetoric authorizes identification with the subject of the topic, not with the subject of the writer. While it would be wrong to draw too firm a distinction between 'abstract' and 'functional' knowledge, everyday expressions and the experiential do give way to an abstract phraseology. Gender discrimination is inevitable in assessment procedures because assessment is the way in which institutions control student subjectivity to give students accredited social status.

Examiners' reports constitute exemplary documents for anyone seeking the criteria by which higher education selects those it considers worthy of perpetuating the tradition. They provide a frame of reference for judging how sexism is institutionalized and how gender selection is hidden under the guise of technical selection.

These are typical comments of my institution's examiners:

> The validation and monitoring of students' studies seems to go too far in accepting students' own inexperienced view of what their educational needs are ... We would be very worried if this principle

reflects the view that whatever is *worthy* is in some way (e.g. skills, products, personal development), ipso facto, Diploma worthy. Clearly this is a mistaken view ... More explicit attention should be paid to the logical and practical procedures involved in task achievement ... Students sometimes have no experience of systematically and properly testing and abandoning false hypotheses, or progressively and systematically reformulating deficient hypotheses.

These criteria of value and formal rhetoric seem totally at odds with one applicant I interviewed recently who hoped that the diploma would help her to be more creative. Examiners' reports are full of military terms ('logistics'), vague morality ('worthy'), and prefer a legal-juridical discourse which seeks 'evidence' to 'identify' problems. But it is not so much what examiners say as what they do not. The examiners are gendered, they come from different disciplines and different institutions but they speak with one voice. They are 'we'. By establishing case-law they try to avoid the plurality of education and the gender of its students. Examiners' reports are like Woolf's characterization of patriarchy as the anonymous 'voice imprinting on the faces of the clerks ... something of its own inexorable gravity, as they listened, deciphered, wrote down' (Woolf, 1922, p. 168).

The category of gender is absent. Yet examiners' reports, unlike novels, are not fiction. Reports influence teaching and admissions. Teachers do not only reject or choose students on the basis of them; they interpret their teaching in examiners' terms: worse still, they actually perceive what happens in the course in the 'mythic' terms that examiners provide. An education that is to respond to the needs of women must make available the values of academic work but also must, quite deliberately, put these values at risk in the context of feminism.

If the equality of women students and women teachers in Women's Studies can depart some way from this prescriptive model we still face a further complication. The very nurturing, consciousness-raising, personal focus of the Women's Studies classroom paradoxically also may make women's experience open to abuse.[5] Assessment takes place within the context of long-term intimate relationships with students with whom we are, even if we hide it well from them, in a position of power. Women students tell women teachers the innermost secrets of their lives at the drop of a hat. So, in this situation, equality and intimacy have social consequences for women's lives and their subsequent careers. The teaching relationship is an artificial relationship, initiated and maintained for a particular purpose within a particular framework. Teachers are, in the main, from powerful groups: the educated, middle-class and white. Simply being a feminist teaching Women's Studies does not enable us easily to eradicate these relationships of power and subordination.

Yet Women's Studies has a particular ethic. This ethic values the moral equality of those who seek education and those who teach. Implicit in this ethic is a further construct that each of us is the first witness, as Catharine Stimpson says, to our experience (Stimpson, 1985). The elasticity of this ethic is at odds with the master narratives of education. The first and foremost contradiction concerns the role of me as a teacher. I ought to be a co-researcher, trying to consider what knowledge is implied by and would clarify students' project work. But I inhabit power. I am a permanent (I hope) member of the institution and the students are more transitory. Eliminating my classroom authority just disguises the power of the institution.

As Bourdieu has told us, institutions work by indirect rules, for example, it is a major issue to get students to question institutional ideas like the one that education needs to be evolutionary. Yet those of us who teach on Access to Higher Education courses as well as to postgraduate MAs know that the quantum leap in knowledge is probably much greater in Access courses and this makes the whole idea of hierarchies and levels very suspect. But I also have power in terms of access to a 'certified' body of feminist knowledge. We need, therefore, to be particularly clear that the complexity of women's experience as a source of analysis is not merely white, heterosexual women's experience nor is regarded as a less sophisticated category than feminist theory. In my analysis, any pedagogic transformations in Women's Studies have first to be understood as belonging to these stubborn structures of invisible power. The very activity of trying to eradicate power serves to remind us how intransigent power is. For Virginia Woolf, in *A Room of One's Own*, a woman's recognition of social power involved a sudden moment of 'consciousness ... when from being the natural inheritor of civilization, she becomes on the contrary, outside of it, alien and critical' (Woolf, 1929, p. 101). How does one adopt the goal of all Women's Studies: to transform education and be an agent for social change while remaining 'alien and critical'? Crudely, the weight of women as statistical numbers has effect because numerical shifts *do* transform social interaction. Second, Women's Studies gives women a hugely increased opportunity to be able to demonstrate their competence. The grand gesture, of course, must be one which enables outward and inner experience to transform both pedagogy and institutional structures.

Fundamental to feminism is the premise that women are not represented in codified knowledge, and the description and the analysis of women's experience is the most significant contribution made by second-wave feminism. The specific issue in this is an attack on the polarized categories of subjective/objective as feminist writers refuse to accept these as discrete categories and make a fresh and feminist encoding of experience. For example, psychoanalysts like Jean Baker Miller and anthropologists like Shirley Ardener are validating the experience of what Ardener calls 'muted groups' as an alternative to Baconian objectivity (see Ardener, 1978, and Miller, 1976).

The experience of women outside the West comes into our classrooms directly from students who are immigrants or who are daughters or granddaughters of immigrant women. This directly challenges the ethnocentricity of traditional sources of evaluation when family histories may be, very often, our *only* source of information given the paucity of Asian and Black studies material in most libraries. Such information demands new methodological approaches as yet under-researched in Britain: alternative models of women's collective action, alternative technologies, alternative models of parenting, childcare and sexuality. For example, most women in PEL's Women's Studies are first-generation students, disparate demographically (18 to 50) and ethnically (Hindu, Bengali, Jamaican, Sri Lankan and white).

Almost all the students are active community women, if not yet actively student women. For example they are experts in the work of church groups, playgroups and nurseries. At the same time they are experts in the sociology of single parenthood, battered wives, and homeless women. In other words, they do not lack knowledge and skills since they can outmanoeuvre benefit and housing offices but they may be suspicious of handed-down explanations of their lives.

For example, as battered wives they know that they do not 'seek out' a battering partner. On the other hand their lack of formal education skills has robbed them of some confidence in their explanatory ability and they need and want to acquire knowledge to demystify the expertise of professionals and become professionals themselves.

It was particularly important for me to find a form of learning which could speak across barriers of age and race. And it was particularly important for the students to be able to assess the value of their experience.

Central to the curriculum, in other words, had to be the view that working-class, Asian, black and lesbian women were not 'deficient' but have developed and distinctive experiences. Using the work of theory, feminist and other, I tried to link the analytic tools of feminism with students' experience, so that they are helped to think critically about their conditions, to redefine their analyses and find solutions.

Devising and instituting a three-year undergraduate programme in Women's Studies to count as one third of a modular degree (now a full degree) was a hard-won event. But what turned out to be more radical for us was the introduction of self-chosen and self-assessed student projects — the presentation.

I start the first class with an apparently very general question: what was your mother doing at this moment in her life, and your grandmother? We share a piece from Tillie Olsen. The issues raised in this first class stay with us throughout the course.

Yet even with what Helen Roberts has called a 'strong' feminism,[6] feminist teaching carries another burden: the problem of how to give students confidence that they are capable of generating their own solutions to life issues. For example, black women students often for the first time spoke comfortably about the connections of race and gender. White women's narrow definitions of feminism were assaulted by the recognition of race. But shaping the content of a Women's Studies course so that it will not be essentially a White Women's Studies course does not prevent the marginalization of black theory nor of experience.

A true transformation of the curriculum requires a fundamental re-evaluation of central concepts and practices. The question we should begin by asking is: What would Women's Studies look like if those typically excluded were not just added but defined as the norm? While this can create distortions of its own, the question and its possible answers can move us more steadily to a curriculum which is genuinely experiential.

There are two writers who describe critical practices which can produce, I feel, a genuinely democratic pedagogy: Audre Lorde and Bakhtin. Lorde argues that learning must take shape from differences (see Lorde, 1984). Lorde's and Bakhtin's theories are complex. In this summary I will simply focus on the concepts that are resonant for feminist teaching.

The project of Lorde's and Bakhtin's writing is particularly relevant to my discussion because it is to transform individual experience through the collective relationship between self and other and between inner and outer. Hard on that assertion is the idea, in Audre Lorde, that black women's contribution must not be additive but part of discussions about any intellectual issue, because 'different' is not simply personal but a shared understanding of social realities. *Sister Outsider*, Lorde's essays dating from 1976 to the present, raise a number of questions about the relation of ethnicity to the psyche in the context of social repression. For example, in 'Poetry is not a Luxury', Lorde insists that we must combine an ancient non-European power of feeling with the European concept that ideas do free us from repression. All of Lorde's essays, particularly 'The Uses of the Erotic', are about the power of what she specifically calls 'deepest non-rational knowledge', or what we could call the experiential. The significance of Lorde's appeal for my argument here is that Lorde claims that this knowledge is likely to be available only in connection between people of difference. The formation of an ethnic identity, by and within the symbolic, has to be in dialogue with an understanding of oneself both as the subject as well as the object of experience. Lorde is very clear that racism depends on privileging experience but by understanding the self to be statements of difference spoken in dialogue Lorde avoids essentialism.

In these statements there is a powerful message for feminist teachers. But at first I used Lorde's theory, interspersed with student work, as if it was something we could work to deconstruct as text. Eventually I realized that much of what I said simply baffled women students because I was asking them to respond to concepts for which they had no frame of reference. According to Lorde 'survival is not an academic skill'; I took this to mean that we cannot teach people what they are not likely to need to experience but I also wanted to avoid a polarization between feminist theory and feminist experience.

I came along this same line to a model for feminist pedagogy in Bakhtin. For Bakhtin, language is democratic, always changing and powerfully regenerative because it is always in dialogue with the unknown, the foreign, the other. But the study of language as an institutionalized formal rhetoric cannot, Bakhtin claims, understand the importance of the role played by foreign words. In *Marxism and the Philosophy of Language*, he said:

On the contrary Indo-European studies have fashioned categories of understanding for the history of language of a kind that preclude

proper evaluation of the role of the alien word. Meanwhile, that role,
to all appearances is enormous ... (Bakhtin, 1973, pp. 75–76)

Language flourishes in ethnic volatility, not in an excess of categoriza-
tion. The chief devices which Bakhtin uses to understand this restless business are 'dialogic' devices and 'extopy' — concepts which help unpack the
self/other difference. Dialogism is not simply the 'taking into account' of the
opinions of others, in other words, liberalism. In 'Discourse in the Novel'
Bakhtin describes a fierce battle in which the foreign word actively contests
the political conservatism of culture or what we might call ethnocentricity.
'Extopy' is active understanding and watchful listening in which knowledge
takes the form of a dialogue where a 'thou' is equal to an 'I' yet appreciated as
different from it.

The student presentation in Women's Studies offers the synthesizing
place for many of these ideas. My pedagogic strategy is to encourage students
not only to include autobiography along with analysis but also to include
dialogue with others in the different contexts of the classroom and the social
context of their research. The seminar provides a framework where analysis,
experience and theory are projected beyond the bounds of individualized
research. 'Watchful listening' is akin to consciousness-raising where empathy
for a white, black, or lesbian experience is crucially preparative but can only
be a transitory role. 'Active understanding' focuses our attention on the
form as well as on the content of each presentation. For example, I ask
students to consider in their presentations work that will directly speak to
(interpellate) students in the group rather than simply give a narrative
account of a researched area like Ageing and Health. Difference is represented
in each presentation when a student changes her analysis, in recognition of
the perspective of other students in the group, not, as traditionally, by
responding to what she thinks I, as a teacher, am likely to assess. Bakhtin's
concept of the moment of dialogue when history, understanding and activity
are the social reality of language calls our attention to the primacy of the
classroom.

For example, students do not hand in presentation materials immediately
because the completion of an individual analysis is dependent on social and
intellectual interaction with the seminar contributions of other students. This
is very opposed to how institutions normally define 'originality'. Radically,
Bakhtin suggests that dialogical forms flourish in moments of transition — in
those times between a dead conservatism and a new social structure. This is a
very optimistic note for students and for feminist pedagogy. The relevance of
Bakhtin for feminism then lies in his recognition of the unequal distribution
of power across language and the need for oppositional tactics. Bakhtin talks
of languages as overpopulated with the intentions of others. The unskilled
speaker or listener, and here Bakhtin describes the Russian peasant, cannot
yet regard one language through the eyes of another.

The point of the student presentation is to enable students to see themselves through other languages. For example, students can try for alternative
endings or solutions in the style of other women in the group. Bakhtin's

theory that language is 'hcteroglot' from top to bottom strengthens our energy to be part of each other's lives — an energy arising in my class's experience from the first seminar which described our mothers' and our grandmothers' lives.

These ideas clearly raise the related issue of the authority of experience and the authority of assessment. Self and peer assessment challenges students to question institutional hegemony but it poses additional problems.

The first problem is increasing students' interest in history, their historical competence, and their ability to move from the context of the contemporary. A second problem is persuading students that the presentation is genuinely more worthwhile than the role or 'banking' method of education they had expected. In their curriculum study for the Mellon Institute, Frances Maher and Kathleen Dunn call this expectation 'dualism', which is when students tend to be impatient with discussions, seeing them as a roundabout way of discovering what they think the teacher should have told them in the first place. I am often tempted to postpone a presentation in order to cover more factual material (see Maher and Dunn, 1984). Clearly the presentation can successfully initiate the process of students' developing new social relations but presentations are very demanding of student time and inevitably a single parent has much less student time than a younger school leaver.

But the presentations did provide crucial information about non-Eurocentric experiences. For example, Florence, a nurse from Zimbabwe, who was describing the bush atrocities committed by Mugabe's troops, made us conscious of the tension between her 'experiential' knowledge and the equally vivid but theoretical account of militarization in the Third World by Cynthia Enloe which we had shared together. Presentations also avoid the victimization syndrome described by Marcia Westkott as 'we are united first of all in our unfreedom'.[7]

Rather than introducing personal history to create a sense of shared vulnerability we use histories as representing our strengths as social agents. In other words each women is both a social representative and a social construct.[8] A good example of what I mean here was Shebahan's presentation about arranged marriages which used the diary of her grandmother who was married at twelve. It was Shebahan's knowledge as a British social representative, not simply the autobiography, which challenged us to reconsider our knowledge of other marriages. But reflection without action is meaningless. An ex-prisoner 'X' described the sexist stereotyping of prisoners (media photographs of women as 'passively' drugged or as masochists, against men as 'active' roof-top demonstrators) set into a history of women in prisons. 'X''s experience was simultaneously a mode and object of inquiry in the women's support group we set up.

In all Women's Studies giving an oral account is very important. It became clear too that the role of the class as a whole in participating in the presentation of each student was of great importance. Students honed their analytical skills while developing their speaking abilities and listening capacities. As we shared our different experiences we dispelled many myths, stereotypes and assumptions that all of us held in some form or other. The

students also developed a group solidarity which heightened their consciousness to the concerns facing ethnic and older women. One student decided to
come out, another revealed that she was a battered wife. It is probably not an
accident that most of the students became deeply involved in Polytechnic
struggles about the staff redundancies. Presentations benefited from the tensions of political activity.

In other words, presentations are an aspect of what in the sociology of
education is called interactive research methodology. This is not just the
study of women as subjects but women as subjects in study. It immediately
focuses a question of epistemology: how do we come to understand what we
are? The *means* of understanding are often not an explicit part of pedagogic
content except in a merely techno-critical sense. Little of the new scholarship
on women has, as yet, explored classroom practices in theoretical terms.
That is to say, the interrogation of, and application of, theory is often part of
our *public*, professional writing but not such a fundamental part of our
private, teaching experience.

For me, the issue was crystallized in one Women's Studies presentation.
Karen made a psychosocial observation of physical touching behaviour in a
day in the life of her best friend in the group. Karen drew our attention to the
theories of Nancy Henley, spoke autobiographically of her own childhood
and asked us to itemize our perceptions of other body languages in the group
(see Henley, 1971). The session was hugely comic but Karen's contribution
also built a complex conceptualization of women's body experiences, one
that both legitimized our individual perceptions and put them in a larger
explanatory model.

Shan, taken out of school at six to work in the fields, began to tell us of
washing rituals in Guyana; Susan, a West Indian midwife, for the first time
saw the symbolism involved in shaving women in labour; Ilona, a Solidarity
member, told us of Polish family patterns. The problem, then, of 'appropriate' knowledge is more complex than whether or not to teach Nancy Henley.
For these women the class was their first opportunity to examine themselves
as women in patriarchal societies. In the Women's Studies course students
were learning about the ideological contexts which have shaped them as
women. The group was, in effect, enacting the central method of Women's
Studies — the act of translation. We were discovering a common language.
In order to understand each other, for an immigrant from Guyana to talk to a
trained health worker, to a member of Solidarity, and to me, we have to find
a language that is at once complex and simple.

The 'language' was the interweaving of theory, autobiography and peer
experience which we had agreed to share. Students used the topics of
women's bodies to speculate, not only on their own ethnic experience, but
also on what this experience could tell them about the interaction between
different cultural and gender expectations and the formation of identity.
These students were able to locate aspects of each other in the context of a
general characterization 'woman'. In short these Women's Studies students
were able to see, and to like, themselves as women.

My version of feminist teaching of course artificially constructs a sense of a coherent project that is usually a much more eclectic event, term by term. None of us know exactly what gender is or how to gauge its effects. This may be because feminist pedagogy tries to include several contradictory interpretations of education. For example, such pedagogy assumes that education is an instrument for gaining power (which artificially valorizes content as knowledge) *and* that education is part of consciousness-raising. The term 'experience' is problematic. We cannot invoke 'experience' without addition since the ways in which we perceive experience are psychosocially constructed — they are effects, produced by historicized binaries of 'natural' and 'unnatural'. The whole ideological underpinning of our experience cannot be understood with a model of experience as the spontaneous product of a gender identity. Rather, any 'experience' is built from internalized social reality (see Eagleton, 1976). Ideology seeks to convert culture into nature, and the 'natural' is one of its weapons. By such means experience or social reality as a natural fact becomes dangerous unless we recognize that it involved social dominance because of its ambiguities and uses.

I think the account of feminist pedagogy in *Gendered Subjects* edited by Margo Culley and Catherine Portuges is a very good case study of all these issues (see Culley and Portuges, 1985). The title *Gendered Subjects* is in itself very revealing. It immediately indicates that subjectivity is the core of feminist studies while gender has, syntactically speaking, at least, a subsidiary role as the appellation of subjectivity. The book collects accounts by American academics of their classroom techniques. In *Gendered Subjects* 'experience' seems to imply intellectual activity. As the editors say in their introduction, once experience becomes an appropriate subject of intellectual inquiry, the classroom is 'forever changed'. The book contains Adrienne Rich's now classic essay 'Taking women students seriously', and it gives far greater attention to black women students and teachers than is the case in British texts. The editors explicitly confront the kind of classroom challenges I have been analyzing by demanding 'a discussion of authority in the feminist classroom'.

So how evanescent is feminist pedagogy? The force of this American feminism, it seems, is to correct the 'academy's traditional myopia'. While important, that focus is as revealing in its way as the revealing title. The focus suggests that the activity of deconstruction is in itself a thoroughly adequate feminist pedagogy, which entails merely a liberal humanist agenda of evolutionary and individual change.

The historian Robert Bezucha bravely set out, at elite WASP Amherst, to introduce feminist history. Feminist history, he argues, will influence the 'most intellectually ambitious' student. The dialectic of experience and theory is lost in Bezucha's classroom. He celebrates feminist history as a cognitive field, making the work of the discipline substitute for subjectivity to appeal to ambitious developing professionals.

In case we might dismiss this as a typically 'masculine' appropriation let me turn briefly to a woman contributor, Catherine Portuges, one of the editors. Her piece 'The Spectacle of Gender: Cinema and Psyche' confronts similar demands. Teaching film from the double perspective of psychoanalysis and feminism is exacting, she claims, particularly because students have multiple emotional identifications with film. Portuges interrogates identification, or experience, by making students come to understand that acts of interpretation are profoundly subjective. The interesting aspect of this account, I think, is how, even in a feminist agenda, students are to deny their social subjectivities and come to see the work of deconstruction, of film interpretation, as their own subjectivity — their new identity. Neither does *Gendered Subjects*, with its accounts of warm and sustaining relationships, treat the structural locations of gendered experience.

This is perhaps why Alice Jardine's book *Gynesis* offers a way out (see Jardine, 1985). What Jardine is analyzing is this breakdown in master narratives. The breakdown has happened in the explanations offered in higher education in relation to postmodernism, or as she calls it denaturalization, that is the proof provided by Derrida, Foucault *et al.* that ideology is based on naturalized categories. This is not new. Over the past century there has been a series of crises in the narratives invented by men — like a succession of kings. What is specific to feminism, and what interests me, is that Jardine points out that this new historicity has been accompanied by a huge increase both in theoretical and in fictional writing by women about women.

Jardine's account is particularly helpful in looking at life histories, because it is part of what Walter Benjamin called a radical re-evaluation of the relation between direct, lived experience and retrospective privileged experience (see Benjamin, 1969).

Feminism, as we know, is rooted in the belief that women's experience is different from men's and is consequently delegitimized, but the bonus of postmodernism for feminism is that postmodernism throws into doubt the enlightenment belief that there is in any case a stable coherent self. Theory can be obscure and ungraceful as reportage, but I found that my placing of educational processes within the field of the literary has helped me to challenge scientism. The technocratic Polytechnic model of education only calculates the unstable and necessarily impermanent collectivities of women in parentheses. The harvest of eclectic theories gathered here from the desires of temporal women can never be stored in some fixed entity, as a permanent education policy. But theory does enable students to reconsider their previously taken-for-granted beliefs and also deepens and increases the range of questions they ask. In abandoning the perhaps illusory neutrality of the teacher, I came myself to experience a new confidence and authority alongside the experience of my students. Clearly feminist knowledge has to be seen as neither an exterior product to be ingested as in 'dualism', nor as a set of personal opinions as in liberalism, but as an evolving construct, created by the self through the analysis of the complex and changing reality of others.

Notes

1 See Woolf (1929).
2 For example, Marcia Westkott in her essay 'Women's Studies as a Strategy for Change' argues that we must move beyond the male definitions and dichotomies

that falsify our experience, without examining the specifics of masculine education which (like women's education) is shaped by particular educational contexts and their relationship to reproduction.

3 For example, feminist scholars call for a pedagogy which will acknowledge the multiple contexts within which knowledge is produced. In 'Memoirs of an Onto-logical Exile', Jill Vickers has identified five feminist rebellions against malestream methods. The first rebellion identified by Vickers is the rebellion against decon-textualization. For example, feminists teach in 'social' areas like rape or domestic violence. Vickers next identifies the rebellion to restore agency. This, of course, is related to contextualization and has been one of the most empowering features of feminist research. One example is feminist peace research in the nuclear industry. The third rebellion is against reversal, that is recognizing practices for what they are, for example, that infantile seduction theories are ideological absolutions of men's moral responsibility. This analyzes practices in terms of who benefits and to what end those practices serve. The fourth rebellion is against objectivity, that is to recognize that the inter-subjective nature of scientific enquiry and the values of the scientist must be part of the knowledge creation process. Vickers's last rebel-lion is against linearity and for epistemological pluralism (see Vickers, 1983).

4 These figures are taken from Williams *et al.* (1989).

5 Janet Finch in 'It's great to have someone to talk to' pinpoints this issue very clearly in the social sciences. Finch argues that women are more susceptible to exploitation when interviewed by other women. Describing her interviews with clergy wives and mothers involved in playgroups, Finch makes three main points. Women give more information to other women because they are women; this makes women interviewees open to exploitation, and this places a particular responsibility on women researchers to 'take the side of' their research population and guard against the abuse of research findings (see Finch, 1984).

6 Helen Roberts in *Social Researching* has given two names to possible forms of the implementation of feminism at least within the social sciences. She calls one 'weak', the other 'strong'. The 'weak' programme takes gender seriously, that is we should not, Roberts suggests, support studies about 'white-collar workers' which exclude women. A 'strong' programme is based on the premise that feminist research actually provides a better sociology (see Roberts, 1984).

7 See note 2.

8 Marie Mies draws this concept from her work in Cologne, where feminist sociologists fought for a shelter for battered women and, together with the women who came for help, started a research project. Its aim was not simply to document individual life histories but to record a collective experience, leading to theories and strategies for change by sharing life histories to relieve women from guilt. Experience was validated in an interesting way by women acting as mirrors of each other, which led Mies into new social methods (see Mies, 1983).

References

ARDENER, S. (Ed.) (1978) *Defining Females*, London, Croom Helm.

BAKHTIN, M. (1973) *Marxism and the Philosophy of Language*, New York, Seminar Press.

BAKHTIN, M. (1981) *The Dialogic Imagination*, Austin, Texas, University of Texas Press.

BENJAMIN, W. (1969) *Illuminations*, Ed. H. ARENDT, New York, Stocken.

BERNSTEIN, B. (1977) *Class, Codes and Control*, Vol. 3, London, Routledge & Kegan Paul.

BOURDIEU, P. and PASSERON, J.C. (1977) *Reproduction in Education, Society and Culture*, London, Sage.

BYRNE, E. (1978) *Women and Education*, London, Tavistock.

CULLEY, M. and PORTUGES, C. (Eds) (1985) *Gendered Subjects*, London, Routledge and Kegan Paul.

EAGLETON, T. (1976) *Criticism and Ideology*, London, New Left Books.

FINCH, J. (1984) 'It's great to have someone to talk to: the ethics and politics of interviewing women', in ROBERTS, H. (Ed.) *Social Researching*, London, Routledge and Kegan Paul.

FREIRE, P. (1970) *Pedagogy of the Oppressed*, New York, Seabury Press.

HENLEY, N.M. (1971) *Body Politics: Power, Sex and Non-Verbal Communication*, Englewood, CA, Prentice Hall.

JARDINE, A. (1985) *Gynesis*, Ithica and London, Cornell University Press.

LORDE, A. (1984) *Sister Outsider*, Trumansberg, New York, The Crossing Press.

MAHER, F. and DUNN, K. (1984) 'The Practice of Feminist Teaching', Wellesley Working Paper, N144, Wellesley.

MIES, M. (1983) 'Towards a Methodology for Feminist Research', in BOWLES, G. and KLEIN, R.D. (Eds), *Theories of Women's Studies*, London, Routledge and Kegan Paul.

MILLER, J.B. (1976) *Toward a New Psychology of Women*, Palo Alto, CA, Stanford University Press.

ROBERTS, H. (1984) *Social Researching*, London, Routledge and Kegan Paul.

SHAW, J. (1976) 'Finishing School: Some implications of sex segregated education', in BARKER, D.L. and ALLEN, S. (Eds) *Sexual Divisions and Society*, London, Tavistock.

SPIVAK, G. (1987) *In Other Worlds*, London, Methuen.

STIMPSON, C.R. (1985) 'Our "Wild patience": Our Energetic Deeds, Our Energising Future', Wellesley Working Paper, N158, Wellesley.

VICKERS, J.McC. (1983) 'Memoirs of an Ontological Exile', in MILES, A. and FINN, G. (Eds) *Feminism in Canada*, Montreal, Black Rose Press.

WESTKOTT, M. (1983) 'Women's Studies as a strategy for change: between criticism and vision', in BOWLES, G. and KLEIN, R.D. (Eds) *Theories of Women's Studies*, London, Routledge and Kegan Paul.

WILLIAMS, J., COCKING, J. and DAVIES, L. (1989) *Words or Deeds: A Review of Equal Opportunity Policies in Higher Education*, London, Commission for Racial Equality.

WOLPE, A.M. (1978) *Feminism and Materialism*, London, Routledge and Kegan Paul.

WOOLF, V. (1922) *Jacob's Room*, London, Hogarth Press.

WOOLF, V. (1929) *A Room of One's Own*, London, Hogarth Press.

Section II

Women's Studies and the Feminist Movement

Introduction

Women's Studies has always been rooted in women's lives and in the women's movement. The questioning of the social and political position of women in contemporary society has thrown up the issues which are the central concerns of Women's Studies. The specialized institutions of education provide a space for the fuller exploration of these questions but with limitations, given the male-dominated nature of many of these institutions. The relationship of Women's Studies and the feminist movement is thus both essential and fruitful, while tension-ridden as well. The papers in this section explore these dilemmas.

Mary Evans critically examines the development of gender studies alongside and as an alternative to Women's Studies. She asks whether this change represents the taming of the radicalism of Women's Studies. Is this a compromise with the academy in which feminists capitulate to pressure from the mainstream to dilute their commitment to radical analysis? Does gender studies grow at the expense of Women's Studies?

Renate Klein argues that Women's Studies came into being as the education arm of the Women's Liberation Movement. It was a development to create knowledge of use to women. Women's Studies has become institutionalized in various ways which have implications for the kind of knowledge that it produces. She argues that diversity should not be used to undermine our solidarity.

Sue Lees argues that feminists need to move into the centre in order to obtain the resources of the mainstream academies to produce better knowledge. The movement out of the margins into the centre is not easy, however, and we will only achieve this through struggle.

Jalna Hanmer argues that Women's Studies is transformative of women's lives — it is a transitional programme. While experience is a key element in Women's Studies we should not reject theory but rather develop it. It is the dominant, male-centred, epistemology which is partial, not that created by feminists.

Chapter 5

The Problem of Gender for Women's Studies

Mary Evans

Any discussion about Women's Studies can begin with the confident assertion that teaching in the area has expanded rapidly in the last ten years. This bold statement then has to be qualified by two points: first, that much of this new learning is in higher and further education and in 'liberal' academic subjects in the social sciences and the humanities; second, it has to be said — in large, capital letters — that academic feminism exists because of the resurgence of Western feminism in the 1960s and the efforts of women to claim for themselves a place in the academy. The women who made this claim, which was almost universally resisted by the relevant institutions, were largely white and middle-class. I shall return to the implications of this later.

But now women are 'on' the academic agenda in a way that they were not ten or twenty years ago. However, now that women have, in a sense, arrived as part of the academic consciousness of the male academy the problem arises of where Women's Studies might go next, and in particular what might happen to that once subversive and radical category of 'women'. The women's movement has come a long way from the days when merely stating the specificity of the female condition constituted a solidaristic and a confrontational act; in other contexts the issues of race and ethnicity have come to challenge the once universal perception and construction of 'women'. In the academy, as much as in the politics of feminism, questions have been asked about the validity of studying a single sex, when every theoretically sophisticated person knows that we are all constructed out of a number of situations/discourses/circumstances. Increasingly, looking back at, or rereading, the great inspirational feminist texts of the 1970s becomes an exercise in reading, sometimes with amazement, works that confidently assume a world of difference between women and men. I would also argue that if we look a little further back — say to 1955 or 1965 — then we would see a world in which women were not just different, they were largely invisible to most academics. Find the woman in British studies of social stratification in the 1960s would be a revealing, if brief, thesis topic.

Nevertheless, today we have, in feminist journals and publications, a sophisticated understanding of what constitutes gender identity and gender subjectivity. Indeed, the word 'gender' increasingly becomes used in the context of work about women or sexuality; the titles of conferences or seminars refer to the issue of 'gender' and a particular context. 'Women', a term in some disarray and some disharmony, appears to have become less acceptable and, in a sense, more controversial. My concern here, therefore, is to explore some of the difficulties in moving away from women to gender. My contention is that women still contribute as much a subject for study as they ever did, and that the identity of women is not the matter of negotiation and personal choice that some enthusiasts of deconstruction insist. Just to cite one piece of what seems to me to be telling evidence: however much individual women may be endlessly constructing or negotiating their personal identity, they are still paid about three-quarters of the wages of men and are still largely excluded from political power. Even if we are not all anxious to take part in parliamentary politics, it is important to remember that political power also includes local, as much as national, representation.

This view of the world may not, of course, appeal to a poststructuralist, postmodernist perception of the world in which some of the lure of the Thatcherite free market seems to have invaded the academy. Voices are raised, inside and outside feminism, which suggest that Women's Studies is no longer necessary, that the category of 'women' is no longer viable and that the apparent maintenance of a concept of sexual division is no longer acceptable. The appeal of theories of a fractured, negotiated, endlessly changing urban consciousness is apparently very considerable; not least because these theories are better able to integrate or to concede differences of race and nationality between women. Unfortunately, the world is not yet postcapitalist (even if in the West aspects of its process, although not its relations, of production have changed), post-racist or post-imperialist. It is because of the continuing existence of material differences and inequalities between women and men within this social context that I would argue for the maintenance of Women's Studies and the use of the category of women. My view about the unchanged structure of the Western world is probably now apparent; in the following pages I would like to elaborate exactly how I think it is a disservice to women to allow the concept of the difference between the sexes to lose its assumption, often tacitly made, of *unequal* difference.

The first claim I would make for the continuing usefulness of the term 'Women's Studies' is that it allows women a space in the academy (and I use the term here to cover all educational sectors, not simply the universities). A space for women in schools (particularly in secondary education) has become an established aim of feminist thinking in education; this 'space' may take the form of a separate institution, or it may take the form of certain kinds of special provision. Whatever its form, what is acknowledged is that girls do better in education if there is some institutional validation of their particular, special needs, needs which tend to disappear in the apparently neutral, but often implicitly male, dominant curriculum. The dominant needs and values of the curriculum are those which relate to men's lives, lives which are premised on the taken-for-granted assumptions that — for example — paid work is uninterrupted by domestic responsibilities. The apparent neutrality of the curriculum can obscure the very real understanding that pupils often have of their own future careers and plans; it is not necessarily the case that the recognition of girls' different 'life scripts' involves a negative assessment of female goals. It may well be the case that girls can more fully develop a sense of their own interests if they are able to do so in their own space and away from constant evaluation and assessment alongside their male contemporaries.

What happens in the school playground, the secondary or further education common room, is not unlike what happens when women and men meet on terms of apparent equality in higher education. Any glance at a primary school playground in Britain will show boys playing football in the large centre space and girls around the edge playing less expansive games or talking to each other. In secondary and further education common rooms the boys/young men occupy the physical space with equal assurance. In higher education the pipe and the conversations about sport are more subtle, if equally omnipresent, reminders of just which sex is in the majority. Yet uncomfortable as this sex-based use of public space can be for women, what is more uncomfortable is the use that men make of academic space. To illustrate this, I want to cite one example, that seems to me to demonstrate how men can assume their rights to the intellectual domination of the world. The case is taken from a discussion in the fascinating conference papers edited by Alice Jardine and Paul Smith called *Men in Feminism*. In this volume there is an exchange between the literary critics Elaine Showalter and Terry Eagleton; Elaine Showalter initiated a dialogue about male feminist writing and Terry Eagleton was asked to comment. He did so by providing a semi-autobiographical account of the British Labour Party. Since Elaine Showalter had used the example of the film *Tootsie* in her remarks, Terry Eagleton may have been making a point of some subtlety about political cross-dressing in the British Labour Party. But this interpretation, favourable as it may be to the intelligence of a prominent critic, still leaves unresolved the issue of a demonstrated attitude — an attitude which suggests that women's remarks are so irrelevant and banal that they are not worth what Jane Austen once called 'rational opposition'. Eagleton, on the evidence of the printed word, did not appear to address *any* of Showalter's substantive points. The point here is not about one individual, but about the habits and assumptions that men assume. The behaviour that they learn is not necessarily anti-women; particularly for middle-class men, the endless competitive rituals of grammar and public school, and later higher education, are about competing against other men. The rewards of success in a labour market are such that they encourage all men to learn patterns of behaviour designed to maximize chances of promotion and elevation in professional hierarchies.

Once learned, these habits are difficult to overcome. But what I would emphasize is, first, that there is a material reason for learning this behaviour, and second, that feminists need to be aware (not to say suspicious) of the pervasive, and seductive, appeal of maximizing individual success. It is quite clear that the interests of Western capitalism would be best served by the universal integration and acceptance of the success ethic. It is equally clear that for some women the rewards of hierarchical success are extremely powerful; when President Richard Nixon remarked that he was 'in power' he revealed the stark reality of the political system of the United States. Since he knew (something) about the formal manners of politics he hastily corrected himself and remarked that he meant to say that he was 'in office'. Unfortunately, the correction was too late; we had all been told quite explicitly what his particular job was about. So it is with women, and men, in far less elevated positions: power does exercise appeal and for feminists there exist complex issues to be discussed and negotiated between being effective and becoming seduced by power. This discussion, it seems to me, is best served if there exists institutional space for women, and a recognition that relationships outside that space have to be approached with some circumspection. And so it is with the conversion of Women's Studies into gender studies, and the greater general integration of Women's Studies into the curriculum of further and higher education.

It appears, on the face of it, that there is a lot to be said for the expansion of further missionary activity into the academic curriculum. It is not as if sexism and/or sexist understanding had disappeared from the world of learning. There is still, as magistrates are fond of remarking about crime, a lot of it about. But two problems present themselves in the early 1990s that were not there ten or fifteen years ago. The first is that Women's Studies — as already mentioned — is under pressure in some quarters to become gender studies. The second is that the institutional situation of higher and further education in Britain has changed; the amount of liberal, 'free' space in the academy (never that substantial) has become even more restricted as a direct result of government policies on education. In this context, false assumptions are made about the kind of accommodation that 'we' have to make with the New Economic Reality. That accommodation assumes that people will learn the subjects that will guarantee them employment and — even more pernicious — that the curriculum will be organized to educate people in what is agreed as 'relevant'. What is presently relevant is the agenda set by the government of economic individualism. It is all too easy within this assumptive world — in which the constraints and imperatives are very considerable — to accept the interests of women and men as similar and agree that women can be considered as non-sexed social actors. Once we begin to think that 'we all have to make a living' and act as if that were the single premise on which social life is organized then it becomes a short step to the uncritical acceptance of the idea that we are all bound by the same values and the same perceptions. Maintaining a clear sense of sexual differentiation in this context seems to me to be immensely valuable; if stated explicitly it maintains a testimony to relationships other than those of the economic market-place and it emphasizes (hopefully over and over again) the social fact of sexual inequality.

It is probably apparent by now that I wish to see Women's Studies remain as that, a study of women and identified as such. Nevertheless, it is important here to consider some of the problems that have emerged about Women's Studies in the last few years. The first issue that I think many of us have become aware of is the complexity of the relationships that have made us distinct individuals. We have fathers, often sons, brothers and male partners, and from these male people we receive, in various degrees, affirmation and support. The history of feminism is littered with examples of women who identified with their fathers, and who in doing so were better able to further the interests of women. The problem with this identification with men is that the very strengths that men often possess are acquired at a cost to women. Women then became involved in a complex situation of defining their acquired strength and competence in ways that do not reproduce the worst excesses of social and sexual privilege.

A second issue — of equal self-consciousness — that has emerged in recent years is that of the nature and construction of female strength. In a poem appropriately labelled 'Heroines', Adrienne Rich puts the question vividly:

> How can I fail to love
>   your clarity and fury
> How can I give you
>   all your due
>   take courage from your courage
> honor your exact
>   legacy as it is
> recognising
>   as well
>   that it is not enough? (Rich, 1981, p. 36)

Valour, courage, fortitude and determination are here all praised in women. But they are also questioned; questioned because a justifiable suspicion has emerged, in feminism as elsewhere, about what people are courageous about. A range of questions has been asked about what is also involved in praise for the heroes and heroines of the dominant culture. Unless we admire anything that women do well on the essentialist grounds that it is good because women do it, we have to be circumspect about what is validated and for what reasons. I would argue that what we should admire, and integrate into our understanding of Women's Studies, is a perception of the world which is highly critical of the structured social and ideological inequalities of advanced capitalist society. Such a perception is alarmingly absent from many aspects of the current academic curriculum; it is acceptable within this curriculum to study such things as 'gender' and 'sexuality' since they do not pose inherent questions about power and can take the form of descriptive accounts of aspects of social life. Without the integration of the concepts of power and inequality the world remains full of people who are just 'different' in much the same way as the people in a children's encyclopedia. Another poem illustrates the possible absences of orthodoxy:

Did you hear about the people they arrested
For burning down the Asian people's houses?
Did you hear about the policeman they put in jail
For beating up the black boy without any cause?
Did you hear about the M.P. they sacked
because he refused to help
his black constituents in their fight
against deportation?
You didn't hear about them?
Me neither. (Bloom, 1988, p. 106)

As Valerie Bloom so powerfully says, we just don't hear much about the events and the processes that are socially inconvenient. Quite clearly, the liberal Western democracies permit a high level of debate and discussion. Nevertheless this is different from positively encouraging the integration into something as central to the interests of the dominant culture as the university curriculum an understanding of the world that disturbs it.

How then does Women's Studies, as opposed to the study of gender, disturb and challenge the dominant culture? First, because asserting the category of woman challenges the classless, genderless, raceless non-problematic person who is the perfect human actor of a consumer society. What this society wants is a person who behaves with perfect obedience within created categories of consumer markets: the housewife, the teenager, the mother, the career woman and so. The distinctions of the market-place between these categories obscure the real similarities between these different women; that all are subject (or potentially subject) to patriarchal expectations about the sexual division of labour and the 'natural' functions of women. When women assert that sex, race and class are theirs, and that their identity is constructed out of a complex interaction between the category of women and the social categories of economic and racial difference, then they challenge created, semi-fantastical categories. Moreover, they make visible to the social and intellectual world the realities of the inequalities that arise from the present social organization of reproduction.

The second reason I would advance for the importance of maintaining (both within feminism and Women's Studies) the centrality of the category of women is that in doing so constraint is given a presence in the ideological world. When we speak of gender, or constructing gender, it is difficult not to think in terms of choice. Once we lose sight of the given in our lives, it is all too easy to assume that each and every social actor constructs the particular social identity that she or he chooses. Over-mechanistic women-as-victim interpretations of the concept of women have rightly been criticized; they make little or no allowance for the ways in which women are 'heroes of their own lives', or the ways in which the situation of women changes from culture to culture. But to abandon 'woman' in favour of a dressing-up-box version of reality is surely dangerous. The political implication is that the potential alliances and sympathies between women are weakened, whilst the ideological implication is that the study of society becomes (yet again) the study of groups of apparently equal individuals. For decades Marxists and socialists have had to struggle to place class on the bourgeois academic agenda, and an enormous amount of academic energy has been poured into attempting to demonstrate both that there is no such thing as class and that class exists. Since it is now the case that both Britain and the United States have seen an increasing polarization between the rich and the poor in the last ten years (a fact of social life that can be seen by reading the material provided by the state bureaucracies of both countries) this argument has the credibility of King Canute's commands to the oceans. But this does not diminish the need of ruling interests in both countries to convince the population that social differences are predominantly those that we choose ourselves.

As it is with class divisions, so it is with sexual divisions. It is all too socially convenient to abandon the uncompromising polarity of woman/man in favour of a more neutral term, a term which seems to suggest that the interests of the sexes have now converged and that the differences in life changes (not to mention economic rewards) that exist between women and men are matters of choice. Indeed, gender is a term of perfect fit with the ideology of the fractured, urban consciousness of postmodernism. In this world the term 'social actor' really comes into the full flower of its maturity, since acting and role playing became the dominant forms of social relationships. Because effective contraception and legal abortion make the control of female fertility apparently unproblematic there appears to be no reason why women and men should not don whatever social disguise they choose. Asserting biological difference in this world of fragile narcissism is almost impolite, if not positively vulgar. Meanwhile, outside this charmed world increasing numbers of women attempt to raise children on inadequate incomes and/or are forced into relationships with men in order to maintain their material survival or that of their children. Negotiating the social meaning of gender in these circumstances is seldom an available option.

The lure of 'gender studies' in the academy nevertheless remains considerable — if only for the usual structural reason of the appeal of being part of the central concerns of the academy rather than the marginalized periphery. Changing Women's Studies to gender studies allows men into the area and seems to add an aura of 'complexity' to what might otherwise be seen as a narrow or restricted field. Since the term 'complexity' is one that academics always use in a positive sense ('a very complex argument', 'a real complexity') studying gender seems to offer an entry to the very heart of the academy. But complexity for its own sake has, for some of us, all the appeal of a thorn bush. Anyone who has studied any feminist work in the last ten years knows that there are differences between women (predominantly of class and race) but some of us maintain that despite these considerable differences (which often lead women to oppress or exploit one another) there remains, particularly in the perception of the dominant culture, an understanding of the term woman, based on biology, which it is in the interests of all women to challenge. This challenge is best maintained, I would suggest, by the continued use of a term which maintains a focus on sexual difference.

Mary Evans

References

Bloom, Valerie (1988) poems in Ngcobo, Lauretta (Ed.) *Let it be Told*, London, Virago.
Jardine, Alice and Smith, Paul (Eds) (1987) *Men in Feminism*, London, Methuen.
Rich, Adrienne (1981) *A Wild Patience has Taken Me This Far*, London, W.W. Norton.

Chapter 6

Passion and Politics in Women's Studies in the 1990s

Renate D. Klein

Passion and politics, in interaction with a politics of curiosity *and* a politics of responsibility, are magic ingredients in the creation and distribution of the sort of feminist knowledge/vision which has the potential to move Women's Studies — and its participants with it — 'out of the margins' in the 1990s and beyond. In this article I first mention some of the dynamics of Women's Studies internationally.[1] Next I list current developments in Women's Studies that I find troubling and perceive as endangering the further growth of Women's Studies. I will end by suggesting some strategies for how, hopefully, Women's Studies will move into the 1990s with a vision of empowering feminist politics towards ending all women's oppressions internationally.

The Idea Power[2] of Women's Studies: Origins and Aims

It is important to remember that Women's Studies came into being as the educational arm of the Women's Liberation Movement in individual Western countries. In the late 1960s and early 1970s, feminists moved from the streets to the classrooms, in and outside higher education, and declared that enough was enough, women had been excluded, made invisible and barred from creating and distributing knowledge for far too long. And what was needed was not just ANY knowledge, but knowledge that helped to *liberate* women, that gave us power to empower ourselves and that gave us strength, based on women's *diversity*. Contrary to what some history-makers are saying now, at that early time feminists wanted the liberation of ALL women of ALL classes, races, sexualities, ages, ethnicities and professions — the collection *Sisterhood is Powerful* edited by Robin Morgan in 1970 is a good example to demonstrate the inclusiveness of the early years. It is also important to remember how many lesbians and how many black women were actually involved in the origins of the Women's Liberation Movement in and outside the academy, and of course how lesbians/black women continue to be a most vital part of Women's Studies which is not emphasized enough in public.

It was the particular position of women — the exclusion from the production and content of male culture — that Women's Studies set out to challenge. Canadian sociologist Dorothy Smith spoke of the 'eclipsing of women' from what is supposed to be 'our' culture (1978). Angry about the perpetuation of the seemingly unquestioned ideology of male dominance that 'omitted, trivialized or distorted' women in what was presented as 'knowledge' (Tobias 1978, p. 88, attributed to Catharine Stimpson), promoters of Women's Studies said that Women's Studies must be an educational experience relevant to and positive for human beings living as women in today's society. Put differently, from its early days, the supporters of Women's Studies stated unequivocally that they were not simply seeking to change knowledge for knowledge's sake — to practice Women's Studies as an academic exercise — but that they were intent on *changing* the lives of *real live* women by improving the political, socio-economic and psychological position of women worldwide. The slogan of the Women's Liberation Movement, 'the personal is the political', thus was extended to '. . . is the intellectual' (Westkott, 1981/1983).

Further, from the outset, Women's Studies made no secret of the fact that it aimed at crossing disciplinary boundaries. Since the drama of 'life' does not take place in a glass-womb (although reproductive biologists would like us to originate there!), subject compartmentalization needs to be broken down in order to both study *and* survive in the *Politics of Reality* (Marilyn Frye, 1987). What was emphasized in Women's Studies were interconnections, continuity and interrelationships: the compartmentalization of knowledge was — and by some of us still is — explicitly opposed.

What these goals make clear is that the 'idea power' of Women's Studies from its origins amounted to a 'philosophy of life' which embraces all human issues — and non-human issues as well. Every issue is a Women's Studies issue and Women's Studies is 'not just a laundry list — it is a perspective on everything from budgets to biogenetics' (Bunch, 1980), and critically evaluates every facet of human existence from interpersonal relationships to established politics, from language to law, from the use and abuse of natural resources to the social construction of reality. Above all, Women's Studies is an *active* force: women are both (and often simultaneously) subject and object of the knowledge generated and transmitted, thus creating a dynamic interaction exemplary of the Women's Studies movement *per se*. Ideally, a common denominator of such work is the shift from a men-centred perspective to a *womened perspective* where women's varying needs and interests following from our diversity in the world are the point of departure; thus, in the words of Dorothy Smith (1978, p. 294), 'taking up the standpoint of women as an experience of being'.

The 'Woman Power' in Women's Studies: The Promise of Diversity

The 'idea power' of Women's Studies is of course both theorized and put into practice by the women who teach and study Women's Studies: the Women's

Studies practitioners.[3] To find out who this group is — the 'woman power' of Women's Studies as I have called them — was one of the main aims of my survey of 158 Women's Studies practitioners (88 teachers and 70 students) in the UK and the USA (including some women in West Germany and Australia) by means of a questionnaire, participant observation and in-depth interviews (Klein, 1986, pp. 104–282). Meeting with all the women was certainly the most enjoyable part of my research: their originality, commitment and hard labour to work for a better future, their originality of research and teaching, of inventing Women's Studies and of 'claiming an education' (Rich, 1977/79), their organizing skills and political 'savvy' were inspiring. It is their diversity — or 'different similarities' — which is most impressive. In tandem with the equally diverse, all-encompassing, holistic 'idea power' (as described above) this breadth and depth is an irrefutable argument why Women's Studies is much more than a new 'subject' which can be integrated into the existing structure of knowledge. It is, in fact, a *new academic discipline* which has already grown a multitude of its own 'side'-disciplines: like a healthy vigorous tree with lots of branches. However, a caveat is immediately needed here: the *ethnic* diversity among Women's Studies practitioners leaves much to be desired, that is, 'white dominance' in Western Women's Studies continues to be cause for great concern and racism unfortunately, exists in Women's Studies too.

The Women's Studies in my study range widely in disciplinary background,[4] age (a substantial number are re-entry women), social class, sexuality, and with varying levels of participation in the Women's Liberation Movement and of identification with women-centredness. Of particular importance in the discussion of Women's Studies as 'discipline' is the fact that the Women's Studies teachers' particular 'brands' of feminisms cover the whole gamut of feminism which in turn greatly influences how they perceive Women's Studies. This means that women who define themselves as reformist or liberal feminists tend to see Women's Studies primarily as remedial: as the 'study of women', as 'adding women on' to the curriculum. A second group, women who identify as socialist feminists, tend to favour the integration of feminist courses into the traditional disciplines and many of them are taken with the development of gender studies. Yet another group, radical feminists, are the main promoters of women-centred, 'autonomous'[5] Women's Studies, preferably organized in independent programmes or, in the USA, in departments. They perceive Women's Studies as an entity in its own right and see knowledge generated in Women's Studies as valid in relation to women.

The Women's Studies students, too, are a very mixed group. As with the Women's Studies teachers their 'life profiles' vary greatly, and this extends to age because a substantial number of Women's Studies students are also re-entry women.[6] A clear difference between Women's Studies teachers and students was the students' greater involvement with feminist activism.[7] They too adhere to many brands of feminism, and their political inclinations influence their view of Women's Studies in relation to its usefulness for their lives. The reformist/liberal feminists perceive sexism as left-over 'prejudice' and expect that Women's Studies will service them in acquiring skills to manoeuvre around remaining sexism and succeed in the world. More socialist-oriented students are deeply grateful for the existence of Women's Studies which often changed their lives profoundly. They regard Women's Studies as a useful tool in contributing to social change including the elimination of racism and classism. Radical feminists perceive Women's Studies as a women-centred power base where they can acquire intellectual and political skills. They are very enthusiastic about its presence and committed to work for its continued existence.[8]

Women's Studies has clearly set itself an ambitious agenda: to try to accommodate, and cater for, the expectations, hopes and 'dreams' of so many different women within the patriarchal reality of higher education is no small goal. Needless to say, Women's Studies classrooms often bristle not only with the dynamics of intellectual excitement but also with emotional energy. Women's Studies courses challenge participants to critically evaluate all knowledge and draw conclusions that often necessitate changes in our political/personal lives.[9]

The Subject Matter of Women's Studies: From Re-Vision to Vision and Re-vision/Vision

Like the 'idea power' and the 'woman power' of Women's Studies, the nature of the subject matter in Women's Studies is by no means monolithic or uniform. I distinguish three main 'types' of Women's Studies scholarship (although of course there are many overlaps):

(1) Re-action, Re-vision:[10] Assessing Women within a
Male-centred World View

This approach is is a critique of male-centredness (androcentricity) and focuses on the absence and distortion of women from the non-feminist structure of knowledge. Whether it is disciplinary or interdisciplinary in nature, women are assessed in relation to the pervasive masculinism in existing scholarship. Examples include feminist critiques of literature, economics, biology, education, psychology, psychoanalysis, sociology and history. Types of courses taught include Women and the Law, Women and Work, Cross-Cultural Studies of Women, etc.

Such work might be summarized as: 'the study of women's oppression — gender roles, gender inequalities, discrimination, exclusion; their causes, nature and effects; women's perceptions of injustice and response to it' (Coyner, 1984, pp. 9–10).

(2) Action, Vision: Assessing Women within a Women-centred World View

Women are at the centre of research and teaching and are researched and assessed in their own right. The male-centred framework ceases to be the point of reference: what happens is a paradigmatic shift, creating new theories and methodologies[11] for teaching and research.

This type of Women's Studies scholarship and course content creates its own women-centred definition of 'cross-', 'trans-', or multidisciplinarity (Bowles, 1983; Coyner, 1983). It is frequently, but not exclusively produced by those who conceptualize Women's Studies as an 'autonomous' entity (i.e. discipline) rather than by those whose main emphasis is to 'transform' the other academic disciplines.

A visionary/action approach is used in courses that focus on similarities and diversities among and between women of various ethnicities, races, nationalities, sexualities, etc. Power differentials are discussed in material as well as ideological terms and the nature of various theories of feminisms is assessed.

(3) Re-vision/Vision, Re-action/Action Combined:
Women's Studies between Criticism and Vision

The most ambitious of the three 'types', this conceptualizes Women's Studies research and curriculum as synthesizing re-vision and vision, i.e. as both critiquing androcentric scholarship and making an 'imaginative leap' towards the creation of knowledge (vision, action).

Janice Raymond's concept of 'Two Sights Seeing' (Raymond, 1986) can be adapted for the Women's Studies curriculum and scholarship which is between criticism and vision: 'At one and the same time, vision is "the exercise of the ordinary faculty of sight" and "something which is apparently seen otherwise than by ordinary sight"' (p. 85).

Examples include research/teaching about the continuing deterioration of women's material conditions ('feminization of poverty'): *Re-visionary* scholarship/teaching exposes its roots (e.g. male devaluation and appropriation of women's work, exploitation of cheap female labour, particularly that of poor women and women of colour cross-culturally); the *visionary* part consists of devising theories for a non-sexist, non-racist international economic system that will benefit women and other oppressed groups (Mies, 1986; Waring, 1989), as well as implementing actions based on networks of 'global feminism' (Morgan, 1984) that will improve women's positions worldwide. Other examples of revisionary/visionary Women's Studies encompass work on violence against women including reproductive and genetic engineering (Klein, 1989b).

Summarizing the three 'types' of Women's Studies scholarship, it is clear that the 're-vision/vision, re-action/action' approach is by far the most exciting, but also the most demanding framework for the production of Women's Studies knowledge. It needs both a combination of 'idea power' and 'woman power' (specialist Women's Studies teaching staff), and, importantly, access to resources (including grant monies to do research which incorporates both an avowedly feminist critique of androcentric research and ideas/theories for creating women-centred knowledge). For example, feminist natural scientists could write research grants as Women's Studies scholars backed up by their programme/division/department of Women's Studies, for women-centred research that does not fall into the 'high-tech' category which presently attracts most of the funding in the natural sciences.

Such research also requires the administrative assurances of continuity that are most secure with independent status; for instance as institutionalised MA/Diploma-granting courses, Women's Studies programmes on the under-graduate and graduate level, or (in the USA) as autonomous Women's Studies departments. As Bonnie Zimmerman, Chairperson of the Women's Studies Department at San Diego State University, USA, put it (personal communication, 20 March 1990):

> The best thing about being a Department is that we all work together and that we are in control. We control the curriculum, that is *we* take the decisions about *what* courses are offered when, and *who* teaches them, and we make all the faculty appointments. Equally important, we have the same access to resources and information as other departments.

Women's Studies Internationally at the Beginning of the 1990s

As we begin the 1990s there is no doubt that Women's Studies is alive and well. In the USA there are more than 30,000 courses and close to 600 programmes including an increasing number of MA and PhD programmes and over 150 research centres. Moreover, in 1990, Women's Studies is a global movement. Without exception, all so-called 'Western' countries — including Australia and New Zealand — have some form or other of Women's Studies. Importantly, Women's Studies has also become a recognized phenomena in Asia with courses in India, Bangladesh, the Philippines, Korea, Japan, China, to name but a few; and there are courses in Mexico and South American countries. In fact I think that Asia and Central/South America are the two continents where exciting developments are taking place particularly with regard to the interaction of theory and practice, and the activist role of Women's Studies practitioners. Korea, for instance, has had Women's Studies courses on an undergraduate level since 1978 and at its oldest Women's University — the Ewha University — it has been possible to get an MA in Women's Studies since 1982 (Chang, 1989). India has an excellent network of Women's Studies courses including some research centres such as the SNDT Women's University at Bombay. Women's Studies in Japan is growing too. In 1983 there were 94 courses; in 1988 there were

280 (and they have had a Women's Studies Association since 1979). A special feature of Asian Women's Studies — and this also holds true for Women's Studies in South America — is the fact that the colonization and exploitation of the so-called 'Third World' by the West — or from within Asia by Japan — are very important topics. The other exciting feature is how well organized and *activist* women in these countries are and how many academics appear to be also involved in some of the many feminist campaigns against sex-determination, pornography, dowry, suttee, sex-tourism, to name just a few. Pilwha Chang pointed out that her Women's Studies graduates frequently become Korea's feminist activists!

So undoubtedly, there is much cause for celebrating the growth and proliferation of Women's Studies. But the undone work weighs heavily. While Women's Studies may be getting stronger and stronger globally, and more diversified, the feminization of poverty and women's illiteracy are increasing worldwide. Sheer survival is getting tougher: women's nutrition, and consequently women's and children's health, are worsening, and male violence against women, be it through sexual abuse, sexual harassment, date rape, rape in and outside marriage, criminal assault at home, pornography and prostitution, is increasing. Increasing too are the many forms of violence committed against our ecosystems, with particularly devastating effects in Third World countries — committed by the West — from which women and children suffer most (see Shiva, 1989). And women's rights to integrity of body and soul are still not recognized as human rights; lesbian existence, for instance, is by no means safe, and women's own decisions whether they wish to be — or can be — mothers or not, are being curtailed even further through the inceasing stranglehold of modern biotechnology be it to restrict reproduction or to enforce it. It is therefore crucial to increase and solidify international networks which must include a strong international feminist Women's Studies movement: a movement which has as its core concept a fervent commitment to *women* across cultural and national boundaries. Yet there are a number of shadows on the wall of such joint feminist theory and praxis which I will examine next.[12]

Obstacles to Feminist Vision and International Sisterhood[13]

One thick cloud on the horizon of Women's Studies is the increasing tendency to rename Women's Studies and call it gender studies. In my view this is the beginning of eclipsing Women's Studies, both by making women invisible (again) — gender is such a neutral term — and by allowing men into feminist space. (The first US chair in gender studies went to Harry Brod.) Promoters of gender studies tell us that Women's Studies is really only about women, that we are marginalizing ourselves, and that what we need is a broader vision. The broader vision they propose is, however, precisely a masculine construction of knowledge that feminists have been fighting against for centuries (see for instance Spender, 1982): the very *limited* idea that the world centres around *hetero-relations* since 'it expresses woman in relation to man — as determined by the concept of gender which relies on *dichotomies*' (Hawthorne, 1989, p. 626; my emphasis).[14] Gender studies thus reinforces the necessity of studying women and men in relation to one another: a much narrower aim than Women's Studies's claim to study the whole world from a feminist perspective! Given the continuing power differences in our patriarchal society — and the increasing number of men interested in (taking over) such 'hetero-relations studies' — my new term for gender studies — with its obsession with the concept of *difference* do not bode well for the future of a strong Women's Studies movement. This new form of hetero-reality might easily become compulsory through community support and financial resources available only to 'balanced' gender studies and not to what they see as 'marginal' Women's Studies.

Indeed, the obsession with 'difference' seems to be a legacy from the 1980s for the early 1990s. Theories of sexualities, especially lesbian sexuality, are now celebrating eroticized power differences among women and ridiculing sexual relations based on equality. Diane Hamer, discussing difference among lesbians in butch and femme sexuality, praises it (1990, p. 147):

> ... as an antidote to the monolithic account of lesbianism within psychoanalysis (as well as to the rather *sexless* emphasis of *sameness* between lesbians supported by a certain current of lesbian feminism dominant in the late 70s and early 1980s see Rich 1980). (my emphasis)

This ideology creates, as Sheila Jeffreys puts it, 'otherness ... through differences of age, race, class, the practice of sadomasochism or role playing' (1990, p. 301). There is much talk about 'individual pleasure' promoted under the guise of 'choice'. Political thought and action is 'out', 'in' is a libertarian ideology that fosters individualism and is centred around 'difference'. And even in the lesbian context, the focus on differences between men and women appears; as Cindy Patton, interviewed by Sue O'Sullivan, says: 'it is possible at this point politically and culturally for lesbians to start looking at gay male porn ...' (O'Sullivan, 1990, p. 132) which is in line with Sara Dunn's comment in the same so-called feminist journal 'to be firmly pro-pornography' (1990, p. 162). When sexual liberals teach such knowledge in Women's Studies classrooms, it defuses the inherent woman-hating nature of patriarchal power and one of its cornerstones, pornography, in the making of which real live women are hurt, indeed sometimes killed. The students' sense of dignity and their/our embodied 'right' to integrity of body and soul may be de-stabilized and numbed: the beginning of another generation of women perhaps, who justify the continuation of woman-hating ideologies with a tyranny of tolerance — anything goes as long as somebody 'desires' it — at the expense of their own freedom?

The concept of difference rules supreme in poststructuralist discourse and deconstructionist epistemology. Through analytical tools, realities are taken apart, turned around, taken apart again and turned around again ... so that in the end what remains is total relativism: a multitude of subjectivities out of which, so the deconstructionist logic runs, it is excitingly impossible to name one as more real than the other. We are left with fragmented bits and pieces, vagueness and uncertainty. As Somer Brodribb puts it, 'texts without contexts, genders without sexes, and sex without politics' (forthcoming). Pluralism reigns supreme and 'nothingness' — when all is deconstructed — precludes us from having clear concepts about, for instance, the power dynamics between the sexes, or feminism.

Soberingly, this 'grand theory' of splitting realities and texts into fragments — all conceptualized in the head without connections to real live women — mirrors precisely what goes on in contemporary science, especially in reproductive and genetic engineering. Here, it is women with a fertility problem — or 'bad' genes — who are split into bits and pieces. They are not conceptualized as whole human beings, but dismembered as 'bad eggs', 'diseased tubes', 'hostile wombs'. These bits are what is looked at — through the pornographic gaze of the 'masters' — and what the 'experts' — the technodocs — will try to 'fix up'. That the other 'bit' surrounding these body parts happens to be a whole person with the complication of a human life, human feelings, fears and longings, does not matter, is not seen as 'real'.

Reproductive and genetic engineering and deconstructionism do represent, unfortunately, the current *Zeitgeist*: a serious threat to everything that is connected, that is interactive and whole, that wants and insists on continuities and commonalities — which are, in fact, some of the cherished values of feminism and Women's Studies. Instead, the cutters with words and knives prefer difference.[15] This not only splits women into non-entities, thereby seriously damaging a woman's sense of self and sense of identity; it also splits women from each other: one of patriarchy's best tools to keep women from forming a joint resistance movement. In fact these ideologies mimic patriarchy as described by Robin Morgan (1989, p. 51):

> If I had to name one quality as the genius of patriarchy, it would be compartmentalization, the capacity for institutionalizing disconnection.... The personal isolated from the political. Sex divorced from love. The material ruptured from the spiritual. The past parted from the present disjointed from the future. Law detached from justice, vision dissociated from reality.

Sisterhood Is Still Powerful — Strategies For the Future

Instead of colluding with such compartmentalized and life-endangering frameworks, what can feminist Women's Studies practitioners internationally do to move 'passionately forward' with our research/lives and keep the Women's Studies movement moving with us right into the centre?

Going back to basics. Remembering that we *do* live in international (techno) patriarchy which continues to oppress and kill women. US philosopher, Janice Raymond, suggested 'putting the politics back into lesbianism' (1989). Paraphrasing her I suggest putting politics back into Women's

Studies: radical passionate politics. Politics that remember the goal of the Women's Liberation Movement to end patriarchal oppression in all its forms: sexism, racism, classism, to name but three — all thriving on 'differences', on separation and division between people. Politics, also, that remember our successes, our empowerment, our pleasures, the joys that often come from working with women, the knowledge that 'sisterhood is *still* powerful' (Klein, 1989a), and that it is, in fact, our lifeline which we cannot afford to sever. Politics, above all, that are emphatic and come from the heart as well as the brain.

Working hard towards making sisterhood more inclusive and validating *all* women, thus truly making the diversity in Women's Studies, as I have described it earlier in this article, into our strength (see also Klein, 1985). Changing and enlarging our limited frameworks by listening to women from other cultures and countries. Reading Vandana Shiva (1989). Recognizing how the increasingly cruel global technology machine is numbing us, swallowing us, killing some of us. Resisting such necrophilic politics with passion, with alliances between women around the globe. Working together if this is what we all want, or respecting our different priorities by supporting one another's actions, if this is preferred. And as western women being careful, also, not to be voyeuristic or to objectify women who are 'foreign' and 'exotic' (Hawthorne, 1989).

Remembering and using the enormous body of feminist knowledge we have generated in the last twenty years including the wealth of empowering fiction, especially writings by women of colour from different continents and countries. Respecting women's 'different similarities' in our own countries based on different abilities, ages, social status, cultures and nationalities. Looking for commonalities instead of differences: it is bonds — often expressed in friendships — not divisions which will make us powerful. For women to disown one another, I think, is suicidal politics. As Kathleen Barry said (1989, p. 572), 'Whenever differences are emphasized without first recognizing collectivity, commonality and unity among women, gender power is depoliticized'.

We have a responsibility to pass on to younger women what has been created in the first twenty years of the Women's Studies movement and we need to work hard to maintain our continuity and continue our growth. As we are reconceptualizing the world, we are reconceptualizing patriarchal geography. We have the imagination, pragmatic shrewdness, endurance and passion to turn 'the margins' into *the centre* through using creative, wild, life-loving lateral thinking, and associating, connecting, and synthesizing the many threads of life into theories which we can put into action.[16] We will succeed if we manage to throw off the patriarchal baggage women throughout the world carry which continues to imprison us in dichotomies, in 'difference', but also in so-called 'gender neutrality'. We need to think and act with truly radical politics — with women's needs and interests squarely at the centre of our work — and believe passionately in the necessity and importance of what feminists globally work for: a strong '*centred*' Women's Studies movement which will contribute to *real* change for the better in the lives of *real* live women, which is, after all, what Women's Studies set out to do.

Notes

1   The first part of this article draws on my PhD dissertation, 'The Dynamics of Women's Studies' (1986); see also Duelli Klein, 1984a and 1984b.
2   I am indebted to Sarah Slavin Schramm for this expression which she created to describe the conceptual origins of Women's Studies as an educational movement for change based on the collective intellectual power of women who are motivated by the ideology of the Women's Liberation Movement to end women's oppression (1978).
3   Florence Howe and Carol Ahlum introduced the term Women's Studies 'practitioner' (1973). I believe it is useful as a common denominator to describe 'those in Women's Studies' in spite of its usual meaning as 'professional or practical worker, esp. in medicine' (*Concise Oxford Dictionary*, 1979).
4   It must be pointed out that no Women's Studies teacher in my study had a degree in Women's Studies. This is changing slowly, but there still is a great need for MA and PhD degree-granting courses in Women's Studies.
5   'Autonomy' within an institution is of course relative and not comparable to autonomy in the sense of being totally *outside* an institution (as the term is used in Germany). Nevertheless I believe it is a useful term, especially when comparing Women's Studies to other academic disciplines which all have their autonomy when it comes to hiring and firing, resources and university politics. For further discussion of the heated autonomy/integration debate of the early 1980s see Gloria Bowles and Renate Duelli Klein, 1983b.
6   I believe the proportion of older women students in Women's Studies is decreasing, and there are more very young women (i.e. in their early 20s). It remains to be seen how this change in balance influences Women's Studies.
7   The lesser involvement of Women's Studies teachers in feminist activism created a considerable amount of tension for many Women's Studies students in my study. They were disappointed that in some cases the teachers' feminism remained aloof and removed from women's 'real lives', in particular with regard to the various forms of violence against women and feminist resistance against it in the form of anti-pornography campaigns or shelters for battered women.
8   The problem with this group is that they are usually overextended as student advocates, leaders in anti-racism workshops, environmental politics, anti-nuclear demonstrations as well as work in feminist organizations (e.g. feminist health centres, rape crisis centres, shelters for battered women, anti-pornography groups).
    There is a fourth student group too — separatist in their political orientation — who do not perceive Women's Studies as an alternative positive education for women. They think that by being part of the academy Women's Studies has 'sold out'. They show no commitment to the continued existence of Women's Studies and the only satisfaction they draw from their involvement in Women's Studies is from getting to know other like-minded women.
9   This is indeed a very different mission from other courses taught at universities. At best Women's Studies 'gynagogy' (a term I prefer to 'pedagogy'; see Klein, 1987) is passionate teaching in order to combine scholarship, reason, intellect, emotion and intuition. Of particular importance are the problems of cross-cultural similarity and diversity; white dominance; heterosexism; the relationship

between Women's Studies and the Women's Liberation Movement; the hidden curriculum (e.g. hierarchies, power differences, grading); men in Women's Studies (see Klein, 1986, 1987).

10   I use these terms as a positive way of 'taking a second look' from a feminist perspective. They are in line with Adrienne Rich's (1975), Mary Daly's (1978), Helen Callaway's (1981) and Robyn Rowland's (1988) interpretations.

11   Feminist methodology is another crucial area of development which I have no time to address in this paper. See Gloria Bowles and Renate Duelli Klein, 1983a, for references, as well as Liz Stanley (1990) and Shulamit Reinharz (forthcoming).

12   I should mention that I will not focus on economic problems which does not mean that I am not aware of the economic plight worldwide and its serious implications for Women's Studies. But I also think it is important to examine obstacles to feminist vision and sisterhood that arise amongst ourselves.

13   The increasing presence of men in Women's Studies, in my view, is another problem. As I have elaborated on this topic at length elsewhere (Klein, 1983) for reasons of space suffice it to say here that whether men appear as 'experts', 'ignoramuses' or 'poor dears' in Women's Studies classrooms, they usually manage to attract undue attention, divide the women on the course, and, importantly, change the climate from one where female students take risks in speaking out, to a hetero-relationally controlled atmosphere. A further cause for concern is the proliferating number of 'Men's Studies' courses in which men are the new experts on women, gender and 'masculinities studies' (Brod, 1987). They manage to thoroughly exploit feminist scholarship by selectively including — and reinterpreting — women's words, followed by the real 'feminist' scholarship: by a male authority of course. For a detailed exploration of this very masculinist phenomenon which in true sexist fashion attempts to render women invisible again, see Jalna Hanmer (1990).

14   Janice Raymond describes *hetero-relations* as a world view (1986, p. 29): 'I use the word hetero-relations to express the wide range of affective, social, political and economic relations that are ordained between men and women by men. The literature, history, philosophy and science of patriarchy have reinforced the supposedly mythic and primordial relationship of *woman for man*.'

15   One of the core concepts of patriarchal (natural) science is the value placed on differences at the expense of similarities. Research results that do not demonstrate differences are usually not publishable as they are not seen as important. Feminists in the natural sciences have thoroughly critiqued this biased method over the last twenty years, particularly in relation to research on sex differences, and pointed to its sexist one-sidedness. It is therefore rather ironical that feminists in literature and increasingly in philosophy, history and education are so taken by the frenzied theorizing of differences and regard it as a positive new conceptual framework (among the many feminist critiques of science see in particular Bleier, 1984 and 1986).

16   Charlotte Bunch's collection *Passionate Politics* (1987) is an excellent example of putting feminist theory into action.

References

BARRY, KATHLEEN (1989) 'Biography and the Search for Women's Subjectivity', in *Women's Studies International Forum*, 12 (6), pp. 561–577.

BLEIER, RUTH (1984) *Science and Gender: A Critique of Biology and Its Theories of Women*, Oxford and New York, The Athene Series, Pergamon Press.

BLEIER, RUTH (1986) 'Sex Differences Research: Science or Belief?', in BLEIER, RUTH (Ed.) *Feminist Approaches to Science*, Oxford and New York, The Athene Series, Pergamon Press, pp. 147–164.

BOWLES, GLORIA (1983) 'Is Women's Studies an Academic Discipline?', In BOWLES, GLORIA and KLEIN, RENATE DUELLI (Eds) *Theories of Women's Studies*, London and Boston, Routledge and Kegan Paul, pp. 32–45.

BOWLES, GLORIA and KLEIN, RENATE DUELLI (Eds) (1983a) *Theories of Women's Studies*, London and Boston, Routledge and Kegan Paul.

BOWLES, GLORIA and KLEIN, RENATE DUELLI (1983b) 'Introduction: Theories of Women's Studies and the Autonomy/Integration Debate', in BOWLES, GLORIA and KLEIN, RENATE DUELLI (Eds) *Theories of Women's Studies*, London and Boston, Routledge and Kegan Paul, pp. 1–26.

BROD, HARRY (1987) *The Making of Masculinities: The New Men's Studies*; Boston, Allen and Unwin.

BRODRIBB, SOMER (forthcoming) 'Discarnate Desires: Thoughts on Sexuality and Post-Structuralist Discourse', in *Women's Studies International Forum*, 14 (2).

BUNCH, CHARLOTTE (1980) 'Global Feminism', talk delivered at Women's Studies Forum, Copenhagen, July.

BUNCH, CHARLOTTE (1987) *Passionate Politics: Feminist Theory in Action*, New York, St. Martin's Press.

CALLAWAY, HELEN (1981) 'Women's Perspectives: Research as Re-vision', in REASON, PETER and ROWAN, JOHN (Eds) *Human Inquiry*, Chichester and New York, John Wiley and Sons, pp. 457–471.

CHANG, PILWHA (1989) 'The Development of Women's Studies in Korea and its Impact on Korean Society', in Proceedings of International Seminar 'Global Perspectives on Changing Sex Roles', published by National Women's Education Centre, Tokyo, Japan, pp. 432–441.

CONCISE OXFORD DICTIONARY (1979) Oxford, Oxford University Press.

COYNER, SANDRA (1983) 'Women's Studies as an Academic Discipline: Why and How to Do It', in BOWLES, GLORIA and KLEIN, RENATE DUELLI (Eds) *Theories of Women's Studies*, London and Boston, Routledge and Kegan Paul, pp. 46–71.

COYNER, SANDRA (1984) 'The Core Concepts and Central Themes of Women's Studies Viewed as an Emerging Academic Discipline', unpublished, January.

DALY, MARY (1978) *Gyn/Ecology: The Metaethics of Radical Feminism*, Boston, Beacon Press.

DUNN, SARA (1990) 'Voyages of the Valkyries: Recent Lesbian Pornographic Writing', in *Feminist Review*, 'Perverse Politics: Lesbian Issues', pp. 161–170.

FRYE, MARILYN (1987) *The Politics of Reality*, Trumansburg, New York, The Crossing Press.

HAMER, DIANE (1990) 'Significant Others: Lesbians and Psychoanalytic Theory', in *Feminist Review*, 'Perverse Politics: Lesbian Issues', pp. 134–151.

HANMER, JALNA (1990) 'Men, Power and the Exploitation of Women', in *Women's Studies International Forum*, 13 (5).

HAWTHORNE, SUSAN (1989) 'The Politics of the Exotic: The Paradox of Cultural Voyeurism', in *NWSA Journal*, 1 (4), pp. 617–629.

HOWE, FLORENCE and AHLUM, CAROL (1973) 'Women's Studies and Social Change', in ROSSI, ALICE and CALDERWOOD, ANN (Eds) *Academic Women on the Move*, New York, Russell Sage, pp. 393–423.

JEFFREYS, SHEILA (1990) *Anticlimax: A Feminist Perspective on the Sexual Revolution*, London, The Women's Press.

KLEIN, RENATE DUELLI (1983) 'The "Men Problem" in Women's Studies: Experts, Ignoramuses and Poor Dears', in *Women's Studies International Forum*, 6 (4), pp. 413–421.

KLEIN, RENATE DUELLI (1984a) 'Women's Studies: The Challenge to Man-Made-Education', in ACKER, SANDRA, *et al.* (Eds) New York, *World Year Book of Education*, Kogan Page/Nichols Publication, pp. 292–306.

KLEIN, RENATE DUELLI (1984b) 'The Intellectual Necessity for Women's Studies', in ACKER, SANDRA and PIPER, DAVID WARREN (Eds) *Is Higher Education Fair to Women?* University of Guildford, Surrey, SRHE and NFER Nelson, pp. 220–241.

KLEIN, RENATE DUELLI (Ed.) (1985) 'Rethinking Sisterhood: Unity in Diversity', in *Women's Studies International Forum*, 8 (1) (Special Issue).

KLEIN, RENATE DUELLI (1986) *The Dynamics of Women's Studies: An Exploratory Study of Its International Ideas and Practices in Higher Education*, PhD Dissertation, University of London, Institute of Education (unpublished).

KLEIN, RENATE D. (1987) 'The Dynamics of the Women's Studies Classroom: A Review Essay of the Teaching Practice of Women's Studies in Higher Education', in *Women's Studies International Forum*, 10 (2), pp. 187–206.

KLEIN, RENATE (1989a) 'The Journey Forward: Sisterhood is *Still* Powerful', in ROWLAND, ROBYN (Ed.) *Girl's Own Annual*, Women's Studies Summer Institute, Geelong, Deakin University, pp. 27–33.

KLEIN, RENATE D. (Ed.) (1989b) *Infertility: Women Speak Out About Their Experiences with Reproductive Medicine*, London, Sydney and Winchester, MA, Pandora Press/Unwin Hyman.

MIES, MARIA (1986) *Patriarchy and Accumulation on a World Scale: Women and the International Division of Labour*, London, Zed Press.

MORGAN, ROBIN (Ed.) (1970) *Sisterhood is Powerful: An Anthology of Writings from the Women's Liberation Movement*, New York, Vintage Books.

MORGAN, ROBIN (Ed.) (1984) *Sisterhood is Global: An Anthology of Writings from the Women's Liberation Movement*, New York, Vintage Books.

MORGAN, ROBIN (1989) *The Demon Lover*, New York, W.W. Norton.

O'SULLIVAN, SUE (1990) 'Mapping: Lesbianism, AIDS and Sexuality', in *Feminist Review*, 'Perverse Politics: Lesbian Issues', pp. 120–133.

RAYMOND, JANICE G. (1986) *A Passion for Friends: Toward a Philosophy of Female Affection*, Boston, Beacon Press; London, The Women's Press.

RAYMOND, JANICE G. (1989) 'Putting the Politics Back into Lesbianism', in *Women's Studies International Forum*, 12 (2), pp. 149–156.

REINHARZ, SHULAMIT (forthcoming) *Social Research Methods, Feminist Perspectives*, New York and Oxford, The Athene Series, Pergamon Press.

RICH, ADRIENNE (1975) 'Toward a Women-Centred University', in HOWE, FLORENCE (Ed.) *Women and the Power to Change*, Berkeley, Carnegie Commission/MacGraw Hill, Berkeley.

RICH, ADRIENNE (1977/1979) 'Claiming an Education', in RICH, ADRIENNE *On Lies, Secrets and Silences*, New York, W.W. Norton, pp. 231–236.

RICH, ADRIENNE (1980) 'Compulsory Heterosexuality and Lesbian Existence', in *Signs*, 5 (4), pp. 631–660.

ROWLAND, ROBYN (1988) *Woman Herself: A Transdisciplinary Perspective on Women's Studies*, Melbourne, Oxford University Press.

SHIVA, VANDANA (1989) *Staying Alive: Women, Ecology and Survival in India*, New Delhi, Kali for Women; London, Zed Press.

SLAVIN SCHRAMM, SARAH (1978) 'Women's Studies: Its Focus, Idea Power and Promise', in BLUMHAGEN, KATHLEEN O'CONNOR and JOHNSON, WALTER (Eds) *Women's Studies*, Westport, Greenwood Press, pp. 3–12.

SMITH, DOROTHY (1978/1989) 'A Peculiar Eclipsing: Women's Exclusion from Man's Culture', in *Women's Studies International Quarterly* 1 (4), pp. 281–295; reprinted in KLEIN, RENATE D. and STEINBERG, DEBORAH LYNN (Eds) *Radical Voices*, New York and Oxford, The Athene Series, Pergamon Press, pp. 3–21.

SPENDER, DALE (1982/1983) *Women of Ideas and What Men Have Done to Them: From Aphra Behn to Adrienne Rich*, London, Ark Paperbacks.
STANLEY, LIZ (1990) *Feminist Praxis*, London, Routledge and Kegan Paul.
TOBIAS, SHEILA (1978) 'Women's Studies: Its Origins, Its Organisation, and Its Prospects', in *Women's Studies International Quarterly*, 1 (1), pp. 85–97.
WARING, MARILYN (1989) *If Women Counted: A New Feminist Economics*, New York, Harper and Row.
WESTKOTT, MARCIA (1981/1983) 'Women's Studies as a Strategy for Change: Between Criticism and Vision', in GLORIA BOWLES, GLORIA and RENATE DUELLI KLEIN (Eds) *Theories of Women's Studies*, London and Boston, Routledge and Kegan Paul, pp. 210–218.

Chapter 7

Feminist Politics and Women's Studies: Struggle, Not Incorporation

Sue Lees

how we dwelt in two worlds
the daughters and the mothers in the kingdom of the sons
(Adrienne Rich)

Women's Studies and the Women's Movement

In this paper I argue that Women's Studies cannot be separated from the contemporary Women's Movement. It evolved out of it and is an integral part of it. Women's Studies did not develop solely or even predominantly from within the academic establishment but in response to demands made by women's groups and the Women's Liberation Movement. Even today the growth of Women's Studies is only possible because students are demanding the right to study from a feminist perspective. Without the demand it would die. Fears are frequently expressed that the adoption of Women's Studies, if only on the periphery, will destroy its challenge to the status quo (see Mies, 1990). It is curious how often Women's Studies is written off as part of the establishment or ignored as irrelevant to the real Women's Movement. When Women's Studies started to grow within universities and polytechnics, there was a concern that developing part of the Women's Movement within male-led academic institutions could lead to its deradicalization. Sheila Rowbotham, for example, argues that

> The Women's Studies courses which emerged out of arguments and struggle have now begun to grow into a little knowledge industry of their own. At the risk of biting the hand that feeds, it is not sufficient to produce for an academic milieu, for this does not engage with the power relations involved in the ranking of certain forms of knowledge and understanding. (Rowbotham, 1989, p. xiv)

This is to overlook the relation between education and struggle. It may not be possible to change the power relations within education in one fell swoop but that does not mean to say that Women's Studies courses cannot be a radicalizing force or that they may not have a political purpose. This view also fails to recognize that education has always been a pivotal demand of the Women's Movement and is still the main route to women's emancipation and the main means of challenging all kinds of knowledge (see Harding, 1986).

A blinkered dismissal of any link with institutions neglects the importance of working for change both from within and without the establishment. It also fails to take into account that the provision of Women's Studies courses, particularly in adult education, opens up new opportunities for women who previously would have been often confined to low-paid work and domestic isolation. The development of Women's Studies outside the higher educational establishment in WEA courses across the country and in adult education provides women with the space to develop their critical abilities, share their experiences and take a critical look at their lives. This dismissal of education is mirrored in a certain anti-intellectualism arising from the importance placed on women's 'experience' as opposed to 'theory' (see, for example, Stanley and Wise, 1983), when both are interdependent. Women's Studies has always had the aim of bridging the gap between the subjective and experiential knowledge on the one hand, and academic knowledge on the other (see Rendel, 1982).

A similar denial of the importance of Women's Studies courses is illustrated by the total absence of discussion about Women's Studies in the journal *Feminist Review*. Even in their special Spring 1989 issue on 'Twenty years of feminism' which covered such topics as trade unionism, lessons from the women's movement in Europe, feminist criticism, race and mothering, no mention was made of the impact of Women's Studies. Instead there has been a tendency to attack any woman-centred analysis as essentialist (see Segal, 1987) overlooking the male-centred nature of much learning. The absence of any discussion about education and Women's Studies by some socialist feminists is particularly curious when so many of them work as academics and have published in the area of Women's Studies. It is almost as though *Feminist Review* contributors need to identify with a politics outside the academic world to ensure their credibility as true 'radicals'.

Isn't it time the connection between Women's Studies and the Women's Movement is fully recognized? The development of Women's Studies rests both on struggling within the mainstream and existing at the margins. Without such parallel development, the Women's Studies Network and the conferences we organize would not have got off the ground. Women are dependent on resources and energy from those working within the academic community as well as from women outside. This third way involves not incorporation into the mainstream, but a foothold in the mainstream with firm links to the grass-roots feminist movement.

The failure to see Women's Studies as part of the Women's Liberation Movement has led to a belief that conferences are no longer held. This is due to the lack of recognition of the roots that Women's Studies has in the Women's Movement which is an important development (see Hanmer, 1989;

Mies, 1990), not just in Britain, but in other parts of Europe and beyond. The links between Women's Studies and the Women's Movement can be seen most clearly in looking at the reasons why women joined Women's Studies courses in the 1980s in such numbers, reasons very similar to those that led women to join consciousness-raising groups in the late 1960s. It is here that the mainstream and the margins can be seen to meet. For example during the last five years we have run Foundation Courses at the Polytechnic of North London, fifteen-week courses that do not demand any qualifications to join or require any assessed work. The courses consist of one three-hour session a week and are run twice a year, once in the evening and once in the day. Women, with varying educational backgrounds, some young, some retired, from different social classes and ethnic groups, flocked to the courses when they were first run in the mid-1980s. Over a hundred attended each course, which we had to divide into numerous seminar groups, and we had to take on a number of part-time women to run them. This year the numbers on the courses have decreased to around thirty but the enthusiasm and the passions expressed by women, many of whom have not been back to education since they were 15 or 16, are just as intense. To teach these courses is a revelation.

Recently, looking at the 1985 application forms, I was struck by how similar were women's reasons for coming on the courses to the reasons we joined consciousness-raising groups in the late 1960s. The following extracts were typical:

> I would like to do the course for the following reasons: Firstly, because of the growing awareness of my interest and commitment towards feminism. My interest in feminism grew with my involvement in a women's miners' support group, a group of women in London linked with women in South Wales coalfield which involved many discussions about differing lifestyles of the two sets of women. Strong links developed between the two groups. My other involvement has been in the ongoing Women and Benefits campaign which started as a Women's signing on Campaign but we found few women eligible for Unemployment Benefit so expanded it to include all benefits. I have learnt much about how discriminating the whole welfare system is against women and how appallingly paid many women are that they do not even qualify for benefit. I would like to do the course to increase my knowledge.

> I cannot claim that I was looking for anything specific when I picked up a pile of leaflets about courses at the library. I looked through them all when I got home. The Women's Studies leaflet stayed on the table. The rest went into the bin. It stayed on the table, nudging me for about two weeks. Even so I turned it over and did nothing. Yes, the lectures sounded interesting but that was not why I applied. It was the conjunction of the apparently irrational and underlying

currents in activities which I am involved with which finally got the form filled in and posted. It is the year of the Tiger, the year I was born in. The second set of influences have a lot to do with what I hear and see as a parent governor of Tufnell Park Primary School. It would be difficult not to be aware of how much of the swimming is done by boys even in a primary school, and how much gentle sinking away by the girls. I am not an ardent feminist, though I am more than interested in how come women and girls have so much disbelief and uncertainty in their abilities.

I hope to come to this course without preconceived points of view, to learn a lot and leave again with an open mind but armed with much greater and deeper understanding. I lived in Leeds and worked for a while in an advice centre helping build up an anti damp campaign in the poor housing around. It was also the time of the Yorkshire Ripper and there was a lot of women's activity and I helped set up a woman's group in my area and invite speakers and arrange self defence classes for people. I helped set up a tenants' association for my estate as well. Then in late 1981 I moved to Islington where I was involved in the Bus Company under fives group, Women's Aid and organized a woman's day for International Women's Day. I am interested in video and just a year ago started a video collective with four friends. We have so far made one video which is about the Barking Hospital Ancillary Workers Strike and are working on a further two on the subject of the portrayal of women in the mass media. This was funded out of our dole money and we then managed to secure a small grant from the GLC.

Since leaving school it feels like my brain has stagnated and I am no longer capable of holding an intelligent conversation about anything more demanding than the weather. It was only at the end of my working life that I came up for air and was able to look at what had happened to me as working woman. Now that I am retired I want to read and study in a structured way. I am a member of the Older Feminist Network and am discovering from meeting other older feminists that we have an enormous amount to learn and share.

I have recently been involved in the setting up of the Bengali and Chinese women's groups and in taking up issues such as the request for parents to send their children to single sex schools, the support of girls and women who found themselves in conflict with parental or community expectations e.g. over marriage, wanting to train, study, or gain employment, secure a divorce. In Tower Hamlets I worked closely with homeworkers in the area, setting up training in machining, English, TU rights in order to strengthen their position in the labour market.

In adult education I have worked closely with working women's groups in setting up a range of education provision appropriate to the women's needs and interests and have contributed to the development and implementation of EO policies. The main reason for doing this course is to learn something for myself not to gain a qualification. So far I've spent most of my working life in Japan and my unsocial working hours made it very difficult for me to take part in activities with other people. What is interesting at the moment is the amount written about women, by women and the flowering of women's groups.

My interest in women's studies has been prompted by the following reasons
1 I am a member of a woman's group
2 I am a member of the peace movement
3 I have been involved in setting up a woman's group in a professional capacity at work i.e. an inpatient psychiatric unit
4 I welcome the opportunity not only to share ideas and opinions on a variety of topics affecting women but also to gain additional concrete information concerning these issues. I am interested in WS from a personal point of view and also to enable me to make a contribution to the women's movement from a more actively political standpoint.

My mother's life, my own experiences, my friend's feeling of inadequacy, the worries and fears of the women I met in the street, of the women I don't know living around the corner, the list is endless. Each one prompts me to find out more and to understand better and hopefully to improve the position and condition of women in today's society. It is a subject which preoccupies me, pains me, uplifts me. It is for these reasons that I want to do the course.

Do these accounts suggest we have reached the period of postfeminism? Over and over again women maintain that they come on courses for themselves, for their own development, rather than to gain any particular qualification. Some are already graduates, some even have postgraduate qualifications, but do not feel their previous education has had relevance to their lives.

Is Women's Studies part of the Establishment?

It is a mistake to dismiss Women's Studies as part of the Establishment or incorporated into it. This is not to say that there are no differences between these courses and consciousness-raising groups. It is important to be clear about the differences between an informal consciousness-raising group which provides a forum for expression of personal experiences which are confidential to the group and usually involves a commitment between members to support each other, and the educational group which is more structured and, though less focused on personal experience alone, often uses such experiences to question concepts and categorizations that leave out women. There are of course contradictions and pressures facing those who are foolhardy enough to attempt working in the mainstream. As Maria Mies points out,

> If Women's Studies is to contribute to the cause of women's emancipation, then women in the academic field have to use their scholarship and knowledge towards this end. If they consciously do so they will realize that their own existence as women and scholars is a contradictory one. As women, they are affected by the sexist oppression together with other women and as scholars, they share the privilege of the (male) academic elite. (Mies, 1983, p. 120)

The pressure to conform or be incorporated into this elite is strong, the danger of being tipped off the soup rim, as Lyndie Brimstone puts it, always there.

I recall an incident in the early 1970s when I was working in a university. The mother of two young children, I joined in a campaign for the provision of nursery facilities. At that time there was more money around for education than is now the case and considerable sums had been spent on new sports facilities, new buildings and equipment. On the other hand, no provision whatsoever was invested in childcare. I was a member of a Nursery Action Group who had been campaigning without success for the setting up of a nursery. In desperation we took eight children into a maths lecture for five minutes to demonstrate the difficulties of studying in the presence of young children. The kids ran around and the lecturer continued to calculate equations on the board. The atmosphere was good-humoured and the incident would have passed without repercussions if the local newspaper had not sent a photographer who snapped a photo of my daughter wearing a mortarboard. She was 3 years old at the time. Her picture appeared in the local press with a report of the demonstration. Pandemonium broke loose. We were, paradoxically accused of interfering with the 'academic freedom' of the university, an unpardonable offence. I was summoned to see the Vice Chancellor, Carstairs, a man renowned for his liberal views. Over tea and biscuits, I was warned that my tenure would be removed should I participate in any political action in future and that the situation would be reviewed in a year's time to consider whether I had behaved myself. I did what I was told and toed the line but this incident was an important factor in my decision to leave a year later. This illustrates that there is not just a danger of being pulled into the mainstream but that the threat of being flung off the rim if you do not conform is always present.

Sue Lees

Women's Studies — A Challenge to the Status Quo

How far is it possible to change the present male-dominated academic world? Mary Wollstonecraft in 1792, in considering education to be the most important pathway to women's liberation, contested the French philosopher Rousseau's statement that if you educate women in the same way as men, women will lose those forms of power they have traditionally been able to exercise over men, and said: 'This is the very point I aim at. I do not wish them to have power over men, but over themselves' (Wollstonecraft, 1792).

To what extent is this possible within a patriarchal capitalistic educational system? This question was originally asked by Virginia Woolf in a book called *Three Guineas*, first published in 1938, and later, in 1979, by Adrienne Rich in her article 'Towards a Woman Centred University' (Rich, 1980). Rich pointed out that feminists can use the male-centred university as a base and resource while doing research and writing books and articles whose influence will be felt far beyond the academy. To quote her:

> Whatever forms it may take, the process of women's repossession of ourselves is irreversible. Within and without academe, the rise in women's expectations has gone far beyond the middle class and has released an incalculable new energy, not merely for changing institutions but for women's redefinition, not merely for equal rights but for a new kind of being. (Rich, 1979, p. 155)

A similar point has been made by numerous other writers (see, for example, Spender, 1982; Bezucha, 1985; Smith, 1988; McNeil, 1987). We set out to develop this ideal at the North London Polytechnic by setting up a centre for Women's Studies in the early 1980s with three aims: to increase access for women students and set up a number of women-oriented courses including a half degree programme in Women's Studies, set up a research base for women and, finally, to attempt to develop an equal opportunities policy and implement it within the polytechnic. The rather eccentric Director at the time, after making the usual cracks about whether we 'hated men' and giving us a few glasses of wine, said 'I am warming to you women' and allowed us to go ahead.

There are a number of reasons why polytechnics and colleges of further education should be more open to change than universities. In spite of the recent managerial income-generation ethos, these institutions are committed to providing education for the less privileged. A higher proportion of their students are female and black. This is increasingly the case as the number of 18-year-olds has declined and the labour force requires more graduates which has led to an expansion of Access courses.

Secondly, the proportion of women lecturers is far higher than in universities. This is not to say that the representation of women is not still very low at management level or even at the level of Principal Lecturer. A recent statistical study of ten polytechnics carried out by Jean Bocock, Assistant Secretary for Higher Education at the National Association of Teachers in

Further and Higher Education, and Mollie Temple, head of access development at Leeds Polytechnic, found that although 49 per cent of lecturers were women, as you moved up the hierarchy the representation of women dropped (see MacGregor, 1990). Only 15 per cent of Principal Lecturers/Readers were women, 12 per cent of heads of department and 13 per cent of senior managers. However when you compare this representation with the universities where, according to the Hansard Report, only 11 per cent of non-clerical staff are women, it does imply that polytechnics are less elitist than universities (Hansard Report, 1990).

Thirdly, polytechnics are more responsive to new developments than the universities. It is at the polytechnics rather than the universities that attempts have been made to put equal opportunity policies into practice. This is perhaps one reason why we were able to set up the Women's Studies Unit. We were ambitious in our aims and now, five years later, I shall try to draw on this experience to evaluate what we have achieved and learned.

We regard Women's Studies not so much as a discipline as a way of transforming the academic world. It is revolutionary in its politics. It is not about adding women on but about bringing women and their experience into education and about reconceptualizing disciplines. It is about allowing women's voice to be heard in the curriculum, integrating the study of emotions as well as the study of cognition into academia. It is about radicalizing institutions, modifying their latent and manifest discriminatory policies, changing the face of education. As Bowles and Klein aptly put it in the preface to their book

> It has the potential to alter fundamentally the nature of all knowledge by shifting the focus from androcentricity to a frame of reference in which women's different and differing ideas, experiences, needs and interests are valid in their own right and form the basis for our teaching and learning. (Bowles and Klein, 1983, p. 3)

Resistance to feminism derives from its radicalism. For example, it seeks to undermine the distinction between the private and the public, between reason and emotion, the objective from the subjective. It is therefore a subversive activity (see Bezucha, 1985).

To what extent is it possible to apply feminist politics to academic life? Academic institutions are concerned with reproducing a patriarchal elite to take over positions of power. Only 15 per cent of the population in Britain have any higher education, one of the lowest proportions in Europe. Only 35 per cent of 16-to-18-year-olds were in full-time education in 1988, which contrasts with 79 per cent in the USA, 77 per cent in Japan, 66 per cent in France and 76 per cent in Sweden. The British educational system is by no stretch of the imagination the most progressive. In terms of sex equality, though there has been an increase in the number of female students at university over the past decade, the proportion of women lecturers, readers or professors has hardly changed over the past half century. Only 16 per cent of university lecturers are women, and a mere 3 per cent of professors. There is evidence too that this is not due to the failure of women to put themselves forward but to the in-built and frequently unconscious biases of appointments panels which are largely composed of white middle-class men. These men are, of course, serviced by poorly paid or unpaid women, not merely at home by wives but also at work where cleaners, secretaries and research assistants are overwhelmingly female. Women, on the other hand, who try to combine child-rearing and career are given no help by the institution and only rarely by husbands. It is difficult to explain how higher education can still be guilty of such discrimination on the grounds of race and sex, while maintaining a popular liberal veneer, what Alison Utley describes in the Times Higher Educational Supplement as 'at best an anomaly, at worst a national scandal' (Utley, 1990). Until it is recognized that positive discrimination operates in favour of men now, and is not something to be introduced 'unfairly' to increase the proportion of female appointments, little can be achieved. Panels are unwilling to recognise their in-built biases to reproduce their own elites, with their own criteria of expertise. It is however possible that postmodernist philosophy will lead to a questioning of such pillars of wisdom and seep scepticism into the employment policies of these elitist institutions. This is unlikely to be sufficient to shake the confidence and self-interest of present power-holders and it is difficult to feel anything but pessimism about the efficacy of equal opportunity policies (see Lees and Scott, 1990).

Women's Studies courses do however challenge this elite from the margins of the academic world and courses are expanding, both at undergraduate level (at the Middlesex Polytechnic, the Polytechnic of East London, the Polytechnic of North London, Sheffield and Lancashire Polytechnics and Lancaster University) and at postgraduate level (at Middlesex, South Bank, Sheffield and Wolverhampton Polytechnics, and Cambridge College of Art and Technology) courses have been set up and are flourishing. At universities too Women's Studies MA courses are proliferating from the first at Kent and Bradford to courses at York, Bristol, Exeter, the Institute of Education and the Open University, to name but a few. Options in Women's Studies are also an integral part of many degree courses, from Cultural Studies and the social sciences to vocational courses for social workers and teachers. Developments are taking place in introducing gender issues into computing (see Griffiths, 1988; Mahony and Van Toen, 1990) and science and technology courses. Women's Studies challenges the unrepresentative nature of higher educational institutions, the academic criteria and processes by which power is maintained. It challenges the separation between the public and the private (see Maynard, 1990) and argues that if women are to obtain equal opportunities, men will have to step out of their ivory towers and take equal responsibility in the servicing of society. This involves men taking on equal responsibility for housework and childcare as well as equal time and opportunities for self-development (Gould, 1984, p. 5). The separation between the public and the private, work and home, will need to be broken down.

I remember when lecturing one day when I had small children, I looked down and saw a nappy pin stuck to my jacket. The incongruity of my two worlds suddenly hit me. This separation between the world of work and the world of domesticity is one which is experienced quite differently by men and women because women are responsible for the domestic realm and are also only accepted in the work world on sufferance; in other words, only if they are able to avoid the domestic world impinging on work. My reaction to the nappy pin was therefore horror, as though my cover had been blown. As we women move between the work and domestic world, hurrying to pick up our kids from nursery, the dirty clothes from the launderette, the food from the supermarket, the prescription from the doctor's, we take on another persona. Meanwhile, our colleagues have retired to the important committees or to the pub or restaurant, where the important decisions are made. A nappy pin on one's lapel will just not do.

Another image flashes into my mind. I am sitting in an examiners' meeting. I am the only woman present. Most of the students we are examining are women and a tutor is asked why one chap's performance has deteriorated over the last year. Eventually another tutor intervenes to say that it was due to pregnancy. The meeting resumes to look at the other 'chaps'.

Is it possible to link these two worlds, the world of learning and the world of domesticity? Is it possible for institutions to take on board the differential responsibilities that men and women have? Change is unsettling and threatening to many. Whether it is changing heterosexist attitudes, conceptual frameworks, sexist or racist attitudes, or the structures of institutions, change is a frightening process. To disregard this and pretend that people are just stubborn and lazy is a mistake. The difficulty of change must be recognized, the slowness of progress accepted. If disillusionment is not to set in, the difficulties should not be underestimated. To quote Adrienne Rich once again,

> Immense forces in the universities ... are intrinsically opposed to anything resembling an actual feminist renaissance, wherever the process appears to be a serious undertaking and not merely a piece of decorative reformism. (Rich, 1980)

With so few women in distinguished positions it is difficult for even committed feminists to have much influence. Women's Studies is at best politely tolerated by the academic community, and any woman interested in furthering her career would be unwise to become too identified with it. Marcia Westkott argued that the realistic course of action was for women within the American academy to stick to writing about women, their historical contexts and creative works but 'employing scrupulously the established methods of the male defined intellectual tradition'. Unfortunately, she argued, this often robbed feminist work of commitment to change (Westkott, 1983).

It is difficult to see how real change could come about unless the proportion of women academics in the universities greatly increases and the proportion of women in managerial positions improves both in polytechnics and universities. The recent report of the Hansard Society Commission for Parliamentary Reform on *Women at the Top* documents how in actuality little change has been achieved in women's access to positions of power in Britain (Hansard Report, 1990). Between 1975 and 1988 the proportion of women in senior academic posts has been derisory and has scarcely increased at all. The report documents discrimination against women in all areas of life, politics, the economy, the law, universities and business. At the launch of the report at the House of Commons, when asked by an MP what was to happen to the men who would be displaced if the representation of women in positions of authority were improved, Lady Howe, who chaired the Committee, answered 'Don't misunderstand me, I am not in favour of positive action'. When advocates of change such as Lady Howe are not prepared to back the only means of bringing about change, little can be achieved.

The Hansard Report argues that all institutions of higher education should appoint an Equal Opportunity Officer who will produce regular audits on the progress of women within the institution, and that this should be combined with the setting of voluntary targets. They go on to argue:

> These targets would not be given any statutory force. Their function would in part be that of consciousness-raising and failure to achieve the target would give rise to questions about whether the institution is adopting the right approach to ensure EO becomes a reality. (p. 6)

Changing the status quo will inevitably be met with resistance. The inevitability of this process of adjustment where some men will be displaced is often denied. By denial, and reassurance that change will only occur through consensus, the possibility of change recedes. A common feature of equal opportunities policy implementation is to deny that its effectiveness involves a loss of power to the present incumbents, a changing of long-standing practices, conflict rather than consensus. The assumption is often made that once the inequality between men and women is documented reasonable men will change.

Exactly the same assumptions have been made on the left, that sympathetic men will support change and that once the evidence of women's inequality is documented the problem will disappear. Similarly, Joni Lovenduski (1986), in her discussion of women in European politics, pointed out that there is explicit male resistance within elites to increasing the presence of women. At the top level, new entrants displace existing power-holders and it is therefore not to be expected that doors will simply open. In state socialist societies, she argues, the best explanation of why women have not entered elites since the establishment of communist party rule is that parties have deliberately and expressly decided that they should not. The position will change only when the parties decide that it should.

Women's networks must acquire the weight to compete with established organizations. Self-organization is essential as sex equality policy does not normally cover political activities. The presence of women has not guaranteed the taking into account of women's interests. The evidence is that many women politicians are surrogate men, that they have no interest in pursuing particular questions of women's rights and even when such an interest is possible, to make any appreciable difference to policy is often impossible.

Scandinavian experience indicates that the number of women must increase dramatically if any appreciable difference is to be apparent. The situation within education is no different. The control of education is firmly in the hands of men. Women's Studies is tolerated at the margins, though it is also infiltrating some main disciplines. At a time when new courses are developing across the country, it is important that we share our experience of teaching. Our experience has been that there are certain prerequisites for the success of Women's Studies:

1   It must have an interdisciplinary base at least in regard to its funding and should not be subsumed into a faculty structure.

2   The question of men's role in Women's Studies, both in teaching and as students should be addressed. Many male members of staff do not understand why it was important to appoint more women to teaching posts in Women's Studies when some men are already integrating feminist theory into their teaching. The threat that 'gender studies' could replace Women's Studies was discussed last year by Mary Evans in the plenary. She emphasized the importance of retaining the category of 'women' and the importance of resisting gender studies (see Evans, in this volume).

3   Financial support and childcare facilities for women with children are vital. The introduction of loans and the increasing cost of education will have a particularly deleterious effect on enrolments of women, particularly black women.

4   Women's Studies should develop hand in hand with equal opportunity initiatives. It should be recognized that such initiatives are often seen as a threat to the reasonable taken-for-granted processes of institutions. In one institution the Equal Opportunity Committee was seen as a staff committee gone wild, totally unrealistic in its demands (Lees and Scott, 1990). At another, the committee was seen as an unrepresentative clique of feminists too militant in their cause, giving too high a profile to equal opportunities and jeopardizing its progress (see Cockburn, 1989). The climate and awareness of such issues has changed dramatically, the change in consciousness a beginning.

At the Polytechnic of North London, there have been many setbacks. The Equal Opportunity Unit that was set up to implement the policy we drew up has been disbanded. The Women's Studies Unit can only now concentrate on courses. It has been transferred to within a Faculty. The ideals we set out to achieve, to transform the academic environment, have not been achieved, but we have taken important steps towards the provision of a different kind of education. It is now possible to specialize in Women's Studies, feminist theory is no longer dismissed as nonsense, as was the case a short time ago. The degree programme has attracted a large number of applicants and the enthusiasm of students grows.

European Initiatives

Increased European cooperation is also likely to boost Women's Studies and the Women's Movement. Already Britain's chauvinism and poor record on women's rights has been shown up by the European Court. Britain has opposed equal pay legislation, maternity and paternity leave, equalizing pension age and rights and improving rights for part-time workers, but is being forced to change. The Women's Lobby in Brussels is far stronger than at Westminster and Women's Studies is taking root at many European universities, particularly in Holland and Scandinavia. The first Western European meeting on Women's Studies, sponsored by the European Parliament section on educational rights, was held in Brussels in 1988, and more meetings are planned. Two European Women's Studies Networks have been formed, the European Network of Women's Studies and WISE, and conferences held with representatives from all over Europe. We have much to learn from experiences abroad. I have just returned from visiting the University of Amsterdam where two recent initiatives have been introduced. A few years ago the government financed a half post in Women's Studies in all eleven universities providing that each university funded the other half post. These posts are now funded wholly by the universities and there are now thirteen professors of Women's Studies.

The other initiative has however not been so successful. At the University of Amsterdam a quota system operates by which women who apply for any post must be interviewed before the men are even considered. The University of Utrecht is considering introducing a similar system. Dr Kea Tijdens told me that the irony was that that it does not seem to have led to an increase in appointments of women. The women applicants are interviewed first but mostly turned down to leave the way open for the men to be appointed. This illustrates the difficulty in bringing about change in elitist institutions. It is difficult for members of appointment panels to recognize their own biases in favour of their own kind. Positive action is regarded as favouritism or not appointing the 'best' candidate.

The reality is that the 'best' is relative to the prejudice of the panel, where an important though often unstated criteria is 'fitting in' with the present elite. Positive action already operates in favour of the status quo; to demand that more women or black people are appointed is only to redress that present bias. This however is no part of the 'liberal' discourse. It is time that equal opportunities became more of a reality.

Conclusion

The expansion of Women's Studies is one of the most exciting developments in the Women's Movement of the 1980s. It is too easy to forget that for centuries women were denied access to education. The one profession that was open to women — marriage — was held to need no education. Education is still provided by and large on male terms, but the provision of Women's Studies courses is an opportunity to make women visible, to challenge the way disciplines have excluded a feminist perspective and the way women have been excluded from the management of institutions and of the curriculum. As long as women can resist incorporation into the mainstream, Women's Studies stands a chance of educating women to resist war and violence and create a new society. It will take a long struggle to change the face of education. It is regrettable how little change there has been since Virginia Woolf wrote:

> Education ... does not teach people to hate force, but to use it ... far from teaching the educated generosity and magnanimity, it makes them on the contrary so anxious to keep their possessions, that 'grandeur and power' of which the poet speaks, in their own hands that they will use not force but much subtler methods than force and possessiveness very closely connected with war. (Woolf, 1938, p. 35)

Womens's Studies seeks to teach people to hate force and to struggle towards a better society.

References

BEZUCHA, R. (1985) 'Feminist pedagogy as a subversive activity', in CULLEY, M. and PORTUGES, C. (Eds) *Gendered Subjects*, Routledge and Kegan Paul.

BOWLES, G. and KLEIN, R.D. (Eds) (1983) *Theories of Women's Studies*, Routledge and Kegan Paul.

COCKBURN, C. (1989) 'Equal Opportunities: the short and the long agenda', in *Industrial Relations Journal*, March, pp. 213–225.

EVANS, M. (1990) 'The Problem of Gender for Women's Studies', in *Women's Studies International Forum*, Vol. 13, No. 5, pp. 457–462.

GOULD, C. (1984) *Beyond Domination: New Perspectives on Women and Philosophy*, Rowman and Lichfield.

GRIFFITHS, M. (1988) 'Strong Feelings about Computers', in *Women's Studies International Forum*, Vol. 11, No. 2, pp. 145–154.

HAMNER, J. (1989) 'Making Waves: Women's Studies and the Women's Movement', paper given at *les cahiers du Grif* European Conference, Bruxelles.

HANSARD REPORT (1990) *Women at the Top*, Hansard Society.

HARDING, S. (1986) *The Science Question in Feminism*, Open University Press.

LANGLAND, E. and GOVE, W. (Eds) (1981) *A Feminist Perspective in the Academy*, University of Chicago Press.

LEES, S. and SCOTT, M. (1990) 'Equal Opportunities: Rhetoric or Action', in *Gender and Education*, Vol. 2, No. 3.

LOVENDUSKI, JONI (1986) *Women and European Politics*, Harvester.
MACGREGOR, KAREN (1990) 'Outlook Bleak for the Female Factor', *Times Higher Educational Supplement*, 7 December.
MCNEIL, M. (1987) *Gender and Expertise*, Free Association Books.
MAHONY, K. and VAN TOEN, B. (1990) 'Mathematical Formalism as a Means of Occupational Closure in Computing — Why 'Hard' Computing Tends to Exclude Women', in *Gender and Education*, Vol. 2, No. 3.
MAYNARD, MARY (1990) 'The Re-Shaping of Sociology? Trends in the Study of Gender', *Sociology*, Vol. 24, No. 2.
MIES, MARIA (1983) 'Towards a methodology for Feminist Research', in BOWLES, G. and KLEIN, R.D. (Eds) *Theories of Women's Studies*, Routledge and Kegan Paul.
MIES, MARIA (1990) 'Women's Studies: Science, Violence and Responsibility', in *Women's Studies International Forum*, Vol. 13, No. 5.
OAKLEY, ANN (1986) *Feminist Thoughts about Jerusalem*, Oxford, Basil Blackwell.
RENDEL, MARGHERITA (1982) 'A Worldwide Panorama of Research and Teaching Related to Women', in *Cultures*, Vol. viii.
RICH, ADRIENNE (1980) 'Towards a Woman Centred University', in RICH, ADRIENNE *On Lies, Secrets and Silence*, London, Virago.
ROWBOTHAM, SHEILA (1989) *The Past is Before Us: Feminism in Action since the 1960s*, Pandora.
SEGAL, LYNNE (1987) *Is the future Female? Troubled thoughts on Contemporary Feminism*, Virago.
SMITH, DOROTHY E. (1988) *The Everyday World as Problematic*, Open University Press.
SPENDER, DALE (1982) *Invisible Woman*, Writers and Readers.
STANLEY, LIZ and WISE, SUE (1983) *Breaking Out: Feminist Consciousness and Feminist Research*, London, Routledge and Kegan Paul.
UTLEY, ALISON (1990) 'Direct Action for a Liberal Code', in *Times Higher Educational Supplement*, 10 August.
WESTKOTT, MARCIA (1983) 'Women's Studies as a strategy for change; between criticism and vision', in BOWLES, G. and KLEIN, R.D. *Theories of Women's Studies*, Routledge and Kegan Paul.
WOLLSTONECRAFT, MARY (1792) *On the vindication of the rights of women*, reissued 1988, W.W. Norton.
WOOLF, VIRGINIA (1938) *Three Guineas*, Penguin.

Chapter 8

On Course: Women's Studies —
A Transitional Programme*

Jalna Hanmer

Women's studies courses are but another venue in which gendered senarios are played out so that teachers, like students, can explore, theorize and work to change their subordination within a sexual hierarchy. This chapter is concerned with the relationship between theory, action and personal experience and uses examples from the University of Bradford MA/Diploma in Women's Studies as many issues for students and teachers are unlikely to be fundamentally different from that of other degree courses. Given the personal and social demands made by developing, maintaining and studying Women's Studies, the question is, why are we doing this?

I decided to begin with myself; not just personal experience, but a biography I suspect is not that much different from that of many other teachers of Women's Studies. The reason for beginning in this way is to locate personal experience within theory as the expression of theory and the base from which theory develops. Personal experience is both embryonic theory and the site for the validation of theory. Expressed this way Women's Studies becomes a form of action, a process, in which theory and experience are explored, separated and merged. The individual teacher, like the student, brings the totality of self to Women's Studies.

As with many of my colleagues in the UK, although I coordinate a Masters in Women's Studies I am not employed to teach Women's Studies. I was a university teacher before I began to teach on a Women's Studies course. I was involved in the Women's Movement, or the Women's Liberation Movement as it was known then, before I was a university teacher. I am a senior lecturer in social work, with a disciplinary background in sociology, but I spend the greater part of my time in teaching, research, publication and administration in the area we call Women's Studies. In Women's Studies in

* A version of this chapter was originally given as a speech titled, 'Making Waves: Women's Studies and the Women's Movement' at the European Conference Women's Studies Concept and Reality, 17–19 February 1989, organized by *les cahiers du Grif*, and published as 'Faire des Vagues: Les Etudes Feministes et le Mouvement des Femmes', *les cahiers du Grif*, Autumn 1990.

the UK, women are almost always employed on a disciplinary basis and few courses have teachers appointed as lecturers in Women's Studies. This personal biography is a comment on the institutional position of Women's Studies in higher education and its relationship to traditional academic disciplines and professional areas.

The organizational structure in which this commonplace personal experience is embedded is illustrated by the Bradford course. During the UGC (University Grant Committee)'s round of cuts in student numbers in the university sector in 1981, Bradford University suffered greater student number losses than many other institutions and, while it may appear paradoxical, this enabled a new educational initiative to get off the ground. So much negativity needed to be counterbalanced with new life and, as the institution had unfilled part-time postgraduate student numbers, we went ahead with a proposal for a postraduate degree in Women's Studies. But care had to be exercised as Women's Studies was not part of the institution's academic planning profile.

Women teachers came together over an eighteen-month period to devise a curriculum that could not be faulted academically and had no resource implications for the institution — that is, no new teachers or books or any other financial imput was required for the programme to be implemented. Even though these basic institutional conditions were satisfied, it is very unlikely that this new degree would have made it though the various university committees without the downturn in the university's fortunes. The UGC 'invited' Bradford University to close a number of courses, including the highly successful as well as the more marginal. Unfilled student numbers offered an opportunity for limited recovery and, while other new initiatives such as management studies were enthusiastically welcomed, every offer had to be seriously considered.

The lukewarm welcome to Women's Studies was expressed organizationally by central academic committees through the imposition of an exceptionally heavy examination structure on students. Even though the course was recognized as innovative, traditional ways of examination were added to the requirement of assessment by essay and dissertation and this had to be accepted by the course team in order for the degree to be offered. Two years later, with the intervention of the external examiner, the examination structure was revised and assessment by essay and dissertation only accepted.

Looking back over the ten years of the degree this was the first of a series of problematic issues facing teachers and students. The list includes acquiring university agreement that full-time students could be accepted, the sometimes muted and sometimes strident complaint that the course was only attracting women students, the raising of part-time student fees so that they are wildly out of step with other institutions offering Women's Studies at postgraduate level, ignoring the teaching needs of Women's Studies that resulted from staff changes and under-resourcing generally. I am confident that other Women's Studies degrees could present their own list, as we are all adversely affected by a structuring of education, as with everything else, so that the gendered interests of men predominate.

The decision to move into Women's Studies on a no new resource basis was unavoidable, but it has implications both for the administration and for the teaching of the degree. Manoeuvring for survival within inadequate parameters needs to be understood as part of the job and one more example of the usual women's life situation of responsibility without authority. To look at administration first, until 1989 I was the only non-professorial teacher of Women's Studies with tenure in applied social studies which meant that the coordinating role could not be rotated as full professors and non-tenured and temporary staff could not be asked to take on the heavy administrative load involved. In relation to teaching, if teachers in other departmental areas offering courses on Women's Studies left, and even in a time when few academics move institution we have had a number of changes, this teaching was not considered when new appointments were made. Sometimes a new member of staff can replace someone who has left, and sometimes not. New members of staff may be able to offer different courses, but there is constant annual worrying which is a key coordinating function. We dare not become a separate academic area, even though this would mean we could receive resources in our own right and not through the good graces of other departments, as these are easier to axe or disband in some other way. The continuation of the degree requires exceptional energy and commitment from its teachers, which is, of course, a plus for students.

We continue from year to year for two reasons. Firstly, because women want to take this course and are prepared and able, often with great hardship, to fund themselves. As it is postgraduate there are no mandatory grants and very few sources of funding, although recently we have received Economic and Social Research Council recognition for studentships and some access funding based on hardship is beginning. As long as we have suitably qualified applicants who will pay whatever the institution demands in the way of full or part-time fees, however this is managed, the university does not object to the course continuing. This must be understood as the major reason for the acceptance of Women's Studies in further and higher education in the past decade and why courses have proliferated in a time of reduced government grants. The reliance by universities on self-funded students, including the higher fees paid by those from outside the Economic Community (EC students pay home student fees), became more compelling as the decade progressed. Secondly, as long as women colleagues in the university are willing to make time, often in addition to their full teaching load, to tutor students and provide courses, this degree will continue. This is of course, another form of institutional fund-raising and yet another demonstration of women's subordination.

As an academic exercise Women's Studies is treated as marginal to the life of the institution even though it is not. It does not have high status within any discipline even though it is a new and powerful theoretical force. This relationship between teachers of Women's Studies, their institution and disciplines is commonplace. The question is: Why do we teach Women's Studies and struggle for the survival of courses when we don't have to?

I suggest it is the relation between theory and action — an overriding concern to be involved in meaningful academic and intellectual work — that is key to the answer for many of us. Women's Studies is the most exciting and lively area in social theory today because understanding about and contributing to social transformation is the heart — the centre — of the enterprise. For example, through the Women's Movement I became involved in research and publication in the area we call violence against women. Once I began to teach in universities I struggled to make a new perspective on violence against women sound 'properly' academic in order to be able to present social work students with a different understanding of family, home-life, marriage; one that was less victim-blaming of women so that the work I and many other women were doing in Women's Aid, the refuge movement for battered women, could be seen as an appropriate agency response and utilized by women in authority over other women who desperately need Women's Aid. This simple example is a tangle of theory and action — of ways of knowing. Intellectual challenges are action.

The early wave of feminism understood theory and practice to be one and the same; the personal is political and the political is theory as well as action. Action gives us the problems we research and identify. Action gives us theory, both middle-range challenges and new ways of knowing what we know. Action gives us the reality against which to assess theories. Action, theory, personal experience, are different vantage points on the material world, and each contains the other. Through Women's Studies these insights become epistemological challenges to dominant ideology and ways of knowing.

Or the process can happen the other way. An intellectual insight may lead to years of study and research and be fed back into that group of scholars working on gender or women, aiding the transformation of a discipline or specific knowledge of discrete areas. My personal example is work around the new reproductive technologies and genetic engineering. Reflection on Shulamith Firestone's belief in a scientific and technological solution to the historic emnity between the sexes (1971), led to an insight more closely approximated by that of Virginia Woolf, 'Science, it would seem, is not sexless, she is a man, a father, and infected too' (1938). The new questions those of us who work in Women's Studies are asking come from the changed social consciousness we call the Women's Movement. Theory gives us the problems we research and identify. Theory gives us action, both middle-range challenges and new ways of being in the world. Theory gives us the reality against which to assess action.

As the Bradford example illustrates, to examine the issue of theory and action for Women's Studies is to ask a series of questions:

1 Where did Women's Studies come from?

2 Are there different types of Women's Studies? That is, are there different basic questions and formulations?

3 Where is Women's Studies located organizationally and how does this affect its development and the access of women?

4   What are the justificatory reasons for Women's Studies? Have these changed over time?

5   What is the relationship of Women's Studies to traditional academic disciplines and specific social theories that cross disciplinary boundaries?

6   And finally, how is Women's Studies contributing to epistemology? That is, the formulation of theory and action, of subjectivity and objectivity, of commonality and difference?

These questions are addressed wherever there is Women's Studies. National culture and the organization of educational systems have an impact on how these questions are approached and introduce difference between experiences in the member states in the European Community and other countries. But there are levels on which similarities exist. Renate Duelli Klein's PhD thesis on the dynamics of Women's Studies explores the ideas and practices of Women's Studies in higher education in the UK, the FRG, the USA and Australia (Klein, 1986). She draws the conclusion that between countries both the theories and practices of Women's Studies in higher education are strikingly similar in that there is a substantial diversity within each country and even within each Women's Studies degree course. Internal diversity is readily apparent within our Women's Studies course through varying teaching styles, theoretical perspectives, research involvement, previous experiences and knowledge of Women's Studies and the Women's Movement, but at the same time there is a commitment and ethos that arises out of a commonality of aims and basic beliefs about the enterprise in which we are engaged.

What has become Women's Studies often began as occasional meetings around specific topics or a series of meetings organized by women in the Women's Liberation Movement. These early days were closely related to consciousness-raising and women took their new understanding and knowledge into a variety of educational organizational forms — however further and higher education was organized within their countries. We also took this new consciousness into traditional disciplines and their degree and higher degree courses and research initiatives. We utilized whatever social space we occupied, or could extend into, to challenge dominant ideology and ways of organizing the world.

Our success in building Women's Studies within adult education, informal education, further and higher education, is primarily the result of the intense interest these courses generate amongst women. The publishing industry we have built as a result of the many women who continue to explore women's position in the social world and what can be done to improve it is supported largely by women who buy these books and subscribe to the many journals and magazines produced by other women. In the UK the publishing industry as a whole is involved in the production of work on and by women. Major academic publishers have established book lists, imprints, and there are several publishers that only produce work on and by women. While Women's Studies is not the Women's movement, the women who create and sustain these courses and the material on which they are based are involved in a struggle against dominant ideology, organization and teaching practice, and ways of knowing.

This commonality exists even though there are important theoretical differences in how the position of women is to be understood and various unresolved problems of access and recognition of the concerns of particular groups of women. In particular black women, ethnic minority women, lesbians and working-class women are marginalized in terms of academic content and as students and teachers in formal educational provision on Women's Studies. Of course the struggles of these groups of women are not the same nor totally separate, but overlap for individuals (Coulson and Bhavnani, 1989). This is also true in terms of the changes women want and the opposition women face. The white, middle-class, heterosexual dominance within Women's Studies in terms of theory, teachers and students is today's orthodoxy in the theory and practice of Women's Studies. For the moment opening Women's Studies to all perspectives, responding to the challenges of black women, of ethnic minority women, of lesbians, of working-class women, overshadows the dispute between radical, socialist/ Marxist and equal opportunity conceptualizations of how to understand the position of women and what should be done to alter it.

But to be specific, in the UK Women's Studies has the example of what happened to Marxism when it was taken up by higher education. Theory became divorced from action even though Marxism is a theory of action. Could what happened to Marxism happen to feminism? How can this outcome be avoided? These became key questions for some of us in Women's Studies at the first Women's Studies Summer School organized by the Women's Research and Resources Centre in 1979, held at the University of Bradford. A major issue was — will moving that part of the Women's Liberation Movement that can be moved into traditional male-led academic institutions lead to the tail wagging the dog — that is, to a deradicalization of the Women's Liberation Movement? Many women thought that it would — to do business with the male-controlled state and its educational institutions could only result in sell-outs and defeat.

These arguments are no doubt familiar. The answers depend in part upon how the issues for women are conceived and how the intellectual struggle to create and convey new knowledge and ways of knowing are pursued within the institution. Is it just a question of adding women on? Of correcting an accidental leaving out of women? The state treats the issue as one of equal opportunities and not systemic inequality. Women's Studies must often comply with this formulation in public statements of aims and objectives. Even the degree I coordinate has the assessment of, and contribution to, issues of equal opportunities in its statement of aims.

Dominant epistemology, or ways of knowing what we know, is based on the core beliefs of positivism, that is, so-called objective knowledge, value-neutrality and a belief in progress. These concepts are the basis of both physical and social sciences' ways of knowing the world and forms an epistemology that has served men well. It has enabled men to retail their views as the only view, as the knowledge of humankind. Using this mainstream scientific view of the world and the methodologies that come from it, women are found inadequate and inferior by learned men, and an occasional woman, via our hormones, brain structure and intelligence, emotions, our biological difference from men a source of explanation for why we do not succeed or why we have personal problems, etc. In brief, biology establishes our inferiority while social relations establishes our blame. Only social superordinates can utilize in their favour this way of knowing the world. Their so-called objectivity is the emergent quality of their position as social superordinates in the sexual hierarchy.

The practice of 'doing knowledge' in this way is the expression of theory, not of objectivity, but of social dominance. Women who began to demand a place for women's voices in social theory recognized the need to replace the androcentric, male-centred, men as representative of human beings, with women as deviant or invisible, ideological construction of knowledge. It is inevitable that feminist scholarship challenged these core beliefs even though initially this was not necessarily the intention nor understood to be the task. To make a place for women in theory and to be included amongst those who theorize, positivistic epistemology has to be moved from centre stage. This is the problematic that led to Women's Studies.

Listening to women is creating an epistemological revolution. In the UK the first concern of women coming from an empirical tradition in the social sciences was with methodology. Feminist empiricism, listening to women, exploring ways to gain better quality data, to incorporate women's experiences more truthfully within theory became the first focus (Harding, 1986). Only by challenging dominant epistemology as male-centred, as partial, could a feminist standpoint be presented as a fundamentally more correct way of understanding women and the world in which we live (Harding, 1986). Only in this way could the charge of non-objectivity, of having values or an axe to grind, of being engaged in politicized activity, be resisted. Theory and action as dualities, as either/or, falls in the demand for the subjectivity of women to be recognized. I often feel I am fighting for my life, literally and metaphorically. I am determined to be recognized as subject, my life experiences so determined by gender, and so shared with other women. To theorize this oppression and exploitation is action.

But our experiences and social locations are not the same. There is more than one feminist standpoint (Harding, 1986). Today the theoretical and action task becomes to recognize and account for difference while not losing sight of commonality. In doing this we are creating a new way of knowing the world, of transforming epistemology, of moving beyond the old dualisms of Western thought, the masculinist, androcentric, positivistic ways of creating and ordering knowledge that render us, one half of all people, theoretically invisible or marginalized, the other, the inferior, the less than human. This is social transformation or action.

And we have to do this in institutions that are not necessarily receptive to Women's Studies, both in terms of curriculum and teaching resources. For example, the only content the Women's Studies course at the University of Bradford has ever been denied is lesbian studies. The option had to be reworded so that it appeared resolutely heterosexist. The dreaded word does not appear once. My protestations that lesbian studies is academically creditable fell on deaf ears, and for a number of reasons. Options that mention racism and anti-semitism have succeeded in passing through the relevant university committees, but teaching resources, that is, teachers, to develop these areas are exceptionally severely curtailed. This is not by design, it appears, but because it just works out that other curriculum needs are given greater priority.

It is important to continually test institutional boundaries. By doing so we make a contribution to theory as well as action. For example, when I was a student at Berkeley, Marx was completely ignored within sociology except in a course on the history of sociological thought where, as I recall, the required textbook dismissed him in a page and a half. Then the professor followed this up by assuring us that Marx was wrong. Outside on Telegraph Avenue, at the gates of the university, anyone who dared to stop to listen to the speakers on their soap-boxes, with their alternative knowledges, were photographed by the security forces (perhaps the FBI as was widely assumed). Then in the 1960s even Marx began the trek through the gates and up the steps of Wheeler Hall, and into social science teaching.

Ideological boundaries of so-called theory are different now. Experience in providing Women's Studies courses and degrees demonstrates that these surround heterosexuality, defining it as the only sexuality that may be openly discussed in Women's Studies at the University of Bradford, and no doubt elsewhere in the UK. One might conclude that this is because lesbianism can no longer be contained within deviance theory, as a sexuality, which leaves it as a critique of heterosexuality as a system of social relations. That is, lesbianism is a direct challenge to the social power of men over women and, as a system of social relations that prioritizes bonds between women, it becomes that which cannot be spoken or known.

Race and ethnicity are different, experience shows, in that the boundary exclusion is not total, but the institution is not clear how they are to be presented, and, therefore, resources are marginalized. These excluded, or partially included, discourses challenging dominant social reality, the ideas and structures in which power relations are embedded. Locating the boundaries and stepping over into that which cannot be spoken or known is a way of identifying subjectivity. The act of doing so is both a challenge to a false objectivity and the exposure of ideology — and the essence of objectivity.

Theoretically Women's Studies is in a transitional phase, moving from the Women's Liberation Movement to becoming a discipline with a body of knowledge, epistemology and methodology. Women cannot be added on to existing disciplines as our marginality is not superficial, but in-built into language, methodologies, approaches, concepts, subject divisions, and hierarchies of disciplines (Hanmer, 1990). Women's Studies can fundamentally challenge academic orthodoxies by including excluded and marginalized knowledges and the differing subjectivities of women. The institutional organization of Women's Studies mirrors this transitional intellectual process.

But what of students? To come on a Women's Studies course is an action — and an action that is redolent of theory. Depending upon the social location of the student the statement that 'I am attending a Women's Studies course' can lead other people with whom the student previously had unproblematic relations to assume that our unsuspecting student now has a new range of beliefs, values and behaviours. 'I suppose you think' begins to get in the way of previously easy relationships. The student may be called names, such as 'women's libber', while argument that seriously contests established power relations can lead to the strongest term of disapprobation, lesbian. Students can be thrown off balance by being treated differently. Sometimes they lose a best friend because her husband makes it too difficult to continue the friendship. How one treats other people, how one should change, the exposure to the world of women and a range of experiences, beliefs, values, histories, challenges what one thought one knew. Race, ethnicity, sexuality, class, become dominant themes, structuring the world of personal relationships as well as theoretical understanding.

The consciousness of incoming Women's Studies students varies considerably. They come because they know, or suspect, something is wrong with the way the world they inhabit responds to women. Incoming students may have virtually none to considerable knowledge of Women's Studies and it may be because of prior knowledge that they seek an opportunity for systematic study. Becoming more effective in whatever direction they are pursuing is an important motivation.

In Women's Studies we are learning, analyzing, theorizing, about ourselves. We are letting the subject into the room — mind, emotions, and personal experience. For students to learn, the knowledge of ourselves and our relations with the world, with men, families, children, other women, cannot be presented in the usual objectified manner. Women students must grapple with 'what does this mean for me?' Women's Studies can lead to new ways of living in the world; the breaking out of ideological strait-jackets. Theory and action are so closely intertwined that to move in one direction is to move in the other.

On Women's Studies courses, women students can behave in new ways. They often feel able to demand, discharge and disclose in ways unthinkable on traditional discipline, or interdisciplinary, or professional courses. This can be critical for student academic development. Taking Women's Studies education seriously at Bradford means both academic and theoretical input, and ensuring that students have their own physical space and time in the programme for student-initiated informal groups with opportunities to sit and discuss anything and everything.

We give our prospective students the equivalent of the UK smoker's Government Health Warning, 'This course can change your life', and tell them not to come if they do not want this. It is intellectually demanding; it is emotionally demanding. Further, students at Bradford are expected through project work to explore ways of applying theoretical knowledge to the everyday world of work, either paid employment or through voluntary groups in which they are involved. Learning how bad it is for women, and by implication for oneself, is painful. Finding ways to make it better for women, often starting with oneself, is gruelling. Theory fuels these processes.

But when theory and action and the recognition of subjectivity are integrated, both teachers and students can be sustained by the processes involved in learning and teaching, and learning by teaching, Women's Studies. Women's Studies is making the waves of transformed consciousness that we call the Women's Movement into systematic study of how to understand and theorize the gendered world in which we live. It is because of the particularities of Women's Studies that the potential for transformative knowledge exists; that is, participation by students and teachers involves both a strong commitment to understanding the gendered world in which we live and the inevitable meeting of deeply embedded social resistance which must be dealt with in some way. For individual women in Women's Studies the reality is that we are 'in for a penny, in for a pound'. The transformative process, however, will not continue inevitably; it could become stagnant and degenerative. But by remaining responsive to excluded and marginalized knowledges and subjectivities, and by striving to include the perspectives of groups of women who question and offer alternatives to current Women's Studies orthodoxies, Women's Studies will remain transformative for individual women, for organizations and for the societies in which we live. Seen at its most optimistic, this intellectual and practical activity is laying the basis for a better life for women everywhere.

References

COULSON, MEG and BHAVNANI, KUM-KUM (1989) 'Making a Difference — Questioning Women's Studies', in BURMAN, ERICA (Ed.) *Feminists and Psychological Practice*, London, Sage.

FIRESTONE, SHULAMITH (1971) *The Dialetic of Sex: The Case for the Feminist Revolution*, London, Jonathan Cape.

HANMER, JALNA (1990) 'Men, Power and the Exploitation of Women', in *Women's Studies International Forum*, 13 (5), pp. 443–456, and in HEARN, JEFF and MORGAN, DAVID H. (Eds) *Men, Masculinities and Social Theory*, London, Unwin Hyman.

HARDING, SANDRA (1986) *The Science Question in Feminism*, Milton Keynes, Open University Press.

KLEIN, RENATE DUELLI (1986) 'The Dynamics of Women's Studies: An Exploratory Study Of Its International Ideas And Practices In Higher Education', PhD, University of London, Institute of Education.

WOOLF, VIRGINIA (1938) *Three Guineas*, Harmondsworth, Penguin.

Section III

Working with Diversity

Introduction

Recognizing the reality of women's diversity — with regard to class, 'race', and sexuality — is an important issue within contemporary feminism, but one which Women's Studies has hitherto tended to neglect. Papers in this section voice the fears that Women's Studies, as it moves towards the 'centre', may itself marginalize lesbian and Black women's experience. Lyndie Brimstone argues for a feminist deconstruction of the very concept of 'margin/centre' as a binary polarization which takes for granted, and thus supports, the configuration of dominant and subordinated discourses. Women's Studies, she concludes, can only be allowed to move out of the margins after it has eradicated from its thinking — and its practices — the notion of marginalization. Shantu Watt and Juliet Cook's paper focuses on the issue of racism within Women's Studies, and calls for the development of a diverse and inclusive feminism, which would accept the reality of difference, and recognize and challenge power differentials between women.

Both Black women and lesbians may be said to have succeeded in making their presence felt more strongly within the fields of feminist publishing than in Women's Studies in recent years. The next two papers in this section discuss recent developments in the establishment of a lesbian voice in fiction and poetry. Paulina Palmer discerns a growing division in the fictional representation of lesbians, between a political approach, focusing on the relation of lesbians to the community, and a psychoanalytical approach, concentrating upon the construction of individual lesbian subjectivity. Her paper also contributes to the debate on the difficulty of amalgamating radical and theoretical feminist perspectives; she argues for the necessity of combining the two approaches, as the only true mode of representing our common, complex reality. Gillian Hanscombe and Suniti Namjoshi's paper, on creating a lesbian voice whilst working within the male and heterosexist traditions of lyric poetry, illuminates the problems confronting all women, and lesbians in particular, as they seek to establish a perspective of their own within the context of patriarchal discourses. Because Women's Studies generally has the task of deconstructing male traditions — the traditions of the various academic disciplines, and of the institutions within which we function — similar analyses could be made of very many other areas of difficulty.

Introduction

Finally, in this section, Avtar Brah's paper on 'Questions of Difference and International Feminism' emphasizes the fact that every woman's experience is necessarily located within heterogeneous discursive processes. She offers the concept of a 'politics of identification', which would work across cultural differences, as a way forward for Women's Studies as it takes on the challenge of women's diversity.

Chapter 9

Out of the Margins and Into the Soup: Some Thoughts on Incorporation

Lyndie Brimstone

Let me begin by saying that 'Out of the Margins and Into the Soup' was not a carefully considered title at all but rather one that came to mind when I saw the publicity for the 1990 Women's Studies Network conference and then, for want of time perhaps, stuck. As it happens, though, I rather like it. In the first place there's the cadence, the rise and ultimate fall aptly expressing the reservations I do have about the direction that Women's Studies would seem to be taking, and the dead-end conceptual frameworks that are being used to get there. In the course of this paper I shall be discussing the centre/margins dichotomy and my suspicions that continued uncritical use of this over-worked model could very well lead us into trouble. Secondly, with its rather peculiar mix of theoretical and colloquial forms, this title serves as a reminder to me and, I would hope, to our Conference, that our purpose here is not to exhibit our academic stature but to communicate, validate and stimulate our efforts. Whilst theoretical abstraction is an essential part of this process in that it allows us to stretch, to flex, to formulate new ideas, it is of little earthly use if we leave it floating around in rarefied air. We are not, after all, angels and some of us have little hope that we ever will be. Finally, on this decidedly human note, I would say that, as a title alone, 'Out of the Margins and Into the Soup' has generated a good deal of curiosity, speculation and, for all its overall seriousness of intent, laughter. This, more than anything else then, makes it a good place to begin.[1]

So, 1990 and Women's Studies is rallying forces. Whether 'out of the margins' indicates an intention, a process or a move that has already been made is far from clear but what this forceful statement does tell us is that Women's Studies will no longer accept its allotted cultural space. There is no doubt that the promise of a new decade is helping to regenerate this much-needed enthusiasm for change: a clean page, a fresh start, a whole new chapter to be actively written, as indeed it was at the start of the 1970s. If it is to be sustained beyond the first euphoric twelve months, however, we might do well to check that we still have access to the basic prerequisites for such a venture, i.e. pens, paper, 'rooms' of our own and something a little different to say. A new time period, yes, renewed hope and vigour, most certainly, but our legacy from the 1980s is dire and cannot so readily be turned over.

How easy it is, in retrospect, to understand the way apparently disparate incidents, issues and events in the political arena all fit neatly together and how hard, even with this potentially empowering realization, not to be paralysed by the unprecedented speed with which legislative change continues to stamp its way, not just onto the statute books, but into our daily lives. What an exhausting business trying to keep up with it all and as for trying to change it, there must surely be a limit to the number of campaigns we can cope with: 'Save Our Health Service', 'Save the Whale', 'End Apartheid', 'Troops Out', 'Support the Miners, the Teachers, the Ambulance Workers', 'No Poll Tax'. . . . If I might be allowed one rhetorical generalization we have, in the last ten years, witnessed restrictions and reductions in just about everything bar rape and the rate of inflation, and each time a cut, a squeeze or a freeze in provision is implemented, it is invariably those furthest removed from the locus of social and economic power who suffer. I don't want to dwell on this but I think we do need to remind ourselves sometimes that academia is not an ivory tower, and a few specific examples of the kinds of interlocking moments I have in mind might help. These can, of course, be interpreted in many ways but my focus here, in keeping with our Conference, is on the glaring relevance of these events to women in general and to Black women and lesbians in particular.

In 1986, the democratically elected Greater London Council (GLC), with its innovatory Womens' Unit, Race Unit and Lesbian and Gay Working Party, was abolished.[2] So too with the enormously influential Inner London Education Authority (ILEA) which also attempted, whatever its limitations, to take equal opportunities seriously at all levels. Contrary to the wishes of the overwhelming majority of parents and guardians who voted for its retention, ILEA was finally disbanded in 1990. The ostensible purpose of this dictatorial exercise? Greater freedom of parental choice! The consequences of these unprecedented Government interventions for smaller organizations have been great. The Feminist Library and the Lesbian Archive, for example, both valuable resources for the pooling and preservation of our knowledge, are threatened. Nurseries, safe transport schemes, law centres, print projects — the list of community casualties is endless.

Meanwhile, Section 28 of the Local Government Act, which prohibits local authorities from 'intentionally promoting homosexuality', became law in May 1988 and is surviving nicely. How on earth a government constantly critical of standards of English teaching could ever have allowed a phrase like 'homosexuality as a pretended family relationship' to appear in a legal document is beyond me — unless, of course, we take into account the fervour with which this rather late in the day final prohibition was added.[3] Nevertheless, there it is and, whilst it remains dubious in law and still to be tested, there can be no doubt that Section 28 is working and that its effects, far from being limited to lesbians, gay men and the children they parent, are considerable. Indeed, I would like to make the point quite clearly here that legislative effects rarely are limited and, because there really is no such thing as a discrete issue, discrimination against lesbians will invariably take its toll, however indirectly, on all women. Against the backdrop of the new social category 'pretended family' the Donor Insemination restrictions included in the current Human Fertilisation and Embryology Bill provide, in fact, an immediate example.

Without ever needing to take a case to court Section 28 serves its ideological purpose by reinforcing, yet again, the inalienable supremacy of the traditional (white) family, whose revitalized and carefully nurtured pre-judices can now be reaped, right across class lines, in the ballot box. Events surrounding the local government elections in the London Borough of Ealing in May 1990 will perhaps demonstrate my point. In this borough, where there is no evidence to suggest that women are safer or more privileged than in any other area, where a gay man was kicked to death on 29 April, just weeks before the elections, and where a black minicab driver was stabbed fifty-four times in a far from isolated racial attack in December 1989, the Conservative Party campaign included a much publicized promise to get rid of the gay problem and give Ealing back to the British: they would eliminate the Race and Women's Units as soon as they took control. Caution was needed before discrediting the work of the former but the latter, linked, in any case, in the public mind as a marginal concern, was easy prey. Hadn't the Women's Unit, after all, been spending voters' hard-earned cash on self-defence classes for lesbians?[4] Money that could have been spent on *our* children's education? Although recent juvenile crime, truancy and pregnant daughter proposals from within the Government make it quite clear whose children they are, the inflammatory Conservative campaign in Ealing work-ed. Within hours of the votes being counted, instructions were given for all files to be removed from the offices of the offending Units and the doors locked. When the workers arrived the following morning they were told their jobs no longer existed. This is an extreme, but not singular, example.

Post GLC and ILEA Labour councillors are not averse to wooing the traditional (white) family vote either, however mythical this family may, in actual fact, be. The difference is simply one of emphasis. No big publicity here, just a quiet reshuffling and, with minimum fuss, the emotive depart-ments disappear, their functions subsumed under 'general administration' and the like. Political manoeuvring, yes, but it's also not difficult to see that a further advantage of this 'low profile' approach is that it makes it a good deal easier for Poll Tax capped and economically crippled councils to freeze these 'sensitive' posts when they become vacant, with little hope of a thaw. However genuinely reluctant previously supportive councils may be, the clear message remains that we are neither high enough on the list of priorities to warrant even minimal expenditure, nor prestigious enough to win votes.

So far I have neither exhausted nor gone beyond changes initiated in the mid 1980s that have had a profound effect on my own 'pretended family' life in London; but perhaps this is enough to demonstrate that, much as conspira-cy theories are decidedly unfashionable these days, there is just cause for concern. How far, in the name of protecting what hard-won privileges we might have accrued, can we let things go and, more to the point, how did they ever get this far to start with? Given that Black people, women, lesbians and gay men, all considered marginal in this society, constitute considerably more than 50 per cent of the voting population something, it would seem, is going drastically wrong and it is on this point that I would like to start making the link between the general issues I have been raising and our specific purpose here.

It is, after all, the idea of having been cast out, rendered insignificant, silenced and denied access to power that informs the title of this conference and, in this conceptual sense at least, it would seem to me that it makes very little difference whether we are talking about women's units in local authorities or women's courses in academic institutions; they are all, in effect, 'rooms'. Just to fix the focus more firmly on our particular area of interest, though, perhaps I might give as a final example of an interlocking issue that will undoubtedly have very real and long-term consequences for women in education, the introduction of the Student Loans Scheme and the concomitant abolition of income support for students.

I, for one, would not be speaking to you now if this had been the state of affairs when I began my first degree in 1981 and being at this Women's Studies Network Conference in Coventry after a fourteen-year absence makes me particularly sensitive to this fact. I was born in this city and expelled from grammar school here. I spent my adolescence in children's homes here and, when I was sixteen, ran away from here to work as a live-in waitress in a hotel. By the time I applied to do a degree in English I had had more bread-and-butter jobs than I can count, and two children. I will return to my experiences as a lesbian student later. What I want to draw particular attention to now is the fact that even with a mature-student grant and housing benefit I have always needed to juggle both part-time work and overdrafts and it has been, make no mistake, a long hard haul. I give you these details because they are not, in essence, my own. I am not singular, a special case or alone but one of the many thousands of women in this country who, one way or another, give the lie to the white, middle-class, heterosexual assumption on which the whole of the British education system is based.

In the broadest sense there can be no doubt that it is working-class children who will be most affected by the free-market approach to education and concomitant changes in the student support system. Children, that is to say, whose families are either unable or, for a variety of class-bound reasons, unwilling to provide further financial assistance, and whose expectations of immediate financial reward once they graduate are, most importantly, greatly reduced. Even when families are willing and able to help, I have little doubt that in the face of competing demands, it's going to be a case of 'Arthur's Education Fund' all over again.

There are two related points, here, that I would like briefly to mention. The first is that whilst the education system has indeed opened its doors and can no longer be accused of directly excluding any able member of society, it must be taken into account that it has also devalued what it has to offer. I am not refering to the standard of education, but to the value of the academic qualifications obtained, for who, nowadays, would expect to join the high echelons, and I use this military reference quite intentionally, with a Bachelors or even a Masters degree? And as for working in or influencing the academic establishment itself, even a doctorate is no guarantee because, with an abundance of applicants holding the same academic qualifications in a diminishing and fiercely competitive field, other factors, like experience, publications, personal presentation and confidence, are then brought into play. Whilst these factors are not overtly discriminatory and it could be and, indeed, often is argued quite convincingly that these 'extras' are necessary to the job, the fact remains that one group is far more likely to have them than another — and I do not believe for a moment that this has never crossed anyone's mind on a selection committee before. All apparent concessions and improvements are in this sense relative and may, in and of themselves, make very little impact in terms of differentials. In other words, all the system has to do to maintain, more or less, the status quo is to keep on moving the goal posts.

The second related point concerns the importance of expectations in a self-perpetuating system. If expectations are based on a concrete imagining of what is possible, the key word here must be *precedence*. It would be interesting to know just how many black/lesbian/working-class identified lecturers we have at this Women's Studies conference and how many students who can say they are being taught by one. I have inserted the word 'identified' because one of the great dangers, of course, of undergoing the rigours of eight years or so of study in order to compete for an academic job is that any such particularity is likely to have been lost, bartered, or buried along the way. The number of lesbians who are still not 'out' in their departments is frightening, for them as well as us.

When I saw the publicity for this Conference, then, all these unruly thoughts came to mind and, as I read the first part of the title to myself again and again, I became more and more troubled. 'Out of the Margins' — what, given the retrogressive conditions I have described, can it possibly mean? Based on the popular analytic model of a centre that not only wields power in an obvious sense but controls, with remarkable elasticity, the production of meaning as well, it is, of course, true that Women's Studies have been allotted a peripheral and rather paltry place on the academic fringe. However exciting, significant and worthy we may consider our work to be and however central we may feel, at times, in relation to each other and, indeed, to society, it is a fact that resourcing for Women's Studies is still as negligible as its status, while for specifically Black Women's Studies it is barely worth keeping an account, and for Lesbian Studies it is simply nonexistent. Small wonder, then, that as the ideologically targeted economic crisis grows, so too do the number of women finding sexual difference, gender studies and representation safer terms than Women's Studies, feminism, and lesbianism — what's that?

But I am getting ahead of myself here. The conference title, 'Out of the Margins', suggests a note of defiant celebration, much as 'Out of the Closet' has done for lesbians and gay men, and I am acutely aware that I have said very little so far in keeping with that spirit. The truth is, to go back to my earlier point, that whilst Out of the Closet has a very precise oppositional meaning, as demonstrated on the 20,000-strong Gay Pride March that took place in London in June this year, I remain confused about what is intended here. If Women's Studies are indeed coming out of the margins then where, I ask myself, are they going? According to my understanding of this formulation there is only one possible direction: the centre.

Of course the very concept of a dominant centre with subordinate margins is, to use that indispensible postmodernist word, problematic. Here's society, pictured very much like a soup dish, with predominantly white, middle-class, heterosexual men occupying the bowl and busily casting out onto the rim all those bits that are both necessary to their self-definition and unsuited to their purpose at any given time much, indeed, as anyone might do with stray hairs, undercooked beans, black beans, les beans, tomato stalks or whatever else we simply don't think belongs in our soup. Is this conference suggesting, then, that like the once maligned potato Women's Studies is now considered safe enough to be incorporated as part of our nation's staple diet? What about the 'beans'? Do we slip gracefully from the rim, too, or will Women's Studies, at this point, join forces with the bailers in order to protect their own, newly elevated interests? When I hear respected feminist academics expressing fears about the (realistically remote) possibility of a 'pecking order' amongst women that would place the boring white middle-class heterosexual at the bottom (their value judgment not mine) and the Black lesbian at the top, I am tempted to think that this may indeed be the case, for there is no essential difference whatsoever between this hierarchical way of thinking and that which the dominant centre has so long employed in the interests of male supremacy. This is the fear of the great take-over endemic to binary logic, which a wholesale acceptance of the margins/centre dichotomy does nothing to dispel. Indeed, as I think of these women, all of whom have worked so hard within feminism, I am reminded of the words that Gertrude Stein gave to the suffragette Susan B. Anthony in *The Mother of Us All* (1947), 'it will do them no good because having the vote they will become like men, they will be afraid, having the vote will make them afraid'.[5]

The two principles that I have raised so far are that if Women's Studies are indeed coming out of the margins, they must make it quite clear just where, exactly, they are going and who or what they intend to leave behind. Until such time as these points can be clarified, I would hold on to the possibility that what we are dealing with here is primarily a conceptual error and that Women's Studies is not, unless it be in puréed form of course, going anywhere at all.

With this in mind I would like to continue by taking a closer look at the centre/margins formulation in relation to my earlier comment on the voting potential of marginal groups. It is quite amazing, in fact, how enormous the margins appear to have grown and how tiny the dominant centre. In recent years the concept has quite rightly found its way into popular discourse and I would imagine that now even the least theoretically minded of us could give a whole range of graphic examples that would seem, superficially at least, to demonstrate the rudimentary workings of the centre/margins pattern. In the course of British history there have, after all, been more than a few 'socially undesirable' citizens banished not only to our shores, but as far beyond them as it was possible to get. Along the same axis we would also take note of stringent border controls that are designed to keep people that the system has no use for out and, indeed, the repatriation schemes intended to rectify earlier 'unfortunate mistakes'. Mid–nineteenth–century attempts to solve the 'surplus' woman 'problem' by shipping half a million Victorian spinsters off to the other side of the Atlantic, where there were surplus men who could use them, also come to mind.[6] And both Hitler and Stalin, of course, had very precise ideas about how to get rid of those 'antisocial' elements — lesbian, gay, dissident, gypsy, Jew — that weren't to their taste. But even these dramatic and apparently unequivocal examples prove, on examination, to be unsatisfactory in a number of important respects.

In the first place an unreal passivity is assumed on the part of the marginalized group which, together with the equally erroneous concept of static dominance, negates our experience of a heavily weighted but nevertheless interactive reality. Secondly, an artificial homogeneity is created both within and between marginalized groups (as demonstrated by the abolition of both the Ethnic Minorities' and Women's Units on the same ticket) which does not automatically exist. And thirdly, having been constituted within dominant culture, the tendency for marginalized groups to reproduce exactly the same hierarchical systems within their own parameters is overlooked — the 'boring white middle-class heterosexual and the Black lesbian' being a fine example and one that also highlights the further difficulty of attempting to locate complex identities, affiliations, loyalties and allegiances within a binary system.

The point that I am trying to make here is that whilst the popular 'them and us' head-count version of centre/margins theory may have limited strategic value, it is not only inadequate as a model of our actual experience but an ultimately disempowering concept as well. Much as we might like there to be at times, the fact remains that there is no straightforward, easily identifiable opposition between centre and margins, oppressor and oppressed, for within the terms of this binary classification system the splittings are so infinite and so unstable that what we invariably end up arguing about is the relative degree of participation each of us has in one or the other position at any given time.[7] Hence the destructive 'ranking of oppressions' that Barbara Smith was arguing against as long ago as 1981;[8] the seeming anomaly of the ineffectual marginal vote; and the equally anomalous idea of Women's Studies marching 'out of the margins' while Lesbian Studies are barely out of the closet.

As presently constituted in relation to dominant culture the interests and concerns of white women and black women, heterosexuals and lesbians are not always the same, but neither are they discrete issues. Not only do we belong to and/or have affiliations with more than one group but it is inevitable that an action against one will to some degree affect all of us. The important phrase here is 'as presently constituted in relation to dominant culture'. To look again at the broader context by way of example, I have no doubt at all that a large number of heterosexual women in Ealing were made to feel extremely, and quite deliberately, uncomfortable by the synonymous use of the terms 'lesbian' and 'Women's Unit' employed by the politicians, and that they would have gone to great lengths to assert their membership of heterosexual culture. I am quite confident, too, that many of these same women feel equally angry and betrayed now that the Women's Unit which did, after all, devote the majority of its resources to their needs, has gone, for in this sense, it is their membership of women's culture that is directly affected. Within an academic focus, it is not difficult to imagine, either, the uncomfortable position of the heterosexually identified feminist (or indeed, the closeted lesbian) on a selection committee who must choose between a male applicant and an out lesbian and neither, given my own undergraduate supervisor's experience, is it hard to understand why lesbian dissertations receive so little support.

Cross-cultural membership isn't easy and dominant culture, fully aware of the manipulative potential of divided loyalties, demands choices and a hierarchical structuring of allegiances, all the time. Neither is it easy to grasp the wide-ranging implications of these artificial choices on every occasion. What is certain, however, is that we must guard well against options that support, however obliquely, the Thatcherite ideal of the traditional (white) family, and when women make a point of distancing themselves from lesbianism, or get angry with lesbians for being so pushy when really it could all be so nice, that is precisely what they are doing.

This word 'pushy', in fact, brings us to another aspect of the centre/margins model and the apparent contradiction between being marginalized (powerless) and assertive (powerful). So, my lesbian student days.

In 1981 I was thirty and setting out to do a degree without even having been to school properly. I was scared and, in this frame of mind, managed to convince myself that my lesbianism was irrelevant. I was, after all, going to study Literature (with a very naive big L) and that had nothing whatsoever to do with my sexual proclivities or politics. After the first few months, of course, I felt more confident but the split in my life was becoming painfully obstructive. Imagine a seminar on *Mrs. Dalloway* and I'm excited. I had tried to read this book in my teens but couldn't make head nor tail of it. Now, with dazzling clarity, I could understand it all! *Septimus was homosexual and ended up killing himself because he couldn't function in the traditional role of husband and the patriarchal medical profession, trying to 'cure' him, made it not only worse but intolerable. Clarissa Dalloway was lesbian but she could function because it was quite acceptable for her, as a middle-class woman, not to engage in sex with her husband but to sleep in her own small bed and dream about Sally Seaton!* Not a very sophisticated rendition, I know, but such was the power engendered by this reading that I just had to tell my seminar group about it. The student response was quite simply cruel, and the authoritative, 'Yes, very interesting, shall we get on?' a burning humiliation. I bit my tongue, swallowed hard, contained myself but, having exposed myself to this degree, things could only get worse. Finally, a typewritten pastiche of an official handout we had received appeared on the department notice board, clearly addressed to me. 'If you want to get a first', it said, 'wear trousers, speak in a deep voice, and do feminist criticism'. No name, no recourse, no institutional support nor any expectation, at that time, that there should be. In that moment, standing in the corridor with a number of other students around, I had a choice to make: come out or get out. I didn't take the notice down. Everyone had seen it anyway and so to not only leave it but write a signed reply on it was an act of defiance, a way of saying I didn't care and that I was indeed as powerful and threatening as the writer clearly imagined me to be. I shook, and in private I cried, but the release of energy that came with that decision to talk and write openly as a lesbian was phenomenal. With the academic support of a feminist supervisor, fully aware that she, by association, had become the object of sneering innuendoes herself, I completed the course, submitted a dissertation with 'Lesbian' right there in the title, and came out with my First. The worm, if you like, had turned using to advantage the same weapons that had been intended to ensure a retreat.

The story so far serves as a slightly skewed demonstration of Foucault's dynamic conception of the centre/margins dichotomy which introduces the notion of 'reverse discourse'.[9] The radicalism of this theory, to be brief, lies in the recognition of the potential for marginalized cultures to challenge the power structures responsible for their creation using, in fact, the very same categories by which they have been disqualified. So, the lesbian student, the marginalized culture, gets pushy, answers back; what then? What is the best an attack from the margins might hope to achieve? Complete reversal? The much-feared take-over? Extremely difficult and given that success, in these terms, would do nothing whatsoever to overthrow the oppressive structure of binary opposition that created the problem in the first place, it is perhaps, in the long term, not even desirable. A few modifications, then? A bigger piece of the pie? Foucault is of little help to us here; in the face of our uncertainty, dominant culture is barely shaken and has all the mechanisms in place to deal with us.

Earlier this year I went back to the same Polytechnic to attend an occasional seminar being given by Jackie Stacey and Richard Dyer, both well-known for their contributions to lesbian and gay studies. I was curious, above all, to find out what had changed since I was there to make such an event possible. On my way in, I asked one of the members of staff what the title of the seminar was (I do, as stated at the beginning of this paper, set great store by titles) and I wrote it down: 'Incorporating Lesbian and Gay Studies into the Humanities Curriculum'. After a stimulating presentation we broke up into groups to discuss ways in which lesbian and gay studies might have an effect on humanities teaching bearing in mind, as Jackie Stacey had suggested, that critical theories as well as reading lists might need to be revised. When the considered response came back that perhaps what we could more fruitfully be doing is looking at the construction of heterosexuality instead, I had the peculiar sensation of being metaphorically eaten alive. Representation, gender studies, sexual difference, the New Man, anything,

anything but lesbianism. I looked at my scribbled title again: *Incorporating Lesbian and Gay Studies*. That would mean uniting them *in* one body, *with* another thing; combining them into one substance. Did Jackie Stacey and Richard Dyer really say that? Lesbian and Gay Studies, in other words, into the liquidized soup? No of course they didn't, but the fact that their title had been paraphrased and remembered like that says a good deal about how dominant culture works.

Far from being a static system or structure, dominant culture is eminently capable of reinterpreting and incorporating just about anything, one way or another, in order to safeguard its own interests. It has to be and, the needs of capital being paramount, there is no doubt that it is these needs which determine, to a very great extent, the timing and the degree of incorporations. Indeed, with this and the demographic time-bomb in mind, post-feminist hype makes a good deal of sense. Women don't want refuges or special units or safe transport schemes or even Women's Studies any more. We're past all that. It's executive briefcases, microwave dinners, BUPA babies, and nippy little cars with a dog in the back we have a *right* to now. Women's Liberation Incorporated. Of course, the need for order and social stability, not unrelated to capital, is also important. Marginal cultures that are getting too assertive and troublesome, however remote their use value to dominant culture, must also be incorporated, sufficiently, at any rate, to diffuse any possible disturbance. This defence mechanism we might call partial incorporation or, if we are not feeling terribly alert, we might call it improvement for that is, indeed, what it sometimes feels like — and goodness me, what a relief, at least for the moment.

It would seem to me, then, that with all this 'coming out of the margins' talk, this is the rather tricky position that Women's Studies is in. There can be no doubt that in recent years we have experienced a number of hard-won, hard-to-hold-on-to 'improvements' and there are, indeed, many Network women who have worked incredibly hard over the last two decades to make conferences such as this possible; but still, even as I celebrate our efforts, our remarkable tenacity, I hear Audre Lorde's words trickling through: 'The master's tools' she said 'will never dismantle the master's house',[10] and I wonder just how much we have changed and how secure those changes are.

So my earlier troublesome question remains: what is the best that marginal cultures might hope to achieve and how will we know when we've got it? This is not an easy one and I do not pretend to have a definitive answer. Taking *integrity* as the keyword, however, helps because one thing I am sure of is that we cannot allow ourselves as individuals, as women, to be fractured and manipulated any more. On a practical level this means putting on our application forms that we have children, even if the only space for it is under 'employment history', and including our waitressing jobs, shop jobs, typing jobs and the rest. By whose standards are these skills and experiences considered irrelevant and how, if we fail to include them, are the gaps in our histories read? It means using the word 'lesbian' when we list our research interests and not converting it to 'women' in the belief that it's only until we get the job/tenure/promotion/funding — there will always be a whole lifetime of reasons to hide, to be afraid, to dis-integrate. To quote Pat Parker who lived and died by the word, integrity means taking all of our parts with us wherever we go and refusing to say to any one of them 'no, you stay at home, you won't be welcome'. It is, as she said, 'a simple dream'[11] but its implications are huge.

Attempting to realize this dream would mean, for example, that we wouldn't be striving for selective incorporation into dominant culture but for the destruction of dominance itself. We wouldn't want to come out of the margins and into the centre, the mainstream, or whatever else we might call it, but to eradicate subordination altogether. We most certainly wouldn't be replicating the pecking-order concepts of dominant culture amongst ourselves but working together to realize the possibilities of a laterally expansive culture. A culture not only open to but dependent upon a full appreciation of the diverse contributions, aspirations and needs of all its members. A culture that would consider itself incomplete without them. So long as we can imagine this possibility, there is no good reason that I can see why we should settle for less. If our theoretical frameworks have grown tiresome and restrictive, then we must rethink them, expand them, bend them to our advantage. Simply exchanging one position for another will get us nowhere. When we leave the margins it must be because they no longer exist. Until that time, they continue to provide the strongest conceptual space we've got.

Acknowledgments

My thanks to Jackie Stacey, who chaired the plenary and took the time to talk with me about the paper beforehand, and to Jackie Nicholls, whose love, support, and critical intelligence has been much appreciated at every stage.

Notes

1 I am conscious of the fact that the style of this paper, originally intended as a plenary address to a large audience of women from a variety of social, cultural and academic backgrounds, is quite different from that generally associated with academic text books. It is written with a very present 'I', employs a wide range of registers, a fair degree of humour, rather more anecdotal and biographical material than is customary and certainly more than is wise. When preparing this paper for publication, however, I could think of no good reason to change it other than to create an illusion of distance between myself and the text and thereby, in some sense, deny responsibility for what's contained within it. A quite inappropriate shift given that the paper works towards placing integrity at the centre of a more embracing discourse for Women's Studies. I am also indebted, here, to Celia Kitzinger's persuasive arguments for a social-constructionist approach to writing (Kitzinger, 1987).
2 See also Tobin (1990).
3 See Colvin (1989).
4 Despite the media distortions, Ann Tobin points out that in 1984 the GLC's expenditure on all lesbian and gay initiatives amounted to 0.8 per cent of the Council's overall budget (Tobin, 1990, p. 62) and although I do not have the

Ealing Women's Unit figures to hand, I understand that the amount there was considerably smaller.
5 Stein (1947), Act II, Scene VII.
   Several heterosexually identified women at the Conference suggested that this paper alienated them and was so intimidating that they couldn't publicly respond. Expressing similar views on other occasions, I have been accused of promoting an 'orgy of guilt'. Although I have no clear answers to offer, other than those contained within the paper itself, I feel it necessary to note these reactions here because it would seem to me that this is a very real problem that we need, in good faith, to address.
6 See Jeffreys (1985), p. 87.
7 For a recent analysis, see Mercer (1990).
8 See Smith (1983).
9 Foucault (1978). For further discussion, see also Dollimore (1986).
10 Lorde (1984).
11 Parker (1985) p. 11; Brimstone (1990).

References

BRIMSTONE, L. (1990) 'Pat Parker: A Tribute', in *Feminist Review*, 34, pp. 4–7.
COLVIN, M. (1989) *Section 28: A Practical Guide to the Law and its Implications*, London, National Council for Civil Liberties.
DOLLIMORE, J. (1986) 'The dominant and the deviant: a violent dialectic', in *Critical Quarterly*, 28, 1 & 2, pp. 179–192.
FOUCAULT, M. (1978) *The History of Sexuality, Volume I: An Introduction*, Allen Lane.
JEFFREYS, S. (1985) *The Spinster and her Enemies*, London, Pandora Press.
KITZINGER, C. (1987) *The Social Construction of Lesbianism*, London, Sage Publications Limited.
LORDE, A. (1984) 'The Master's Tools Will Never Dismantle the Master's House', in LORDE, A. *Sister Outsider: Essays and Speeches*, New York, The Crossing Press Feminist Series, pp. 110–113.
MERCER, K. (1990) 'Welcome to the Jungle: Identity and Diversity in Postmodern Politics', in RUTHERFORD, J. (Ed.) *Identity: Community, Culture, Difference*, London, Lawrence and Wishart, pp. 43–71.
PARKER, P. (1985) *Jonestown and Other Madness*, New York, Firebrand Books.
SMITH, B. (1983) 'Introduction', in SMITH, B. (Ed.) *Home Girls: A Black Feminist Anthology*, New York, Kitchen Table Press.
SMITH, B. and SMITH, B. (1983) 'Across the Kitchen Table: A Sister to Sister Dialogue', in MORAGA, C. *et al.* (Eds) *This Bridge Called My Back: Writings by Radical Women of Color*, New York, Kitchen Table Press, pp. 113–127.
TOBIN, A. (1990) 'Lesbianism and the Labour Party: The GLC Experience' in *Feminist Review*, 34, pp. 56–66.
WILLIAMS, R. (1977) *Marxism and Literature*, Oxford, Oxford University Press.

Chapter 10

Racism: Whose Liberation?
Implications for Women's Studies

Shantu Watt and Juliet Cook

Racism is central to the experience of the majority of women in today's world. This simple truth is still controversial in many contemporary (white?) feminist arenas. Women's Studies, as the main educational representation of feminism, needs to demonstrate an ownership of racism as a central concern for all women — that is to say, Women's Studies needs to take responsibility for challenging racism alongside challenging sexism.

Out of the literature and practice of Black feminism worldwide comes an emphasis on the overwhelming impact of racism on the lives of Black women in a multitude of societies, as a result both of past oppressions — the reverberating impact of slavery, colonialism and neo-colonialism — and the development of new 'global, international oppressions' (Brah, 1990). Racism is therefore both central and international. The literature, experiences and practice of Black feminists in Britain and the USA (to draw on our most accessible sources) demonstrates these points only too clearly. It is a position stressed in Bryan, Dadzie and Scafe's key book on the Black British experience (1985). It is also expressed powerfully in the following way by Lorde (1984):

> The oppression of women knows no ethnic nor racial boundaries, true, but that does not mean that it is identical within those differences, nor do these reservoirs of our ancient power know these boundaries. To deal with one without even alluding to the other is to distort our commonality as well as our difference. For then beyond sisterhood is still racism. (p. 70)

We choose to use the term 'race' to denote that we are talking about a group whose identity is *socially* constructed by another more powerful group, frequently on the basis of some allegedly inherent physical characteristics that are seen as undesirable and inferior. We define racism in the following way: 'Racism is a process of systematic oppression directed towards people who are defined as inferior, usually in pseudo-biological terms such as skin colour' (Cook and Watt, 1987). We choose to use Black to signify that the term refers to much more than skin colour; it refers to a shared experience of racism through which oppressed people are joining together to turn that experience to positive and powerful effect. It is used, in other words, as a political term.

Our own research on Black women and Social Services Departments (Watt and Cook, 1989) reinforced the centrality of racism in the lives of Black professional women. It was from a comment by one of the women we interviewed about her experiences of being the only Black woman in a workplace women's group that our current work on developing new working strategies for white and Black women began. Racism did not come onto the agenda of the women's group and the Black social worker said that she felt she did not have 'permission' to raise it although it was her main concern at work. Other Black women in many different contexts have documented similar experiences (see e.g. Hooks, 1984). Our own experience (with others) of trying to put racism on the agenda at the 1989 Women's Studies Network Conference was not a happy one, despite the organizers' efforts to include both our session and one by Kum-Kum Bhavnani and Margaret Coulson on 'race' and gender issues. Fortunately, the format of the 1990 Conference indicated a stronger commitment to marginalized issues by giving racism more prominence throughout the conference programme. Such developments are very much to be welcomed. However, no one at the 1990 Conference as far as we are aware acknowledged the similarity between the Conference title (now the title of this book) and the name of bell hooks' pioneering book *Feminist Theory: From Margin to Centre*. Whilst there are indeed reasonable concerns about the margins/centre dichotomy (Brimstone, this volume), nonetheless hooks' exploration of 'attempts by white feminists to silence black women . . . in conference rooms, classrooms, or the privacy of cozy living room settings' (Hooks, 1984, p. 12) has a strong resonance for us in Britain in the 1990s.

A cursory glance at the feminist literature available in Britain reveals that it deals overwhelmingly with the experience of white women, often white women of middle-class background. Issues of class are dealt with but frequently in the form of theoretical debates about Marxist or socialist feminism, the underpinnings of which are currently under radical review. What is still conspicuous by its absence is the issue of racism, and the 'race'/gender dimension. In the 'race' relations literature, discussion of 'race'/gender issues is largely absent in a body of work still dominated by white, male writers. In both cases, where references to Black women occur, they are usually presented in highly stereotypical ways. It has therefore been left largely to Black women writers and activists to make public the need to study and improve their lives. In so doing, they have set a new agenda for all thinkers and actors in the field, namely to consider 'race', gender and class oppressions in all their interrelatedness and complexities. The title of Angela Davis's 1982 book *Women, Race and Class* makes this agenda explicit. In her fascinating analysis of early women's rights campaigns in nineteenth-century America, Davis shows how class and 'race' divided Black and white women in ways that were very damaging to the movement. She also points out that Black women such as Sojourner Truth were concerned to make alliances between all women. Her famous question 'Ain't I a woman?' captures this position most tellingly.

The concept of 'triple oppression' has become a shorthand way of referring to these theoretical developments. It is a term that at once highlights the issues but at the same time creates the danger of oversimplification. As Anthias and Yuval-Davis (1983) point out, it is necessary to develop sophisticated theories to account for the various ways in which 'race', gender and class interlink over time and in different societies. To create a hierarchy of oppressions, to try to add oppressions to each other, is profoundly misleading. One immediate danger is that Black women will be conceptualized in stereotypical ways as the ultimate victims, or as some kind of superwomen for daring to survive (Chigwada, 1987). The dangers of a spiral into competition between individuals and groups about who is the most oppressed is a feature of the 'identity politics' that Parmar (1989) has recently warned about. She says:

> Such scaling (i.e. developing hierarchies of oppression) has not only been destructive, but divisive and immobilising. Unwilling to work across all our differences, many women have retreated into ghettoised lifestyle 'politics' and find themselves unable to move beyond personal and individual experience. (p. 58)

Theorizing shared and different experiences, including the oppression of women by other women on grounds of 'race', and developing a positive practice for the future by developing a basis for action against structures of racial inequality is therefore becoming an urgent priority for the 1990s. But theorizing 'race', developing anti-racist practice, and owning racism are daunting tasks, for many white women have little experience of taking on these issues, which involve seeing ourselves (JC — i.e. white women) as both oppressors and oppressed, as both powerful and powerless. Hard intellectual and emotional work is involved.

Nonetheless, the message is clear from Black women — that the task is vital and that it can be undertaken by Black and white women working together (with space for Black women to work separately) if the notion of some form of shared sense of womanhood is to begin to be a reality. The effect and impact of racism on the lives of Black women renders problematic the very fundamentals of 'feminist theory' — for example, notions that the family is *the* site of women's oppression; reproductive rights when they mean only or primarily the right to abortion; notions of paid work as necessarily liberatory for women; and the significance of domestic labour in women's lives (for discussions see for example Carby, 1982; Parmar, 1982, 1989; Williams, 1989; Barrett and McIntosh, 1985; Ramazanoglu, 1989). Racism clearly divides us as women in our daily lives — where we live and where we work. Westwood's (1984) study of factory women shows that women work together on economic issues but that racism divides them in other ways both inside and outside the workplace. Racism renders Black women both visible and invisible — visible as targets, scapegoats and sexual objects by white society; invisible as human beings, as women, as people with things to say and demands to make. For Black women, therefore, visibility is a challenge, whereas for white women it means individual variety. Black as a label imposed from the outside always involves generalization.

Without putting Black women back into the ultimate victim/ superwoman trap, hooks (1984) argues that there is a uniqueness about the position of Black women in society that makes their views essential to the development of feminist theory and practice. Precisely because Black women bear the brunt of 'race', class and gender oppressions, they are 'the group that has not been socialised to assume the role of exploiter/oppressor in that [they] are allowed no institionalised other that [they] can exploit or oppress' (p. 140). There are a number of important implications that can be drawn from this insight. Black women have generated a wide variety of ways of surviving, and countering the oppression they experience. The richness of these responses and the very women-centredness of many of them is reflected in the growing body of literature, music, art and other forms of expression that are now available. It is also illustrated in the many practical projects to improve their lives that Black women worldwide are involved in. Walker (1985) has called this new form of Black feminism 'womanism' and she defines it as follows:

> Usually referring to outrageous, audacious, courageous, or willful behavior. Wanting to know more and in greater depth than is considered 'good' for one. . . . A woman who loves other women, sexually and/or non-sexually. . . . Appreciates and prefers women's culture. . . . Committed to survival and wholeness of entire people, male and female. (p. xi)

Black women therefore bring new perceptions and new forms of feminism to the fore. Their contribution to the development of feminist theories and practice for the benefit of *all* women is absolutely central. As hooks (1984) again puts it:

> It is essential for the continued feminist struggle that black women [we would add, and white women] recognize the special vantage point our marginality gives us and make use of this perspective to criticise the dominant racist, classist, sexist hegemony as well as to envision and create a counter-hegemony. I am suggesting that we have a central role to play in the making of feminist theory and a contribution to offer that is unique and valuable. The formation of a liberatory feminist theory and practice is a collective responsibility, one that must be shared. (p. 15)

The task as we see it is to generate ways of moving forward positively towards a position within feminist theory and practice that is inclusive rather than exclusive, and that recognizes and challeges power differences (of which racism is a very important example) between women and seeks to remove those power differences. The goal is to create a variety of forms of solidarity (Jordan, in Parmar, 1989) between women that will enable differences and similarities to be enjoyed and developed in an anti-oppressive environment. An idealistic goal we agree, and one that needs to be made much more concrete and specific. We found much common cause with Ramazanoglu's recent (1989) plea for women to begin to theorize both oppression *and* liberation. Similarly, Jordan (in Parmar, 1989) asks women to consider why, to what end should groups of women unite? Alliances, coalitions for what?

It is our view that as women, we need to ask ourselves not only what we want to be liberated *from* but also what we want to be liberated *to*. Specifying shared goals and developing the means to achieving them in concrete and practical ways have not been feminism's strong point, particularly when issues of 'race' have been at stake. It is to this task, in a preliminary way, that we turn our attention in the second part of this chapter.

When as a Black woman and a white woman, we agreed to offer a workshop at the Women's Studies' Network Conference in 1989, we were determined to make Lorde's statement ('for then beyond sisterhood is still racism') CENTRAL to the theme of such an historical event for Women's Studies in Britain.

We had both entered the 'struggle' separately and from different locations and social networks. As a Black woman (SW), I have often listened to a number of theoretical positions being discussed and debated. I tried to understand these in relation to myself and my experiences, remembering that at the end of the day (certainly in the last fifteen years or so) it is usually up to me to raise '. . . And what about racism?'

Often when this was discussed, another woman in the group might ask why we were spending so much time again on racism. A plethora of thoughts and feelings surround me as I remember to keep calm in order to give a sound rationale. How do I then 're-enter' the struggle to minimize oppressions?

Through our joint work, we have had the opportunity to discuss and share ideas about different ways of tackling the issues, particularly the issue of whose responsibility is it to tackle racism? So many questions came to mind and our aim has been to clarify at least *one* stage of what has to be a long and complex process. Here are some to consider:

- How do all women collectively ensure that RACISM IS CENTRAL to every discussion, policy and procedure for Women's Studies?

- For whom is the issue of racism a 'problem'?

- How can women make tackling racism a *norm* in feminist analysis and make the resistance *less*?

- What are the problems involved in conceptualizing when so many factors are at stake such as class, culture, heterosexism . . .?

- How is it possible to take responsibility for exploring and engaging with the issues in order to make a positive transition from challenges to practical changes?

- How can we make sure that there is concrete support for individual anti-racist, anti-sexist acts from institutional structures?

- What are our experiences and understandings of the structures of institutional 'equal opportunitism'?

- How can we open up issues of inclusion and exclusion, delegated and 'authorized' power?

- Where does the *need* for change come from?

- What are the costs and benefits of change?

Our research on Black women and Social Services Departments (Watt and Cook, 1989) had highlighted forcibly for us their systematic oppression and their strategies for survival and resistance against marginalization. Their struggles involved the establishment of mechanisms to consolidate their position, and to voice experiences and knowledge of Black people's lives in Britain. The research confirmed our view that the major challenge is for women of the dominant group (white) to develop their (our — JC) under-standing and willingness to change oppressive, exploitative practices; and to recognize and own the consequences of the actions of the dominant group towards another group.

1989 — Making a Start

It was our aim to raise some of these ideas at the first conference in 1989. However, we were concerned at the notable absence of Black women on the day and when only ten women signed up for the workshop, we felt that we were going to be a long way from making racism central in 1989. The dilemma for us was then to accept that elsewhere racism would be addressed as central — we acknowledge individual choice and diversion. One of the participants in the workshop wrote in her evaluation: 'It was undeniably noticeable and affecting for those who attended this workshop that we were so few in number. It set a sombre tone for the proceedings as we felt the weight of the issues even before the discussion.' In spite of these difficulties, very positive work was done in the session.

The participants were divided into three discussion groups, two white and one Black. They were invited to examine the ways in which Black women could begin to permeate mainstream structures on an equal footing. To what extent are Black women used in a tokenistic way to ensure the 'correct' number for monitoring purposes, for example? Black workers en-tering the system are very well aware of the actions and practices that ultimately determine who gets what, how and where. These are the areas of tension when Black and white women talk of resources, job opportunities, status (established or recognized), power (recognized), lines of communication and knowledge.

The main question, we suggested, is how to make alliances. Empowering has become associated with patronage. Empowering for us should entail overcoming and changing the obstacles so that 'outsiders' can become 'insiders'[1] if they wish; and 'giving up' the power that prevents the process of self-actualization for others. The groups considered this process of permeation with white women as the insiders, trying to examine their own oppression in a white male-dominated system and developing their own strategies. White women in such situations may not always be a homogeneous group. Black women can be seen as outsiders, with a strong racial identity, trying to get on the inside either individually or collectively.

The three groups shared their discussion ideas and feelings. The Black women's group had focused their discussion on:

- prioritizing issues

- deportation

- the centrality of domestic violence

- the centrality of state violence for Black families

- feelings of lack of trust *vis-à-vis* white women.

For the Black women, such an opportunity to meet other Black women and to share experiences from a commonly understood baseline was paramount. It was about affirming the effects of oppression which were daily experiences, without having to justify. It was an opportunity to consolidate and to be reassured in order to continue with strength in the struggle. To voice experiences of racism and of sex-ploitation, and to think of redefining their own boundaries in spite of the pressure and resistance from the dominant group.

The two groups of white women's discussion included the following:

- why should Black women trust us?

- white women being 'led' by white men

- issues about social contact/lack of it

- being accepted as a white women by Black women

- feeling that there isn't much to go on in this enterprise

- trying not to be divisive

- being aware of the power relationship

- making allies and friendships with Black women

- the context of alliances

One of the participants said 'As a white women, I don't feel oppressed by Black men'.

Another woman expressed feelings around 'questions of seeing oneself as an oppressor becomes difficult'. The October 1989 Women's Studies Network Newsletter contained the following comments from a participant:

> In particular we saw the importance of SOCIAL contact outside work.... This shows the interconnectedness of employment/ workplace experience and wider social issues.... For Black women a key issue at work is how to PERMEATE the structure. In the context of a sharp social/cultural demarcation outside work, this process can be seen as more than merely a matter of numbers and professional opportunities.

There was some discussion within the whole group about issues of mis-management at work and the way that anti-racist policy and practice opens up all other areas of work that are being badly managed and handled in oppressive ways. There are many important issues for management arising from our discussions.

The experience of running the workshop and of the 1989 conference as a whole was that there are many challenges for women of the dominant group that have to be taken up for the Women's Movement and Women's Studies to begin truly to be open to all women. We suggested that there might be a three-staged process involved for white women in particular:

1 owning the issue of racism, our (JC) power, our conscious choices and our ability to make changes

2 recognizing and valuing differences — amongst white women but also amongst Black women; supporting different ways of working, and separatism

3 working together as Black and white women *for* different kinds of liberation as well as against different kinds of oppression

1990 — Moving Forward, Gently?

For the July 1990 Women's Studies Network Conference, we offered a workshop on 'Organizational Contexts: Developing Working Strategies for Black and White Women'. Efforts had been made to give racism a higher profile in the 1990 Conference by offering other sessions in addition to ours on, for example, Black women and education (Claudette Williams), and Black women and the law (Selina Goulbourne). Our experience of the 1990 Conference was certainly a better one. We decided to focus on organizational contexts more generally because organizations are usually the main arena in which Black and white women operate in the same physical environment. If the 'solution' was to be equal access to paid work and equal treatment for both Black and white women, then what is the 'problem'?

There was a very positive response in terms of numbers to the workshop in 1990. There was also a very positive response in terms of the atmosphere, the hard work and the enjoyment that we certainly felt was a striking aspect of the session. As a Black woman and a white woman working together, it was important to acknowledge the dilemmas and constraints of our own development. Again to state that my (SW) own Blackness was not about skin colour but about a journey to change those distorted perspectives. After all, as we pointed out in our introductory section, it is in Black women's lives and daily experiences that the power dynamics in society are more clearly exposed.

In our introduction to the workshop, we gave an example to illustrate some of the assumptions and some of the pitfalls at work. A white woman within an academic setting was reminded by a Black woman of feeling used and exposed. A verbal apology was made and accepted and so at one level there was some clear communication. However, in the apology letter that followed, the white woman ended by writing '. . . but please let me know what I can do . . .'. This was about giving a dual message: one was about placing the responsibility on the Black women, and the other, about unconsciously stating that 'I have the authority'.

We expressed the view that there is some kind of stigma attached to Black/white feminist issues which serve as part of the process that seeks to divide women by devaluing their work. As a result, finding common cause may become harder. We suggested that rather than feeling conflict, we wanted to work with the energies to produce NEW thinking. The workshop was to be a beginning within the Women's Studies Network setting, an attempt to 'break the silence'. In order to create a *climate* of *change*, we need to be able to reach:

- an acceptable perception of each other's REALITY

- personal commitment of *ownership* and *outcome*

- ability to take risks

- sharing and supporting

- listening and learning from each other's experiences

- an understanding of the dilemma for Black women of a possible choice between involving themselves in research and locating their energies in their communities

- acknowledging achievements and tangible outcomes

- developing a clarity about our own action.

The participants worked in six small groups including one Black women's group. They were asked to consider, in the context of an organization with an equal opportunities policy, what were the obstacles to promoting women's interests in the organization. Secondly they were asked to determine what their own priorities for change would be. All of the discussions were shared. The Black women's group said that they didn't get beyond their first point because there was so much to discuss. The consensus from the group mirrored many of the concerns raised in the 1989 Workshop by the Black women's group, and we urged participants to act on these issues together and separately.

There was considerable common ground amongst the suggestions from the other white women's groups. Obstacles centred on hierarchical structures dominated by white, male, heterosexual power, and the resulting differences between the interests of the organization and the interests of the women who work in it. Priorities for change included changing the 'rules' or the principles on which the organization operates, increasing access for women, and breaking down the barriers between 'work' and 'home'. Some groups made specific reference to 'race' issues and the difficulties involved in Black and white women becoming united. There was perhaps a sense that if we got the other things right, the 'race' issues would resolve themselves. Certainly, it would have been useful to explore this point in more depth.

In spite of the constraints of time, the positive energies around in the session ensured that we were working towards a clearer understanding and more open communication. Our concluding review consisted of reminders to all of us about:

- clarity of action around issues of INCLUSION/EXCLUSION; white women need to be aware of the risk of colluding with white men to exclude Black women

- issues of VISIBILITY/INVISIBILITY for both groups within the organizational culture; how Black women might be shunted around to endorse the organizational numbers game in order to become a visible symbol of the 'success' of an equal opportunities policy whilst remaining invisible in the career hierarchy

- establishing a baseline to challenge the organizational CULTURE

- working towards a common, collective purpose

- ownership and conscious choices

- building alliances

- personal definition and clarity around areas of responsibility and authority, for example, job descriptions: Black women are often expected to carry additional, unspecified duties such as training, expert advice; how aware are white women of the mechanisms that sustain these expectations?

- equal opportunities policies and their 'paper policy' syndrome

- awareness of organizational ethos or is there a *culture* of *confusion*?

Conclusion

There is clear evidence from the two workshops of a positive commitment from Black and white women to move forward on the project of a diverse and inclusive feminism that can create new forms of liberation which we have been trying to develop. For us, there is an urgency about taking up these issues in both theoretical and practical arenas. We are also clear that the issue of owning racism for white women is still the major obstacle to this liberatory process, and that this need *not* be at the expense of Black women. Talking feminism and anti-racism is not enough. It is about ensuring that a personal/political commitment finds expression in taking initiatives and risks and in being persistent.

Note

1 This distinction was developed by the Black Perspectives Committee of the Central Council for Education and Training in Social Work (CCETSW) in 1988 when trying to raise the issue of its position *vis-à-vis* the central committee of CCETSW.

References

ANTHIAS, F. and YUVAL-DAVIS, N. (1983) 'Contextualising feminism — gender, ethnic and class divisions', in *Feminist Review*, No. 15.

BARRETT, M. and MCINTOSH, M. (1985) 'Ethnocentrism and socialist-feminist theory', in *Feminist Review*, No. 20.

BRAH, A. (1990) 'Questions of Difference and International Feminism', plenary session, Women's Studies Network Conference, Coventry.

BRIMSTONE, L. (1990) 'Out of the Margins and into the Soup?', plenary session, Women's Studies Network Conference, Coventry.

BRYAN, B., DADZIE, S. and SCAFE, S. (1985) *The Heart of the Race*, London, Virago.

CARBY, H.V. (1982) 'White woman listen! Black feminism and the boundaries of sisterhood', in CENTRE FOR CONTEMPORARY CULTURAL STUDIES *The Empire Strikes Back*, London, Hutchinson.

CHIGWADA, R. (1987) 'Not victims, not superwomen', in *Spare Rib*, 183.

COOK, J. and WATT, S. (1987) 'Racism, women and poverty', in GLENDINNING, C. and MILLAR, J. (Eds) *Women and Poverty in Britain*, Brighton, Wheatsheaf.

DAVIS, A. (1982) *Women, Race and Class*, London, Women's Press.

HOOKS, B. (1984) *Feminist Theory: From Margin to Centre*, Boston, MA, South End Press.

JORDAN, J. (1989) cited in PARMAR, P. 'Other kinds of dreams', *Feminist Review*, No. 31.

LORDE, A. (1984) *Sister Outsider*, Freedom, CA, Crossing Press.

PARMAR, P. (1982) 'Gender, race and class: Asian women in resistance', in CENTRE FOR CONTEMPORARY CULTURAL STUDIES *The Empire Strikes Back*, London, Hutchinson.

PARMAR, P. (1989) 'Other kinds of dreams', in *Feminist Review*, No. 31.

RAMAZANOGLU, C. (1989) *Feminism and the Contradictions of Oppression*, London, Routledge.

WALKER, A. (1985) *In Search of Our Mothers' Gardens*, London, Women's Press.

WATT, S. and COOK, J. (1989) 'Another Expectation Unfulfilled — Black Women and Social Services Departments', in HALLETT, C. (Ed.) *Women and Social Services Departments*, London, Harvester Wheatsheaf.

WESTWOOD, S. (1984) *All Day Every Day*, London, Pluto.

WILLIAMS, F. (1989) *Social Policy: A Critical Introduction*, Oxford, Polity.

Chapter 11

The Representation of Lesbianism in Contemporary Women's Fiction: The Division between 'Politics' and 'Psychoanalysis'[1]

Paulina Palmer
For Cambridge Lesbian Line

Introduction

Lesbian fiction produced in the past twenty years, the period following the advent of the lesbian feminist movement in the 1970s, is, in terms of the themes and genres which it treats, notably varied and diverse. The experimental nature of this fiction and its capacity for growth are illustrated by the fact that in a relatively brief time it has already passed through several different phases and exhibited a number of different trends and stylistic modes. Writers such as Rita Mae Brown, working in the 1970s, generally utilized the genres of the *bildungsroman* and confessional novel, and concentrated, somewhat narrowly, on the theme of Coming Out. In contrast, Aileen La Tourette, Barbara Wilson, Jeanette Winterson and other writers working in the 1980s and 1990s encompass in their texts a far wider range of themes and genres. The construction of lesbian subjectivity, lesbian continuum, lesbian feminist community, relations between mothers and daughters, and crimes of violence perpetrated against women, are, as I have illustrated elsewhere, themes which contemporary writers introduce (Palmer, 1990). The topics of lesbian sexual practice and desire also receive attention in works of fiction. Genres which writers employ include the thriller, science fiction and fantasy. While the realist mode continues to be popular, a move towards anti-realism is apparent in a number of novels.

However, despite the developments which have occurred in lesbian fiction in the past twenty years and the increasing diversity of themes and genres explored by writers, one particular feature of this fiction has changed very little. This is the division which it reveals between an explicitly political approach to lesbianism and a psychoanalytic approach. In treating the topic of lesbianism in novels and stories, writers tend to adopt either an approach which focuses on lesbian feminist community or, alternatively, an approach which foregrounds the individual female subject and the construction of her psyche and sexuality. They appear to experience considerable difficulty in reconciling and combining these approaches — with the result that a pronounced rift exists between the two. The existence of this rift, and the bifurcation of the fictional treatment of lesbianism into 'political' and 'psychoanalytic' categories to which it gives rise is, in my view, unsatisfactory. It promotes an unreal divorce between two areas of experience which, as we know from our own lives, are interrelated and interdependent. While having complex subjectivities and being involved in personal relationships and partnerships, we also participate in the lesbian community and in social and political groups such as women's centres, study groups and lesbian help-lines. To think in terms of a rigid division between these different areas and activities is inaccurate and false.

However, although the rift between the two alternative approaches to lesbianism which writers of fiction adopt is by no means desirable, it is none the less understandable — and relatively easy to explain. As I shall demonstrate, it does not reflect the limitations and inadequacies of individual writers, the majority of whom are highly talented, but, on the contrary, stems from the theoretical and discursive context in which they work. It mirrors and reproduces, in fact, the rift between a focus on the political significance of feminist community, and a psychoanalytic emphasis on female subjectivity, which is a divisive feature of feminist theory in general. It illustrates the incompatibility between the different discourses associated with these two perspectives, and the difficulty which theorists and writers encounter in reconciling them. I make reference to this rift and its ideological and literary implications in certain of my earlier publications (Palmer, 1989, pp. 125–148; 1990, pp. 54–56, 61–62). Here I shall explore it in greater detail.

In investigating in this essay the division between an explicitly political approach to lesbianism and a psychoanalytic approach I do not mean to imply that one is superior to the other. On the contrary, I see both approaches, and the discourses and strategies of representation associated with them, as equally fruitful and valuable. I aim to illustrate their differences and incompatibilities and, by so doing, shed light on and account for the difficulties which writers experience in trying to reconcile them and bring them together.

The Division between 'Politics' and 'Psychoanalysis' in Feminist Theory

Before examining the division between 'politics' and 'psychoanalysis' in lesbian theory and fiction, I shall explore, as a preliminary step in my argument, the effect of this division on feminist theory in general. As Lynne Segal and Elizabeth Wilson point out, the division is a source of discord and controversy both in the Women's Movement and in contemporary feminist discourse (Segal, 1987, pp. 56–69, 117–133; E. Wilson, 1986, pp. 60–74, 122–133). A political perspective on feminism, as Segal and Wilson illustrate, is markedly at odds with a psychoanalytic one. The two perspectives have little in common. Their differences hinge on contrary attitudes to women's community and on contrasting definitions of that problematic figure 'the female subject'.

A focus on the political significance of women's community is generally identified with the popular, radical feminist branch of the Women's Movement. Women who are committed to this approach prioritize the topics of feminist collectivity and work-projects. Highlighting the importance of the dialectic of sex, they emphasize the challenge which feminism directs at male power. They concentrate attention on the struggle which women wage to resist and combat patriarchal structures and forces. As for woman herself, she is portrayed as an autonomous, rational, self-determined agent, who is capable ideally of making informed choices and controlling her own life and destiny.

This radical feminist model of female autonomy, rationality and agency has obvious attractions for women, and appears at first sight to be wholly positive. However, it is a highly idealistic model, one which fails to recognize the irrationalities and contradictions of the psyche. The difficulty which many women experience in living up to it, and the problems they encounter in controlling and mobilizing their lives, can make it, in the long run, counter-productive, giving rise to feelings of despondency, self-criticism and disillusion.

A psychoanalytic approach to feminism, on the other hand, originates not in the popular, radical feminist branch of the Women's Movement but in the more elitist realm of academia. Exponents of it pay little attention to themes of women's community and acts of resistance to male power. They concentrate instead on themes of female subjectivity, the fractured self and the construction of femininity. Rather than emphasizing female autonomy and agency, they portray woman as a subject — a subject who is controlled by both cultural and linguistic structures, and by the pressures of her own psyche. As Lynne Segal observes, the problem with a psychoanalytic representation of femininity is that, taken to the extreme, it depicts women as excessively passive. Seen from this perspective, 'Women are merely "subjects", and subjects are denied autonomy, trapped within the operation of linguistic structures and laws' (Segal, 1987, p. 131).

Another feature of the psychoanalytic approach to feminism which merits comment is the emphasis which it places on 'the fractured self' — and the rejection of the concept of 'the unitary woman' to which this gives rise. Elizabeth Wilson points out that people who accept this model of subjectivity maintain that 'There is no such thing as a unitary "woman" — we are all bundles of contradictory atoms and impulses. The idea of the unitary self is a fiction. Leading on from this there is no such thing as "women's oppression" in any unitary sense ...' (E. Wilson, 1986, p. 70). While the rejection of the concept of 'the unitary woman' does not, of course, negate the facts of women's oppression it does complicate their theorization. Moreover, as is often the case in academic seminars, it serves to deflect attention from them.

Emphasis is placed on the complexities of female subjectivity and the fractured self, rather than on women's social experience, and the material and economic aspects of their lives.

Comments expressed by Denise Riley are also relevant here. Riley points out that if, as the Lacanian theory of the fractured self implies, there is no such thing as 'a unitary woman', then 'women' as a category is destabilized. The concept of women's community, which radical feminists regard as the centre of feminist struggle, is thus rendered problematic (Riley, 1987, pp. 35–44). It ceases to provide a firm centre for political organization and action.

The challenge which psychoanalysis poses to the concept of 'the unitary woman' is not, of course, the only factor to destabilize the idea of women's community in recent years. An increased awareness among feminists of the significant differences which separate and divide women — differences of race, class and sexual orientation — has had a similarly destabilizing effect.

The notion that fragmentation is a crucial aspect of both individual and collective identity, fundamental to psychoanalytic theory, is disconcerting and disturbing. It can give rise to contradictions in feminist theory and politics.

The Division between 'Politics' and 'Psychoanalysis' in Lesbian Feminist Theory

The division between a radical feminist emphasis on women's community, and a psychoanalytic focus on the individual subject and her psyche and sexuality, as well as being a feature of *feminist* theory, is also a feature of *lesbian feminist* theory. In theoretical accounts of lesbianism the rift between the two positions and perspectives is strikingly evident.

Theorists who highlight the political value of lesbian feminist community, many of whom wrote in the 1970s and early 1980s, emphasize the challenge which lesbianism and lesbians as a group direct at patriarchal, heterosexual power. I cite as examples of this perspective the New York group Radicalesbians, and the American theorists Charlotte Bunch and Adrienne Rich. All three regard lesbianism in predominantly political terms, while underemphasizing and playing down its sexual and personal aspects. They also portray lesbian relationships in a somewhat idealized light, turning a blind eye to their conflicts and tensions.

Radicalesbians in their influential essay 'The Woman Identified Woman' describe the lesbian identity as constituting the centre of women's community. They depict it as representing a challenge to male-defined images and expectations of femininity. They are of the view that:

> Only women can give to each other a new sense of self. That identity we have to develop with reference to ourselves, and not in relation to men. This consciousness is the revolutionary force from which all else will follow, for ours is an organic revolution. For this

we must be available and supportive to one another, give our commitment and our love, give the emotional support necessary to sustain this movement. Our energies must flow toward our sisters, not backward toward our oppressors. (Radicalesbians, 1973, p. 245)

In her essay 'Not for Lesbians Only' Bunch argues that the lesbian critique of 'the institution and ideology of heterosexuality as a cornerstone of male supremacy' is relevant to all feminists, irrespective of their sexual identification. She sees 'a commitment to women as a political group' as a fundamental feature of lesbian feminist thought (Bunch, 1981, p. 68).

In 'Compulsory Heterosexuality and Lesbian Existence' Rich investigates what she sees as the enforced recruitment of women into heterosexuality. She discusses the concept of 'lesbian continuum' and depicts woman-bonding as an act of resistance to patriarchal power (Rich, 1980).

Very different from the political account of lesbianism put forward by Radicalesbians, Bunch and Rich, is the psychoanalytic analysis of the topic. Although psychoanalytic accounts of lesbianism display marked differences, they none the less display a number of common features. Instead of giving priority to the political aspects of lesbian community, they focus attention on the construction of lesbian subjectivity and sexuality. Themes which they frequently treat include: the fractured self; the psychic contradictions stemming from the unconscious; the analysis of lesbian relationships as a displaced version of the mother/daughter dyad in the pre-oedipal stage; and the thesis of an alternative economy of female desire. Theorists who concentrate on these themes generally interpret lesbianism in terms of the libertarian concept of 'the freedom of the individual'. They pay little, if any, attention to the political importance of lesbianism as a challenge to patriarchal power. Instead of idealizing lesbian relationships, they scrutinize their areas of conflict and tension, and seek to explain them.

Two theorists who take a psychoanalytic approach to lesbianism are the British Joanna Ryan and the French Luce Irigaray. Ryan in her essay 'Psychoanalysis and Women Loving Women' comments on the emphasis which psychoanalytic theory places on the precarious nature of female heterosexuality. She points out that 'A strength of most psychoanalytic accounts is that they do not see a girl's pathway to heterosexuality as either straightforward or inevitable'. On the contrary, by highlighting the fact that in order to become heterosexual a girl has to transfer her love from a female object (the mother) to a male one, they give us 'a view of women as pushed and pulled out of their original homosexual intimacy into an ambivalent and very incomplete heterosexuality, where men may be the exclusive and primary erotic objects but are for the most part emotionally secondary to women' (Ryan, 1983, pp. 203, 206). Developing the ideas of object-relations theorists such as Nancy Chodorow, she argues that the analysis of lesbian love in the light of the mother/daughter dyad in the pre-oedipal stage is vital to an understanding of its emotional complexities. Refuting the accusation that to approach lesbian relationships from the point of view of mother/daughter relations is necessarily reductive and pejorative, Ryan argues that, on the contrary, it helps to shed light on, and explain the intensity and ambiguity of the emotions they involve (p. 208).

In 'This Sex Which Is Not One' Irigaray concentrates on defining a separate economy of female desire. She argues that woman's desire cannot be analyzed within male parameters and claims that 'Her sexuality, always at least double, is in fact *plural*' (1981, pp. 101–102). Irigaray associates the diffuse, multiple nature of female sexuality with the imaginary realm of the pre-oedipal mother/daughter dyad. Describing female desire as a 'Minoan realm' which is repressed and concealed by the structures of a phallocentric culture, she argues that 'it is recuperated only secretly and in hiding' (ibid.)

Here I need to make clear that, in discussing Irigaray's ideas, I disagree with the approaches of Janet Sayers, Kate McLuskie and Toril Moi, who interpret Irigaray as a 'biological essentialist', and with the perspective of Lynne Segal who reads her as a 'psychic essentialist' (Whitford, 1989, pp. 106–108). On the contrary, I agree with the views expressed by Margaret Whitford, who merits our gratitude for enabling Anglo-American readers to achieve a more accurate understanding of Irigaray's thought. As Whitford convincingly demonstrates, Irigaray 'addresses herself to the construction of femininity by the symbolic' and, in consonance with this, places 'a stress on the determing power of the symbolic order' (Whitford, 1989, pp. 122, 108).

Few theorists combine a political approach to lesbianism with a psychoanalytic approach. However, Irigaray and the British theorist Diane Hamer attempt to do so. Utilizing different approaches and lines of thought, they argue that lesbian identity, far from being a pathological condition as patriarchal culture has traditionally claimed, represents the psychic repudiation of phallocentric expectations of femininity and a challenge to patriarchal power. Irigaray in 'When the Goods Get Together' explores the role of object of exchange which patriarchal culture assigns to women. She advises women to resist and elude this role by rejecting relationships with men and, instead, relating to one another (Irigaray, 1981, pp. 107–110).

Hamer argues that a correspondence exists between lesbianism as a psychic position and feminism as a political one. Both positions, she maintains, represent forms of 'refusal'. Feminism in terms of social relations, and lesbianism from the point of view of psychic life, refuse to accept the belief in male superiority, which is promulgated by a patriarchal culture (Hamer, 1990, p. 145).

Irigaray and Hamer are, in fact, unusual in attempting to reconcile and combine a psychoanalytic approach to lesbianism with a political one. On the whole the two approaches remain discrete. Moreover, not only is there a pronounced division between them, but also women who are committed to one approach frequently denigrate and fiercely criticize the other. An example of this occurred at the Women's Studies Network Conference (Coventry Polytechnic, 7–8 July 1990), where I presented this paper. After I had spoken, several radical feminists in the workshop took the opportunity to attack a psychoanalytic perspective on lesbianism as unacceptable and pejorative. In their opinion, a radical feminist perspective, which presents the lesbian feminist identity and community as a political challenge to patriarchal power, is the only acceptable position and point of view for lesbians to adopt. Far from seeking to reconcile the two approaches, these women seek to resist and undermine the psychoanalytic one, and make the political dominant.

Another example of the division between political and psychoanalytic approaches to lesbianism, and the heated arguments and debates it can provoke, is provided by some of the essays in the current issues of *Feminist Review* (34, Spring 1990) and the radical feminist magazine *Trouble and Strife* (19, Summer 1990). While the writers in *Feminist Review* tend to adopt a psychoanalytic or apolitical approach to the topic, those in *Trouble and Strife* employ a political one. In some cases they criticize and attack one another's positions and points of view.

The Division between 'Politics' and 'Psychoanalysis' in Lesbian Fiction

When we move on to consider the representation of lesbianism and relations between women in fictional texts, we find that the writers reproduce with varying degrees of fidelity the division between a political emphasis on women's community and a psychoanalytic focus on individual subjectivity which, as I've illustrated, is a feature of both feminist theory and lesbian feminist theory.

The American novelists Marge Piercy and Barbara Wilson, writing in the 1970s and early 1980s, set the agenda for a political approach to lesbianism in fiction. They foreground in their narratives themes of women's community and feminist work-projects, depicting them as the base of resistance to patriarchy. They tend to treat lesbianism in terms of woman-bonding, while underemphasizing its sexual aspect. The goal of the protagonists in their novels is to achieve a strong, unified identity, in order to survive and to resist acts of patriarchal oppression. They also seek to integrate themselves socially in the lesbian feminist community and to find a partner.

Piercy's *Small Changes*, published at the early date of 1973, illustrates this political approach at its simplest and most clear-cut. Piercy structures the novel on the contrasting positions occupied by the two central figures, Beth and Miriam. Beth is working-class and, in the course of the action, comes to identify as lesbian. Miriam is middle-class and identifies as heterosexual. The novel has a moralistic slant. This reflects the attitude of lesbian chauvinism current in the 1970s. Heterosexual Miriam, unwisely investing her energies in relationships with men, ends up by both losing her independence and becoming emotionally isolated. Lesbian Beth, on the other hand, chooses to support the burgeoning Women's Movement — and wins the twin reward of independence and a lover. Feminist community is represented in the novel by the women's communal housing project which Beth helps to organize and the theatre-troupe led by her lover Wanda.

In treating the dichotomous themes of the affinities and differences between Beth and Miriam, Piercy appropriates and inventively re-works certain well-known motifs from fairy-tale and fable. The motif of the quest, the 'Cinderella Motif', the contrasting figures of the princess and the beggar maid, and the fable of the race between the tortoise and the hare, play a key part in the novel.

Piercy's subsequently published novel *The High Cost of Living* (1978) also centres on the topics of lesbian relationships and lesbian feminist community. The protagonist Leslie, a graduate student studying History in Detroit, is portrayed struggling hopelessly to resolve the conflict between her working-class perceptions and lesbian feminist consciousness, and the middle-class, male-dominated values of academia. Piercy's treatment of lesbian relationships and groupings, the reader notes, is much less idealized than in *Small Changes*. Differences of class, economic privilege, and sexual orientation have a disruptive, divisive effect on relations between women.

In her novel *Ambitious Women* (1982) and her thriller *Murder in the Collective* (1984) Barbara Wilson develops the themes of lesbian feminist community and work-projects which Piercy introduced into fiction. Highlighting the complexity and ambiguity of female relationships, she affirms the value of lesbian community while at the same time pinpointing the conflicts and tensions which it displays. The narrative strategies which she utilizes to represent these contradictions resemble those adopted by Piercy in *The High Cost of Living*. For example, the acts of cooperation performed by the central characters in the novel are depicted as taking place against the backdrop of the antagonisms and infighting of the lesbian scene.

The problematization and destabilizing of the categories 'women' and 'women's community', which occur indirectly in the novels of Piercy and Wilson, receive explicit expression in Wilson's thriller *The Dog Collar Murders* (1989). In this text female identity is portrayed as shifting and unstable, while lesbian feminist groupings are disrupted by divisions and hostilities. A disturbing feature of the novel is that incidents of female exploitation and crimes of violence against women are described as perpetrated not by male characters but by female ones.

Altogether Elsewhere (1985) by the British writer Anna Wilson also contributes to the problematization and destabilizing of the idea of feminist and lesbian feminist community. The novel, set in the London inner city, is deliberately bleak and depressing in mood, and austerely minimalist in style. Wilson takes as her theme women's efforts to combat and challenge male violence. She concentrates on a group of women, some lesbian and others heterosexual, who, worried by the increase in violent crime, unite to form a band of vigilantes. They patrol the streets at night, protecting women from molestation and assault. While emphasizing the political value of feminist community and lesbian identity, Wilson avoids idealizing either the group itself or the personal relationships of its members. Both units are disrupted by tensions and conflict. Achieving a sense of community and maintaining personal relationships appear, in the fractured and alienating conditions of contemporary urban capitalism, a painfully uphill struggle. Women have to contend with both the facts of female difference and the internal stresses of their own psyche.

It is interesting to note that the value which writers such as Piercy, Barbara Wilson and Anna Wilson, who depict lesbianism as constituting a political challenge to patriarchal power, place on woman achieving a strong, unified identity affects their treatment of bisexuality. They portray the bisexual woman as an unreliable, disruptive figure. Her shifting desires and allegiances are shown to have a destructive effect on lesbian relationships and the feminist community. Examples of bisexuals who are depicted in this manner are the journalist Magda in Barbara Wilson's *Ambitious Women* (1982) and Jenny in Nancy Toder's *Choices* (1980).

Aileen La Tourette, Harriet Gilbert and other writers of fiction who adopt a psychoanalytic approach, represent lesbianism in a very different light from that described above. Underplaying the themes of lesbian feminist community and the explicitly political aspects of lesbianism, they concentrate instead on exploring its personal and sexual aspects. They examine the tensions, as well as the harmonious facets, of lesbian relationships. Although they do not depict lesbianism as constituting a deliberate challenge to patriarchy, they frequently foreground its transgressive aspects and highlight its capacity to disrupt the patriarchal status quo. The emphasis these writers place on the individual female subject influences their view of Women's Liberation. Adopting a libertarian perspective, they envisage Women's Liberation more in terms of the subject's free play of multiple identities and heterogeneous desires than in social or economic terms. In consonance with this viewpoint, they present bisexuality in an attractive, sympathetic light, even while acknowledging its disruptive, divisive effect.

Writers such as La Tourette and Gilbert appropriate and re-work themes and configurations from feminist psychoanalytic theory in a strikingly imaginative manner. One theme which they successfully re-work is the representation of lesbian desire and relationships in terms of a displaced version of the bond between mother and daughter in the infant, pre-oedipal stage. This appears frequently in fiction with a psychoanalytic slant. Gilbert's *The Riding Mistress* (1983) and Penelope Farmer's *Standing in the Shadow* (1984) are two novels which are structured on it. The theme, though attacked by radical feminists as being reductive and giving a pejorative view of lesbianism, is, in my view, very fruitful. The recognition by object relations theorists such as Chodorow and Dorothy Dinnerstein of the contradictory nature of mother/daughter love in the infant, pre-oedipal stage, the fact that it is the source of both immense fulfilment *and* immense frustration and distress, offers writers a vehicle and source of imagery to describe the intensity and ambiguities of lesbian love. It enables them to explore the contradictory pleasures and pains inherent in lesbian relationships, as well as examining the links between the two poles.

This theme is treated very powerfully by Gilbert in *The Riding Mistress*. The passionate and intensely possessive involvement which the narrator Charlotte forms with Helen Taylor, her former teacher, has strong preoedipal resonances.

Another motif which recurs in fictional texts adopting a psychoanalytic approach to lesbianism is 'the alternative economy of female desire'. Emma Tennant in *The Bad Sister* (1978) and La Tourette in *Nuns and Mothers* (1984) employ different strategies to represent it. Interweaving in her narrative Gothic imagery of witchcraft and vampirism, Tennant describes lesbian desires and relationships as constituting a transgressive, irrational, subterranean realm — one associated with dreams and the unconscious. She treats lesbianism symbolically, depicting it, from a psychoanalytic point of view, as representing the unconscious of patriarchal culture (see Farley, 1980, pp. 269–272). Its appearance signifies, as Sonya Andermahr has pointed out in her helpful comments on my analysis of the novel, 'the return of the repressed'. Patriarchal society, using weapons of pseudo-rationality and logic, strives in vain to obliterate it and stamp it out.

The Bad Sister, as my discussion suggests, is a controversial novel. Whereas I detect in Tennant's treatment of lesbianism a strong element of homophobia, my colleague Gill Frith disagrees. She believes that the novel 'is not an *attack* on radical feminism; rather, it is a heightened, surrealistic account of the *challenge* represented by feminism, which presents it as a new, disruptive and radically different way of seeing the world' (Frith, 1989, p. 372).

Aileen La Tourette's *Nuns and Mothers* (1984), while concentrating primarily on the subjectivity of the central characters, also focuses attention on the transgressive aspects of lesbianism and its destabilizing effect on phallocentric culture and discourse. La Tourette wittily subverts Christian imagery by appropriating it to describe lesbian sexual practice. The protagonist Helena and her lover Georgia have been educated together at a Roman Catholic convent. Kissing Georgia between the thighs, savouring what La Tourette sensuously describes as 'the glistening clitoral pearl', she thinks, 'Worship and receive this communion on my outstretched tongue' (La Tourette, 1984, p. 65). This mingling of sacred and profane imagery, which is achieved with exceptional delicacy, continues a tradition employed with subversive effect by lesbian and gay writers such as Djuna Barnes and James Kirkup.

Attempts to Reconcile and Combine 'Political' and 'Psychoanalytic' Approaches in Lesbian Fiction

Up to now I have concentrated on discussing the division between a political focus on lesbian feminist community, and a psychoanalytic emphasis on female subjectivity, which is a feature of feminist, and lesbian feminist, theory and fiction. I shall conclude this essay on a different note — by considering certain fictional texts which attempt, with varying degrees of success, to reconcile and combine the two perspectives.

An interesting example of a novel which attempts, unsuccessfully in my view, to bring together political and psychoanalytic perspectives is Michèle Roberts's *A Piece of the Night* (1978). *A Piece of the Night* is Roberts's first novel to appear in print. Uneven and over-ambitious though the text is, it none the less contains many admirable features. Roberts sensitively explores the protagonist Julie's discovery of her lesbian orientation, and her relationships with her mother Claire and her lover Jenny. In exploring these topics, Roberts brings together the psychoanalytic motif of the pre-oedipal mother/daughter dyad, with the political theme of the lesbian feminist communal household. She understandably encounters some difficulty in combining a psychoanalytic discourse with a radical feminist, political one. For example, the representation of woman as 'subject', which characterizes psychoanalytic discourse, conflicts with, rather than complements, the radical feminist portrayal of her as autonomous agent.

The story 'The Threshing Floor' (1986) by the black writer Barbara Burford also attempts to combine a radical feminist focus on women's community with a psychoanalytic view of lesbianism. Burford interweaves the idea of lesbian continuum, represented in the text by the various relationships which the protagonist Hannah forms with her co-workers at the Cantii Glass Co-operative, with the psychoanalytic theme of the link between lesbian subjectivity and the mother/daughter dyad. As a child, Hannah was rejected by her mother and brought up in an institution. When, as an adult, she forms a relationship with the poet Jenny, she unconsciously projects upon her the image of surrogate mother. Jenny, however, resents the imposition of a maternal role. She encourages Hannah to cultivate the art of self-nurture.

One of the most successful attempts to combine psychoanalytic and political perspectives on lesbianism is found in Jeanette Winterson's acclaimed *Oranges are not the Only Fruit* (1985). The interplay which Winterson creates between the two discourses is of vital importance to the novel. It helps to account for the impression of social and psychological richness and density which it displays. A psychoanalytic perspective is apparent in the emphasis Winterson places on the theme of the fractured self and the narrator's multiple identities. These identities are represented by the series of fabulous episodes, based on fairy-tale and *The Arthuriad*, which intercept and fragment the main narrative line. A psychoanalytic perspective is also reflected in the contrasting images of motherhood interspersed throughout the text. Images of the mother-figure as tyrannical witch are juxtaposed with images of her as benevolent nurturer.

However, *Oranges are Not the Only Fruit* does not treat lesbianism merely in terms of personal preference but also reveals a political slant. Winterson depicts the narrator's lesbian desires and identity as constituting a form of resistance to phallocentric expectations of femininity. They enable her to stand up to and eventually reject the homophobic attitudes of the pentecostal church group to which she and her mother belong.

Conclusion

As I have illustrated in this essay, neither the theorist nor the writer of fiction find it easy to successfully negotiate the rift between political and psychoanalytic approaches to lesbianism, and reconcile these two contrary perspectives. The viewpoints and emphases associated with each position are very different. In certain respects they appear, perhaps, incompatible. How can one link the radical feminist view of woman as autonomous agent, in control of her own life and destiny, with the psychoanalytic view of her as the subject of psychological and cultural structures? How can one combine a psychoanalytic focus on female subjectivity and the fractured self, with the political theme of feminist community resisting and challenging patriarchal power? Now that the concept of 'the unitary woman' has been rejected by academics, and the idea of 'women' as a unified group destabilized, is it possible for writers to represent women's community in a positive, unproblematic light? And what about the controversial topic of bisexuality? The radical feminist view of the bisexual as merely a disruptive presence in the lesbian community seems naively simplistic and moralistic. It is at odds with the psychoanalytic acceptance, even celebration, of bisexuality as an example of the female subject's free play of identities and heterogeneous desires.

This essay, as well as drawing attention to and exploring the contradictory perspectives on lesbianism, female subjectivity, and women's community, which confront writers and theorists at the present time, also raises some interesting points about the relationship between fiction and theory. It illustrates the importance of the creative writer's appropriation and re-working of theory, and indicates her dependence (either unconscious or consciously acknowledged) on the work of the theorist. Although it is possible for an unusually talented writer such as Jeanette Winterson to successfully negotiate the division between political and psychoanalytic perspectives, and to combine and reconcile the two within a single text, Winterson is the exception in this respect. It seems likely that only when the dichotomy between 'politics' and 'psychoanalysis' has been resolved in the field of theory or, at any rate, the tensions and contradictions which it involves fully analyzed and understood, will it be possible for more writers of lesbian fiction to achieve a similar feat.

Note

1 I am indebted to Sonya Andermahr and Jackie Stacey for comments on this essay.

References

BROWN, RITA MAE (1973) *Rubyfruit Jungle*, Vermont, Daughters Inc.
BUNCH, CHARLOTTE (1981) 'Not for lesbians only', in BUNCH, CHARLOTTE and STEINEM, GLORIA (Eds) *Building Feminist Theory: Essays from Quest*, (1986) New York, Longman, pp. 67–73.
BURFORD, BARBARA (1986) 'The Threshing Floor', in BURFORD, BARBARA *The Threshing Floor*, London, Sheba, pp. 87–210.
CHODOROW, NANCY, (1978) *The Reproduction of Mothering: Psychoanalysis and the Sociology of Gender*, Berkeley, University of California Press.

DINNERSTEIN, DOROTHY (1977) *The Mermaid and the Minotaur: Sexual Arrangements and the Human Malaise*, New York, Harper and Row, 1977; London, Souvenir Press, 1978.

FARLEY, PAMELLA (1980) 'Lesbianism and the Social Function of Taboo', in EISENSTEIN, HESTER and JARDINE, ALICE (Eds) *The Future of Difference*, Boston, Mass, G.K. Hall, pp. 267–273.

FARMER, PENELOPE (1984) *Standing in the Shadow*, London, Gollancz.

FRITH, GILL (1989) *The Intimacy which is Knowledge: Female Friendship in the Novels of Women Writers*, with 'Supplementary Chapter', PhD dissertation, University of Warwick, publication forthcoming.

GILBERT, HARRIET (1983) *The Riding Mistress*, London, Methuen.

HAMER, DIANE (1990) 'Significant Others: Lesbians and Psychoanalytic Theory', in *Feminist Review*, 34 (Spring), pp. 134–151.

IRIGARAY, LUCE (1981) 'This Sex Which Is Not One' and 'When the Goods Get Together', in MARKS, ELAINE and DE COURTIVRON, ISABELLE (Eds) *New French Feminisms: An Anthology*, Brighton, Harvester, pp. 99–110.

LA TOURETTE, AILEEN (1984) *Nuns and Mothers*, London, Virago.

PALMER, PAULINA (1989) *Contemporary Women's Fiction: Narrative Practice and Feminist Theory*, Hemel Hempstead, Harvester Wheatsheaf.

PALMER, PAULINA (1990) 'Contemporary Lesbian Fiction: Texts for Everywoman', in ANDERSON, LINDA (Ed.) *Plotting Change: Contemporary Women's Fiction*, London, Arnold, pp. 42–62.

PIERCY, MARGE (1973) *Small Changes*, New York, Doubleday.

PIERCY, MARGE (1978) *The High Cost of Living*, New York, Harper and Row; London, Women's Press.

RADICALESBIANS (1973) 'The Woman Identified Woman', in KOEDT, ANNE, LEVINE, ELLEN and RAPONE, ANITA (Eds) *Radical Feminism*, New York, Quadrangle, pp. 240–245.

RICH, ADRIENNE (1980) 'Compulsory Heterosexuality and Lesbian Existence', in *Signs*, 5, 4 (Summer), pp. 631–660; London, Onlywomen Press, 1981.

RILEY, DENISE (1987) 'Does sex have a history? "Women" and feminism', in *New Formations*, 1 (Spring), pp. 35–45.

ROBERTS, MICHÈLE (1978) *A Piece of the Night*, London, Women's Press.

RYAN, JOANNA (1983) 'Psychoanalysis and Women Loving Women' in CARTLEDGE, SUE and RYAN, JOANNA (Eds) *Sex and Love: New Thoughts on Old Contradictions*, London, Women's Press, pp. 196–209.

SEGAL, LYNNE (1987) *Is the Future Female? Troubled Thoughts on Contemporary Feminism*, London, Virago.

TENNANT, EMMA (1978) *The Bad Sister*, London, Gollancz; London, Picador, 1979.

TODER, NANCY (1980) *Choices*, Watertown, MA, Persephone Press.

WHITFORD, MARGARET (1989) 'Rereading Irigaray', in BRENNAN, TERESA (Ed.) *Between Feminism and Psychoanalysis*, London, Routledge, pp. 106–126.

WHITFORD, MARGARET (1991) *Lucy Irigaray: Philosophy in the Feminine*, London, Routledge.

WILSON, ANNA (1985) *Altogether Elsewhere*, London, Onlywomen Press.

WILSON, BARBARA (1982) *Ambitious Women*, New York, Spinsters Ink.; London, Women's Press, 1983.

WILSON, BARBARA (1984) *Murder in the Collective*, Seattle, Washington, Seal Press; London, Women's Press.

WILSON, BARBARA (1989) *The Dog Collar Murders*, Seattle, Washington, Seal Press; London, Virago.

WILSON, ELIZABETH, with WEIR, ANGELA (1986) *Hidden Agendas: Theory, Politics and Experience in the Women's Movement*, London, Tavistock.

WINTERSON, JEANETTE (1985) *Oranges are Not the Only Fruit*, London, Pandora.

Chapter 12

'Who wrongs you, Sappho?' — Developing Lesbian Sensibility in the Writing of Lyric Poetry

Gillian Hanscombe and Suniti Namjoshi

The scope of this paper is a retrospective analysis of the attempt to arrive at a lesbian perspective in our own work over the past twenty-five years. Three main stages in perceptual and technical development are discernible. The first is the humanist stage: can a lesbian poet belong, even on the margins? Can she, too, be 'human'? Can she contribute insights to the 'human condition'? The second is the centralist stage: endorsed by feminism, can a lesbian poet make a lesbian perspective central? The third is the creaturehood stage or the prophetic stage: having found possibilities for identity, audience and a 'common language', can a lesbian poet include in her vision all that is *not* lesbian?

The Humanist Stage

In this section we propose to address the two principal problem areas confronted at the outset: these were dilemmas caused for the lesbian poet by the nature of lyric itself; and dilemmas caused for the lesbian poet by the doctrines of liberal humanism.

As young poets, particularly stimulated by the lyric tradition of poetry in the English language, we inherited certain formulations: connotations fixed by traditional images, for example, the rose, the garden, or the chase; and the traditional roles assumed by the lyric persona, the 'I' who speaks the poem. The 'I' — the lover, the pursuer, the wooer, the thinker, the speaker — was assumed by convention to be male; whereas the 'you', who was addressed, but who — of course — remained silent, was assumed to be female. Alienation from the lyric tradition was, in the beginning, acutely painful and confused, since the most obvious explanation for it was simply to assume that one wasn't 'good enough'. If one's poems didn't seem to fit in or to resonate with work being written by others, and if one's work seemed discontinuous with its own roots (i.e. the lyric tradition), then surely it simply meant that one wasn't a 'good' poet.

Irony is fundamental to a lesbian life. But a young lesbian poet's amateurism is particularly ironic, given that the ground on which she attempts to place her feet is necessarily chimerical. How could she, that is, write from the perspective either of the hunter, or — indeed — of the hunted, of the pursuer or the pursued, of the speaker or the silent one? On the one hand, the passive role of the hunted might be deemed by traditional lyricists to be quintessentially female: but such a stance, such an image, does not connect with a young lesbian's experience of being in love or with her experience of romantic passion. Nevertheless, all young lesbians know both that they're female and that their experiences of passion and eroticism are as fully human as those claimed by men. On the other hand, the images of the hunter or of the pursuer or of the speaker were also unusable, although initially they seemed more promising: partly because the prevailing mythology about lesbians was that they were Stephen Gordon lookalikes; but crucially, for a poet, because these prototypes could act in the world, and had the blessed gift of utterance.

The difficulty was that despite the richness of the poetic tradition, its whole universe was a rigidly heterosexual one, at the centre of which was a long continuity of male consciousness, which was itself patriarchal in its assumptions about all forms of order: the divine order, the meaning of history, the social order. In other words, it wasn't simply that pronouns were gendered, but also that imagery itself was gender role stereotyped. Not only was this a complex enough problem intellectually, but it was also the case that hardly any analytic language existed which could be helpful for deciphering the real problem. The real problem was not the lesbianism of the lesbian poet, but the male-centred heterosexualism of the lyric tradition.

Sex itself is an image and in lyric love poems is a central metaphor for figuring the relation between the 'I' and the 'you'. In other words it embodies an entire ideology, and in the lyric tradition this ideology is the ideology of patriarchal heterosexuality. In the prose novel, sex is presented as experience; but in a lyric poem, it is a signifier. The popular notion that delimits being a lesbian to sexual orientation only is useless from the poet's point of view. It is the significance attached to sexuality, rather than sexuality divested of significance, that concerns poets. This means that a lesbian writing a love lyric in her own voice, i.e. not in an encoded voice, necessarily either subverts the lyric tradition or ruptures it every time she writes such a poem, because she is the unimaginable: the woman speaker as lover addressing a fellow woman lover.

Similar difficulties arose with other features of lyric technique. The use of language in lyric poetry proceeds from the basis that an 'I' addresses a 'you'. In the novel, by contrast, the use of language proceeds from the assumption that human characters extraneous to the 'I' who is the author and the 'you' who is the reader will be brought into being, and may serve a plethora of functions. Characters can be used as alibis, they can be used as preachers, as symbols, as case studies, as vehicles for a whole range of philosophies and psychologies of human behaviour. The 'persona' of lyric poetry does not function in the same way. Ironic distancing is always possible, and in a good lyric poem always occurs, but in lyric poetry the gender and stance of the persona are supremely important, because the 'I', the persona in a lyric poem, controls the relationship between the 'I' and the 'you' (since the 'you' is almost always silenced) and it is this relationship between the 'I' and the 'you' which embodies in itself at least some aspect of the basic relationship between the 'human' and the 'other' and therefore lays claim to universality.

All this raised problems for us as young lesbian poets, in particular the notorious pronouns problem, and the question of whether to use male or female personae. This was not simply a matter of taking male or female attitudes, but also involved the use of figures from myth that carried a concentrated weight of meaning helpful for the purposes of lyric, but disastrous in their heterosexual overtones. In 'Prologue 4' from *Hecate's Charms*, GH tries to circumvent all these problems by deliberately conflating the genders both in the 'I' and in the 'you' of the poem, in an attempt to arrive directly at 'universality'. Here are the first and third stanzas:

> If I come across you then
> in the terrors of the Himalayas,
> in Beirut, in St. Helena,
> then, when the world has got to know us,
> we shall be one another's sinner.

> Why you come across me then
> only I shall know. And the place
> will be fire and the earth will be so much water.
> My charred fingers will harden in praise
> and never again will my eyes falter.[1]

SN in 'Homage to Circe' attempts a different device by giving the weight of mythological reference to the 'beloved' and leaving the gender of the 'I' unclear in most of the poem; but since this presents the problem that the 'I' will be presumed to be male unless otherwise indicated, she throws in one line that makes the gender of the speaker clear: 'I could sit cat-like and gaze sisterly' (*The Jackass and the Lady*, p. 45).

However, the most fundamental problem posed has to do with the inability of the lesbian to take over the basic assumption of the 'otherness' and 'non-humanity' of the 'other' as opposed to the inherent humanity of the male persona.

These are not problems shared by male homosexual poets, since, being men, they could assume the gift of utterance as men, and could also assume the active stance without that presenting an ambiguity about the nature of maleness. Therefore it was much less problematic for Auden to write lines like 'Lay your sleeping head my love/Human on my faithless arm' since the reader of lyric assumes the speaker to be male. Shakespeare's sonnets often elicit a similar response. The gender of the silent beloved is assumed to be female, but since he/she never speaks, the reader's response to such poems isn't unduly unsettled by disclosure that the beloved may be male. But try it the other way around: imagine a female persona speaking the lines, 'Lay your sleeping head, my love', or 'Let me not to the marriage of true minds' and something quite different happens. First and immediately, the reader/listener experiences surprise and a jolt that the authority of utterance has been assumed by a speaker who is unquestionably female. Once a lesbian learns that that jolt is going to occur every time she writes, then she begins to learn how to use her own voice. Simultaneously she understands that whatever she writes, even the purest lyric, cannot be other than subversive. In this practice she has come to terms with the meaning of her alienation.

All these dilemmas took shape with reference to the prevailing tenets of liberal humanism, which formed the basis of the teaching and reading (and therefore the definition) of English literature within the universities and within the intellectual milieu in general. The unstated tenet was what feminists later disclosed to be the equation human = Man, which actually meant the centrality of male consciousness. The supremely important explicit tenet was the doctrine of ultimate realities or the universality of human nature and of the human experience. This tenet completely ignored the facts of imperialism and was therefore unconscious of its assumption of power. Diversions from European liberal humanism in the languages and cultural systems of all the rest of the world were not deemed relevant, since all the rest of the world was unconsciously deemed inferior, i.e. other. For a lesbian to identify with the cultural norm developed historically from the unconscious self-glorification of white male conquerors was seductive, but absurd.

The power of this set of ideas had presented enormous, sometimes overwhelming problems for earlier women writers, even if they were heterosexual; but for the lesbian poet they presented a crisis. Women writers either had to prove that they had male minds (George Eliot for example) or they had to construct elaborate theories which could extend male consciousness to subsume female consciousness, e.g. Virginia Woolf's exposition of the artist as an androgynous figure. But these strategies are not available to the writer of lyric, whose materials derive solely from the poetic capacities of the language and who does not create what Susanne Langer calls virtual histories or virtual societies as does the novelist. The conventions of lyric poetry are tighter and more constricting quite simply because they are much older, and the weight of the tradition is considerable. On the one hand, any new lyric poet needs that weight and richness; but on the other hand, the lesbian has the peculiar irony not only of belonging to the 'otherness' of the humanist equation (which she shares with all women), but also of being excluded from the central heterosexual metaphor.

It eventually became evident to us as lesbian poets that liberal humanism didn't actually exist. What did exist in the tradition was patriarchal humanism, which does not accord full humanity to women and which has certainly elided the humanity of lesbian utterance. It was therefore not possible intellectually to accept that the experience of sexual love and passion was the 'same' for all individuals (i.e. Man) and at the same time to accept a displacement to an ill-differentiated margin. After all, experience — anybody's —

was, according to humanism, not marginal, but indeed universal. It was also the case that according to humanist canons of great lyric poetry, or even good lyric poetry, hardly a woman was to be found; and in a thousand years of English lyric writing not a single lesbian voice was listed. Logically this meant either that lesbian experience wasn't human, or it meant that no lesbian by definition could ever write a good lyric.

The answer therefore to the question — can a lesbian poet belong to the humanist tradition — was 'no'. At this point in our consciousness — fortunately for us — contemporary feminism arrived; and within the space of ten years it offered a sense of audience, frames of reference which made sense of our perceptions and experiences as women, and uniquely an unambivalent recognition of the existence and importance of lesbian perspective. Unlike humanism, feminism could and did include us. It remained for us to explore what a lyric poem to which a lesbian consciousness was central might actually be.

The Centralist Stage

In the centralist stage the lesbian poet makes a lesbian awareness and a lesbian perspective central to her writing. A lesbian 'I' and a lesbian 'you' are no longer problematic, but this is not simply because of an increase in her skills. The fact that an audience now exists for whom a lesbian persona is not grotesque and to whom a lesbian perspective actually matters is crucial.

Neither SN nor GH had an overnight conversion. The climate of ideas influenced them as it did many other women. Most of the poems in *The Jackass and the Lady* (Namjoshi, 1980) were written between 1972 and 1976. In *The Authentic Lie* (1982), which was written between 1976 and 1978, SN had begun to use a female persona with more confidence and skill. Her politicization in 1978–79 gave her an assured sense of audience for the first time and resulted in the writing of *Feminist Fables* in 1980. *From the Bedside Book of Nightmares* and *The Conversations of Cow*, as well as much of the verse in *The Blue Donkey Fables*, had already been written when SN and GH met in June 1984.

GH's development was different. *Hecate's Charms*, written between 1972 and 1974, marked a clear departure from all earlier work where every attempt to solve 'the pronouns problem' had failed. The device used in *Hecate's Charms* was to create two personae, both female, who could conduct a dialogue within the terms and parameters of a lyric poem. Between 1974 and 1984 GH wrote two further sequences: *Jezebel Her Progress* and *Mary/ Martha*, where again a kind of internal dialogue and commentary is shared between voices. In GH's case, the influence of feminism on her poetry was less direct than it was for SN. For GH, feminism's immediate impact had to do with other forms of writing, in the three prose areas of literary/academic criticism (*The Art of Life: Dorothy Richardson and the Development of Feminist Consciousness*) (1982a), journalism (*Rocking the Cradle: Lesbian Mothers*) (1981, with Jackie Forsler) and a foray into polemical fiction (*Between Friends*) (1982b).

Our meeting in 1984 and subsequent relationship profoundly influenced our poetry. One result was the writing of *Flesh and Paper* between 1984 and 1986. The reciprocal exchange, poem for poem, clarified for us, as nothing else had, that an attempt to extend liberal humanism to include lesbians was a waste of time. Together we claimed the central ground for lesbian consciousness in the 'Introduction' to *Flesh and Paper*, part of which reads:

the worlds we inherit ... are essentially commentaries on experience; and a lesbian woman does not inhabit the worlds that make sense to heterosexual men. Nevertheless, she is clearly human and sentient; she lives and speaks; she most definitely invents the world. The difficulty, as feminists and others have been showing for a good while now, is that all worlds are not equal ... It is our lived experience as lesbians that the 'universal truths' of the human heart, which are claimed as knowledge by the male heterosexual literary tradition, are not 'universal' at all ...

Who, in lyric poems, is addressing whom and in what capacity? And who is overhearing? And who has authority and credentials to comment on what is being said? ...

... we lesbians ... now have a new understanding. We can speak in public. That means we can take the central 'I' and 'you' and 'we' of the language of lyric poetry to mean ourselves, without compromise. It is lesbians who write and hear and overhear and understand. We have the awareness of a lesbian context and a lesbian audience ...

These formulations were arrived at after the experience of writing the poems which was unique for both of us, i.e. neither of us had ever been confronted with a 'you' who literally spoke back. The process began with SN's epigraph to the first poem she sent GH: '"Writer requires active accomplice." Want Ads. Saturday Times.' Both of us were writers and both of us were acutely aware of the technical difficulties surrounding the writing of lesbian poetry. It is not surprising that this awareness forms one of the underlying themes of the sequence.

As it became clear that we were, in fact, producing a coherent sequence of poems, and not just writing letters, it became possible to write poems that harked back to earlier poems and picked up the themes developed in them. For example, the following lines from the second last poem refer back to the notion in the earlier poems that words invent reality (up to a point):

We can compose an ocean if we like;
deck it about with sand dunes, a
mountain or two, some trees.
Or we can compose ourselves.
But a politics? To invent, just we two,
a view? How to think? What to do?
And a country?

(Flesh and Paper, p. 63)

We were happy writing this sequence of poems. We thought we had solved the problems set by the humanist tradition for lesbian poets because the 'I' and 'you' were now equal, equivalent and interchangeable, since each could utter, respond and refer to previous utterance. One of the things this meant technically was that the persona within the poem could reach outside it. In the traditional lyric, the convention is that the 'you' who is being addressed actually hears what is said, but it is merely a convention, since the 'you' never replies. In *Flesh and Paper* it is quite obvious that the 'you' has heard, since she literally answers back. A further convention in the traditional lyric is that the real reader, i.e. the eavesdropper, is male and that the male persona is speaking for him and in a sense to him rather than to the silent female 'you' in the poem. In *Flesh and Paper* we felt that we were speaking for and to all lesbians and that not only had the barrier between the 'I' and the 'you' disappeared, but so too had the barrier between poet and listener. For example, the poem 'Now, flick the folds of your robe' has the lines:

The watchers are women like us — complete
with diverse histories. And if some look askance,
and some are here by chance or circumstance,
their purpose is only to discover
how women might speak, lover to lover,
and offer the exact, the right response.

(*Flesh and Paper*, p. 33)

It seemed to us that in this lesbian universe (as opposed to the liberal humanist one) we had obviated the 'otherness' of the other. It is true that the lesbian universe was surrounded by a powerful and inimical heterosexual one, even in the context of the poems, and that the language itself had to be manipulated since it still carried its patriarchal, heterosexual past; but we felt that the years of learning how to use the language and the tradition, together with the structures afforded by a genuinely lesbian 'you' and 'I', had at last allowed us to contribute something towards the development of lesbian lyric poetry.

For the lesbian lyric poet the problem of the 'disposal' of men is primarily a technical one; it has to do with the subverting of patriarchal literary conventions in such a way that they work for us rather than against us. The view that the problem of men is largely one of content led to what we think should properly be seen as polemical poetry. One characteristic of the flood of verse released in response to lesbian feminism was the assumption that what really mattered in poems was the content: i.e. the content should express the authentic experiences of lesbian women, and should consign men to the margins or elide them altogether. This emphasis on content alone couldn't, for the complexity of reasons we've outlined, produce true lyric; what it did produce was polemical poetry. The characteristics of this poetry are a passionate rhetoric, a content of personal narrative, and a declarative 'I' who addresses the audience directly. Its weaknesses, in our view, involve abandoning, to a greater or lesser extent, the principal features of lyric writing: i.e. the development of imagery; the control of shifts in tone by means of ironic distancing; and the awareness of resonances with and subversions of traditional practice. Had women actually been the true inheritors of the mainstream tradition, such an emphasis on content might merely have produced bad lyrics; but since men have never been marginalized in reality, the best of such work strikes an authentic polemical note because it has justice on its side.

Flesh and Paper was published in 1986; but between 1986 and 1990 (the time of writing this paper), the climate changed. What happened next is perhaps characteristic of all liberation movements. The lesbian audience did not remain static and the growing dislocation between feminism and lesbianism made both of us uneasy. The very proliferation of difference within the lesbian sense of identity tended to reduce the word 'lesbian' to merely a matter of sexual orientation. To speak of *the* lesbian perspective became impossible, and of *a* lesbian perspective problematic, since there were 'lesbians' who were making it clear that almost any perspective could be lesbian.

For us, new problems arose as a result of lesbian pluralism. Some of the underlying values seemed less than attractive. And the vision of lesbian leaders, under the banner of lesbian solidarity, making war on everything deemed 'other' was utterly unsound, both aesthetically and politically. Surely our great gift had been our ability to identify with the rest of creation since it too lay under the oppression of patriarchy. Considerations such as these, together with questions of lesbian responsibility, have preoccupied us for the past few years.

The Creaturehood Stage? Or the Prophetic Stage?

In this stage what becomes a major preoccupation is not the quest for identity, so much as the way in which identity and identifications are formed. In addition, being a lesbian raises questions which have to do with the problem of power, with proper relationships and with an ethically sound way of life. It is the premises and the approach that are likely to characterize a lesbian sensibility — in so far as the word 'lesbian' can be used in this way any more — and to offer a perspective that extends beyond a plea for ordinary human rights and for permission to survive. What this leads to, of course, are the ancient moral and religious questions, including some of the questions asked under liberal humanism, but with the difference that what is at stake is the welfare of life itself rather than merely the welfare of the white male.

In this stage SN and GH have tended to formulate the questions in terms of their original cultural backgrounds: Hindu, Indian with a strong dose of J. Krishnamurti for SN; Christian, Australian for GH. For SN it makes sense to call this phase the creaturehood stage, because it seems to her that what has gone wrong is that we have lost our sense of creaturehood. Since Hinduism is pantheistic, she finds the notion unproblematic. For GH it feels more natural to call this phase the prophetic stage since the 'prophetic' voice, as opposed to the solitary voice of the Romantic lyric, is an attempt to admit and to solve ethical dilemmas that arise within society, i.e. an attempt to save the world, rather than a turning away from it. For both GH and SN the central questions are ethical ones: i.e. a shift from 'Can a lesbian live?' and 'Can a lesbian poet write?' to 'How shall a lesbian live?' and 'How shall a lesbian poet write?' though differences in temperament and cultural background have resulted in different strategies and formulations.

The rise of lesbian pluralism has raised two sets of problems. Opinions are stated and stances taken by 'lesbians' with which we cannot agree at all, e.g. the endorsement of sadomasochism (SM) or of lesbian pornography. It then becomes awkward to claim that we are speaking as and for all lesbians. The other set of problems has to do with the quest for identity and with what happens when some sort of collective identity is at last formed; what seems to happen is war against other collective identities and a simple-minded, jingoistic attempt to proclaim that we are best. The difficulty is that neither GH nor SN can honestly say that we are best, and in any case, arguing about who is best simply re-invents a hierarchy of power, whether actual or intended. What is startlingly clear is that the ego's will to survive, if need be at the expense of other egos, inevitably raises ethical problems. To phrase it in Christian terms, sin remains; and sin of its nature needs atonement (literally *at-one*-ment).

GHs response has been to explore further the process of identity formation in order to discern where the flaws lie. For GH, having moved the lesbian persona centre stage, the poetic challenge has had two interrelated strands: one has to do with trying to tell *all* the truth; and the other has to do with fidelity to the feminist axiom that the personal is political. By trying to tell *all* the truth, including the truth about the dark sides of lesbian humanity, the poet becomes implicitly ethically prescriptive. It is no longer adequate to hold to the earlier polemic that cried for justice for an oppressed people. The 'universalizing' undertaken by a lesbian lyric poet must try to diverge from the recent Romantic past, in which the lyric 'I' is deemed emblematic of all the other 'I's' who eavesdrop, so that the 'I' of her poetry can subsume the collective 'we'.

In GH's recent work this has led to the use of the tone of prophecy, where although the speaking voice is characterized as an 'I', it contains within it the strands of many voices. In ancient custom both poets and prophets spoke for the people; and it has been the case, in contemporary feminism, that poets and polemicists have spoken for women. One implication of all this is that if the process of establishing lesbian identity has been a collective one, then the recognition of flaws and failures and the poetic challenge to tell all the truth also take place in a collective context.

For SN the problem of lesbian responsibility has meant a turning inwards to see which aspects of the ego and of the process of identity formation are destructive and indeed dispensable. In both instances, the effort is towards a moral perspective, if not moral authority, which can examine the failures within the ego and within the lesbian collective, as well as within the hetero-patriarchal system, which after all continues to exist.

In *The Conversations of Cow*, which can perhaps best be described as a lyrical satire, SN had already explored some aspects of the notion of identity and alienation. For a Hindu, the idea that identity is arbitrary, is familiar rather than startling. The metaphor of reincarnation indicates that who you are is merely who you are this time round. Loss of identity, i.e. freedom from having to be someone, rather than achieving personal immortality, is the ultimate aim. Combined with the experience of alienation, these ideas lead easily to the perception that who you are at any particular moment in time has a great deal to do with who you are perceived to be. *The Conversations of Cow* is not concerned with the quest for identity, so much as with dispelling the fear of the 'other' and with understanding that it is not 'other'.

The Mothers of Maya Diip takes up the problem of lesbian responsibility and lesbian childishness, just as several of the *Blue Donkey* fables raised the problem of warring egos. If a lesbian matriarchy did indeed exist, would a lesbian be happy in it? This is the superficial point. The real point is that myths and legends and even 'poems' can be constructed both to endorse and to generate prevailing systems, and that such systems in one way or another legitimize power in the name of authority. Since questions are raised about the morality of this, some answer has to be found to the unquestioned authority of the bigger and better gun.

Perhaps what is at the heart of all these questions is fear. The 'St Suniti and the Dragon' sequence which SN is working on at present may be an attempt to deal with some of these questions. The point about St Suniti is that she's afraid; she's a creature and doesn't know how to live morally with other creatures; she wants to know how to save her soul and how to be good, but she doesn't want to be too good, because that is too hard and perhaps also because it's too dangerous. That is why the sequence contains a series of 'Failed Prayers'. For example:

> If I could pluck out the eye of malice,
> bury it deep, let it lie;
> if freed of malice, I could breathe freely
> (let earth resolve the luckless lie);
> if I could watch a tree sprouting,
> barren and beautiful,
> and stand there casually while its golden apples
> poisoned the air;
> then I could say, 'Ah, Malice worked.
> Malice did it,'
> as I walked away, breathe a sigh.

But if the deconstruction of identity, and not just of male identity — though that is urgent — and if questions about whether a morality of powerlessness is at all appropriate, have become central concerns, then on the face of it, at least, it has become difficult to speak for and to and with the voice of an oppressed people. Oppressed, we certainly are, but perhaps not only in the ways that we had first thought.

GHs sequence *Some of Sybil* constructs a lesbian universe in which lesbians, too, inherit original sin. The voice of Sybil is taken from the patriarchal past, thus literally claiming that there is nothing new in the phenomenon of lesbianism. But Sybil is also a contemporary voice, sometimes arguing with other lesbians, sometimes advising them, sometimes abandoning them, sometimes in love with them, sometimes boasting to them and — finally — grieving for them. The poems, that is, have shifting personae and a multiplicity of 'yous'. Mistakes are admitted, confessions of inadequacy made, pettiness revealed; while at the same time it is acknowledged that the burdens of patriarchal supremacy and the corrosion of powerlessness both continue. The underlying lesbian leitmotif remains, however: the urgency of desire and the celebration of sexual idealism.

Two of Sybil's 'abolition' poems may make these points a little clearer.

So, Sybil, might we together answer? We haven't died. Why don't we abolish the hideaway houses the walled gardens where girls make love among poppies and lady lovers tend hibiscus? When the gardens were planted, women of pleasure abolished men altogether and mated only in season. (I say come when you say pain when you say rage I receive your breasts.) And they kept their babies for tomorrow. (My hands are fish my head is a young ewe butting.)

We could abolish assemblies and scripted complaints. And we could abolish fashion again; relent in the grim cause of individual incident, of the divisions of the freedom to dissent; and come again to the collective supper not knowing who is for us and who against.

For GH it remains important to continue the search for an ethical stance that makes sense of the diversity of lesbian experience and of the adversarial situation lesbians still confront day after day. To SN it seems imperative that we re-examine the concepts of identity, identification and the moral attitudes arising from powerlessness so that the struggle for liberation does not end in a frittering away of the initial idealism. What technical demands these approaches may present remains unclear, but common sense would indicate that lyric poetry demands a combination of them both. Or to put it in ethical terms, in the end, love is the law:

Back in the garden (between utterances) where we're (bent on) existing oh well we lay out phrases thin down rows of sentences (they must be cleaned they must be vacuumpacked for supermarkets) we subvert the weather with all manner of devices (pleats to the knee and nipples altogether hidden) because the sisters require to know the authentic pain, the acceptable ethic (the origin of idioms, the precise inflection) so that words betoken neither governed nor governing

and if flaws

nevertheless appear, our Rule allows no unpicking of syntax without confessional credentials (she says pain I was — and I say rage
because —)

                        and so shall we
ever love one another

                                           (Some of Sybil)

Note

1 All the poems quoted in this essay, whether or not previously published, are the
copyright of Gillian Hanscombe and Suniti Namjoshi.

References

HANSCOMBE, GILLIAN (1975) *Hecate's Charms*, Sydney, Khasmik Poets.
HANSCOMBE, GILLIAN (1975–78) *Jezebel Her Progress* (unpublished).
HANSCOMBE, GILLIAN (1979–82) *Mary/Martha* (unpublished).
HANSCOMBE, GILLIAN (1982a) *The Art of Life: Dorothy Richardson and the Development of
Feminist Consciousness*, London, Peter Owen; Ohio, Ohio University Press.
HANSCOMBE, GILLIAN (1982b) *Between Friends*, Boston, Alyson Publications; London,
Sheba, 1983; London, The Women's Press, 1990.
HANSCOMBE, GILLIAN (1986–88) *Some of Sybil* (unpublished).
HANSCOMBE, GILLIAN and FORSTER, JACKIE (1981) *Rocking the Cradle: Lesbian Mothers*,
London, Peter Owen; London, Sheba Feminist Publishers, 1982; Boston, Alyson
Publications, 1982; new ed., 1987.
NAMJOSHI, SUNITI (1980) *The Jackass and the Lady*, Calcutta, Writers Workshop.
NAMJOSHI, SUNITI (1981; 1984; new ed. 1990) *Feminist Fables*, London, Sheba Feminist
Publishers.
NAMJOSHI, SUNITI (1982) *The Authentic Lie*, Fredericton, Canada, Fiddlehead Poetry
Books.
NAMJOSHI, SUNITI (1984) *From the Bedside Book of Nightmares*, Fredericton, Canada,
Fiddlehead Poetry Books.
NAMJOSHI, SUNITI (1985) *The Conversations of Cow*, London, The Women's Press.
NAMJOSHI, SUNITI (1988) *The Blue Donkey Fables*, London, The Women's Press.
NAMJOSHI, SUNITI (1989) *The Mothers of Maya Diip*, London, The Women's Press.
NAMJOSHI, SUNITI (1989–) *St. Suniti and the Dragon* (in progress).
NAMJOSHI, SUNITI and HANSCOMBE, GILLIAN (1986) *Flesh and Paper*, Canada, Rag-
weed; UK, Jezebel Tapes and Books.

Chapter 13

Questions of Difference and International Feminism[1]

Avtar Brah

'Why do we have to be concerned with the question of Third World women? After all, it is only one issue among many others.' Delete 'Third World' and the sentence immediately unveils its value-loaded cliches. (Minh-ha, 1989, p. 85)

For several hundred years now a global economic system has been in the making. It evolved out of the transatlantic trade in human beings, it flourished during the Industrial Revolution, it has been nurtured by colonialism and imperialism, and now it has achieved a new vitality in this age of microchip technology and multinational corporations. It is a system that has created lasting inequalities both within nations and between nations.

All our fates are linked within this system but our precise position in it depends on a multiplicity of factors such as our gender, class background, colour, ethnicity, caste, whether we live in a rich industrially advanced society or a poor country of the Third World. Given the global nature of this system it is axiomatic that questions of feminism cannot be framed without reference to this international context. This point may seem self-evident. But the ongoing debate surrounding questions of Eurocentricism, racism and feminism shows that these issues are far from settled.

The feminist slogan 'sisterhood is global' that was commonly used by the women's movement in the 1970s signalled the centrality of an international dimension to feminist practice but as many critics have since pointed out the slogan failed to acknowledge the heterogeneity of the condition of being a woman. What does it mean to be a Native American or Native Australian woman whose land rights have been appropriated and whose cultures have been systematically denigrated by the state as well as by the dominant ideologies and practices within civil society? What precise meaning do questions of 'domestic labour' hold for peasant women in the poorest areas of Kenya, who not only are responsible for caring work at home but also have to undertake long hours of strenuous work on the land as well as carry water and firewood for long distances to ensure daily survival? What are the realities facing low-paid women workers employed by multinational companies in countries such as the Philippines, Hong Kong and Sri Lanka? What are the similarities and the differences between their life chances and those of women doing similar work in Britain? How do patriarchal ideologies articulate with international relations of power in the formation of sex-tourism as a growing industry? What are the points of convergence and divergence in the lives of black and white women in Britain? Such questions point to major differences in the social circumstances of different groups of women, and this will mean that their interests may often be contradictory. How will feminism in the 1990s address the contradictions underlying these different womanhoods?

How do we ensure that as we grapple with the construction of strategies which would give women greater economic independence and political control, which would alleviate the burden of childcare and domestic work, rid society of patriarchal violence, and allow women to have control over our sexuality and freedom of choice over childbearing — how do we ensure that these strategies do not reinforce and reproduce existing inequalities? I do not believe that we can begin to develop these strategies unless they are grounded in an understanding of the ways in which issues of class, racism, gender, and sexuality are interconnected and inscribed within the global social order.

Of course these questions are not new. But they take on new meanings in the context of major changes both in the global economy, and in the political and cultural map of the world. This period of momentous events in Eastern Europe, the Soviet Union, South Africa, Central and South America and the Gulf — to mention a few examples — calls for an urgent assessment of the implications of these changes and new alignments within the global social order for different groups of women, men and children the world over. What implications will the predicted 'triumph of the market' economy have on vulnerable social groups in Eastern Europe? How will women's lives be affected by the resurgence in ethnic conflict and racism? Will consolidation of a new European identity strengthen the racisms through which Europe and its diasporas have constructed the non-European 'others'?

The present crisis in the Gulf illustrates both the strength and the inherent instability of the emerging new configuration of world alliances. It is interesting to note how vested economic interests have converted those who have previously been strongly opposed to economic sanctions in South Africa into staunch supporters of an economic blockade in the Gulf. Governments and peoples who have consistently ignored the decades of struggle for self-determination of the Palestinian people are now vehemently in support of Kuwait's right to exist as a sovereign state. This is not to suggest that the invasion of Kuwait is justified but to point out the double standards that characterize particular political positions on the Gulf crisis.

The role of labour migration in lubricating the world economic system is graphically illustrated by the events in the Gulf as we watch television pictures of thousands of Asian women and men workers stranded in the desert with little food or water. Their plight had been all but ignored in the early stages of the crisis when only the Western citizens in the Gulf were a focus of concern. It is also worth noting how Western residents in the Gulf have been socially constructed as heroic and valiant bearers of a 'civilizing mission' against an 'oriental despot' bent on using Western women and children as a 'human shield'. On the other hand, when the world attention did ultimately shift to the appalling living conditions of Asian workers, this collectivity has been represented not as subjects with human rights but as objects of Western charity. Racism, class and gender dimensions are all combined in the unfolding of these events.

The Gulf crisis reveals elements of conflict as much as collaboration between the superpowers. Simultaneously, it brings into relief the rivalries among the nations of the Middle East and internal class contradictions in these societies. The massive military build-up, costing billions every day, underlines the perniciousness of the growing militarization of a world in which millions still do not have enough to eat. Women may not be very visible on the world stage of politics but we are part and parcel of the system. Women's labour both inside and outside the household is central to the sustenance of the system. The social representation of women in nationalistic discourses as carriers of the 'race', of male honour, and as dependants of men, renders women (and children) as ideological fodder in competing nationalisms on the world political stage. We are also thoroughly implicated in the system through our own political positions which determine how and in what ways we collude with, accept, resist, or challenge international hierarchies of power. We need visions, critical perspectives, that enable us to come to grips with this complex reality.

But the complexity of global relations does not imply that we are not able to develop strategies for concrete political intervention.

We may use abstract concepts such as gender, racism, or class to analyze social phenomena but these abstractions have very real, concrete effects, albeit of a differing order, on different groups of women. Returning to the Gulf crisis, for instance, we may take the example of Asian and white British women stranded in the region. At the more visible level the difference in their accommodation has been striking — the latter in hotels, whereas the former have been kept in makeshift tents. Several white women interviewed on television described how they had left behind most of their material belongings. The Asian women too are leaving for their countries of origin practically empty-handed. But the consequences for the two groups will be rather different.

The majority of the Asian women have been employed in the Gulf doing low-paid menial jobs as domestic workers with very few political or social rights. Their wages have been a major, if not the sole, source of income for their extended families in Asia. Their loss of livelihood is likely to result in considerable hardship and poverty since they are faced with prospects of almost certain unemployment upon their return. The Western women have been in the Gulf region either as wives of diplomats, military personnel, professionals, technicians or businessmen, or, to a lesser extent, have themselves been engaged in these well-paid occupations. Whilst their return to Western countries with established welfare systems may in some cases result in a drop in the standard of living it is nonetheless unlikely to lead to impoverishment.

Of course, we will wish to sympathize with the personal losses suffered by all women. But we need feminist theories which enable us to develop understandings of why, for instance, the rich and the poor countries of the world supply different types of labour to the Middle East, and why this present crisis is expected to have a far more devastating impact on the economies of South Asia than on those of richer countries because of such factors as the loss of migrant workers' remittances which constitute an important source of foreign exchange with which to service the foreign debt, higher oil prices, and the cost of sanctions and repatriation of workers. We need accounts of why certain sectors of the world economy become feminized, why certain categories of women perform particular kinds of paid work, and how these different groups of women are differently represented within different political, religious, academic and commonsense discourses (cf. Mitter, 1986; Mohanty, 1988; Enloe, 1989).

We can find equally pertinent examples in Britain. As is now well known, it is not a matter of coincidence but rather a result of the history of colonialism and imperialism that the post-war labour shortages in Britain were met via the recruitment of workers from the former colonies in Asia and the Caribbean. Research evidence shows that although the employment profiles of African–Caribbean and South Asian origin women are not identical (and there are differences between different categories of South Asian women) nonetheless these women are predominantly concentrated at the lowest rungs of the gender-segregated labour market (cf. Brown, 1984; Brah, 1987; Bruegel, 1989).

Black women's experiences of racism in the labour market, the education system, the Health Service, the media, and with respect to a variety of state policies such as those on immigration, policing and social welfare, means that, even when black and white women share a broadly similar class position, they constitute distinctive fractions within that specific class location.[2] Their everyday life experiences will therefore be characterized by certain commonalities but also by crucial differences. But all this begs the question of how 'difference' is to be conceptualized. I believe that discussions around 'differences' may be conducted at cross purposes unless we attempt to clarify how the notion of 'difference' is being deployed within a specific context.

How may 'difference' be conceptualized? At the most general level 'difference' may be construed as a social relation constructed within systems of power underlying structures of class, racism, gender and sexuality. At this level of abstraction we are concerned with the ways in which our social position is circumscribed by the broad parameters set by the social structures of a given society. Some of the examples I have so far given refer to our positioning in such social structural terms. It is extremely important to address this level as it has a crucial bearing on shaping our life chances. Difference may also be conceptualized as experiential diversity. Here the focus is on the many and different manifestations of ideological and institutional practices in our everyday life. These everyday practices constitute the matrix against which we make and remake our group, as well as personal, histories. But we need to make a distinction between 'difference' as representation of the distinctiveness of our collective histories and 'difference' as personal experience, codified in an individual's biography. Although mutually interdependent, the two levels cannot be 'read off' from each other. Our personal experiences arise out of mediated relationships. How we perceive and understand our experience may vary enormously. For example, we may experience subordination without necessarily recognizing it as such. The same social practice may be associated with somewhat different meanings in a different cultural context. There may be psychic and emotional disjunction between how we feel about something and how we believe we ought to feel from the standpoint of our analytical and political perspectives. The group histories that chronicle our shared experience will also contain their own measure of contradictions but there is no simple one-to-one correspondence between collective experience and personal biography (see Brah, forthcoming). To state the obvious, collective experience does not represent the sum total of individual experiences any more than individual experiences can be taken to be a direct expression of the collective.

Hence we need to make distinctions between, for example, 'black' and 'white' women as historically contingent analytical categories constructed within and referring to specific historical processes of colonialism, imperialism, and anti-black racism, *and* black and white women as individuals. Whilst the former describes a social division, the latter draws our attention to human subjects as complex beings who are sites of multiple contradictions, and whose everyday praxis may reinforce or undermine social divisions.

It is now widely accepted that 'woman' is not a unitary category. The question remains whether it can be a unifying category. I believe that it is possible to develop a feminist politics that is global, but it demands a massive commitment together with a sustained and painstaking effort directed towards developing practices that are informed by understandings of the ways in which various structures of inequality articulate in given contexts, and shape the lives of different groups of women. We need to address how our own position — in terms of class, racism, sexuality, caste, for example — locates us within systems of power *vis-à-vis* other groups of women and men. For example, as an Asian woman living in Britain I am subjected to racism, but as a member of a dominant caste within the specific community from which I originate I also occupy a position of power in relation to lower-caste women. From my standpoint, a feminist politics would demand of me a commitment to opposing racism as much as casteism although I am positioned differently within these social hierarchies, and the strategies required of me in dealing with them may be different.

Similarly, we may take the example of Irish and black women in Britain. Both black and Irish people have a history of being colonized, both occupy predominantly working-class positions within the British class structure and both have been subjected to racism. But anti-Irish racism and anti-Black racism have different histories. We must recognize that as white Europeans Irish women are constructed as a dominant group *vis-à-vis* black women in and through the discourses of anti-Black racism, even when they themselves are in turn subordinated within anti-Irish racism. Alliances that would empower both groups must not only take into account the similarities in their material circumstances but also involve commitment to combating the differing racisms to which the two groups are subjected. Black and Irish women would need to examine the ways in which their 'womanhoods' are both similarly and differently constructed within patriarchal, racial and class relations of power.

As a consequence of the major restructuring of the world economy, the dominance of multinational capital, the impact of the new communications revolution, and the profound political upheavals of recent times, we are witnessing global tendencies that are simultaneously complementary and contradictory. On the one hand, the ever increasing globalization of cultural industries is leading to homogenization of cultural consumption across transnational boundaries. On the other hand, we are faced with the parallel tendency towards greater fragmentation; the resurgence of local aesthetic, political and ethnic tradition; and the assertion of difference. Under such circumstances it is important to identify when 'difference' is being organized hierarchically rather than laterally. We need to disentangle instances when 'difference' is asserted as a mode of contestation against oppression and exploitation, from those where difference becomes the vehicle for hegemonic entrenchment. In practice this exercise is not clear cut. For instance, nationalistic discourses may be employed by liberation movements as well as by racist and chauvinistic groups and organizations. Moreover, both sets of discourses may be constituted around, and/or be constitutive of, representations of women which reinforce rather than undermine women's subordination. In these instances feminist practice would require that we pay careful attention to the historical and social circumstances which underpin a given nationalism, and its consequences for different economic groups and for different groups of women.

A distinction between 'difference' as a process of differentiation referring to the particularities of the social experience of a group, from that whereby 'difference' itself becomes the modality in which domination is expressed, is crucial for several reasons. Firstly, it draws our attention to the fact that 'difference' need not invariably lead to divisions amongst different groups of women. Secondly, it reminds us that our experiences are not constituted solely within oppressions. They encompass an immense range of emotional, psychological and social expressions. In this sense, cultural diversity — as expressed, for example, in art, music, literature, science and technology, traditions of political and cultural struggle against domination, and different modes of human subjectivity — may be acknowledged and, depending upon the social perspectives within which these formations are embedded, affirmed and celebrated. But we need to be aware that the notion of 'cultural difference' can be appropriated by social tendencies which seek to construct impervious boundaries between groups. Contemporary racism in Britain provides an instance of such appropriation of 'cultural difference'.

A subordinate group may also mobilize symbols of cultural difference as an expression of pride in its social identity. Such a political assertion of cultural identity could potentially constitute a progressive force, although it too cannot be assumed to be invariably unproblematic simply because it is a form of struggle by a subordinate group. Particular expressions of cultural pride may emerge as a cause for concern if cultural practices are treated as reified symbols of an essentialist historic past. Hence, the meaning of cultural difference — whether inscribed within the specificity of male and female cultures, class cultures, or cultures defined on the basis of ethnicity (and these are overlapping categories) — is contingent not only on the social context, but also upon the extent to which the concept of culture is posited in essentialist or non-essentialist terms.

The issue of essentialism seems to call for conceptual clarification between:

(a) essentialism as referring to a notion of ultimate essence that transcends historical and cultural boundaries;

(b) universalism as commonality derived from historically variable experience and as such remaining subject to historical change; and

(c) the historical specificity of a particular cultural formation.

It should be possible to recognize cultural difference in the sense of (c) and acknowledge commonalities that acquire a universal status through the accumulation of similar (but not identical) experiences in different contexts as in (b) without resorting to essentialism. It is evident that as women we can identify many commonalities of experience across cultures which none the less retain their particularity. In other words, historical specificity and universalism need not be counterposed against each other. My own use of the term 'universal' in the way described above is somewhat of a departure from the general usage of the term. I am arguing the case for a non-essentialist universalism; that is, for a concept of universalism as a historical product.

We would be in a better position to address the need for mutual respect for cultural difference without recourse to essentialism if cultures were to be conceived less in terms of reified artefacts and rather more as processes. This may also circumvent the issue of cultural relativism. If cultures are understood as processes instead of fixed products, it would be possible to disapprove of a particular cultural practice from a feminist standpoint without constructing a whole cultural group as being inherently such and such. For example, we may condemn the practice of 'suttee' without following in the tradition of colonial and post-colonial discourses (such as the television film 'Far Pavilions') which seek to represent such practices as the symbols of the inherent barbarism of Indian cultures. This would require that the racialized discourses and practices are challenged equally vehemently and persistently.

Similarly, we may condemn racist practices in Britain without assuming that British cultures are inherently racist instead of racism being a particular (albeit a strong) strand which is an outcome of historical and contemporary social factors.

A corollary of the above argument is that human subjects are not fixed embodiments of their cultures. Since all cultures are internally differentiated and never static, though the pace of change may be variable, our subjectivities will be formed within the range of heterogeneous discursive practices available to us. Hence, a variety of subject positions will emerge within a single cultural context offering the possibility of political change as we move from one subject position to another — from a non-feminist to a feminist position, for example. But, far from being a smooth transition, a shift in subject position may be accompanied by all manner of emotional and psychic ambivalences and contradictions. These must be addressed if feminist visions that take account of issues of racism, class and sexuality are to make a lasting impact. It is essential to examine the loci of power which produce and sustain specific forms of subjectivity. For instance, we may ask questions about the nature of power that surrounds white subjectivity in a society where non-white people are subjected to racism, or heterosexual subjectivity in a society where lesbian and gay sexuality is subjugated. Critical perspectives developed from such enquiry should enable assessment of the personal implications for us as individuals of adopting anti-racist or anti-heterosexist positions.

A sense of ourselves as located within heterogeneous discursive practices shows not only that we inhabit multiple and changing identities but that these identities are produced and reproduced within social relations of 'race', 'gender', class and sexuality. The degree to which we can work across our 'differences' depends on the conceptual frameworks and political perspectives from which we understand these differences. It is the nature of our political commitments and perspectives that can provide the basis for effective coalition building.

I believe that coalitions are possible through a politics of identification as opposed to a 'politics of identity' (cf. Adams, 1989; Parmar, 1989). We develop our first sense of community within a neighbourhood, but we soon learn to see ourselves as part of many other 'imagined communities' — imagined in so far as we may never actually meet those people face to face. But we learn to identify with these groups, their experiences, their struggles. These processes of political identification — these processes of formation of 'communities in struggle' — do not erase the diversity of human experience; rather, they enable us to appreciate the particular within the universal, and the universal within the particular. However, this politics of identification is only meaningful, indeed, only possible, if based on understandings of the material and ideological basis of all oppressions in their global manifestations; of the interconnectedness as well as the specificity of each oppression. And it is only meaningful if we develop a practice to challenge and combat them all. We can work locally in our own groups, organizations, workplaces, and communities but we need to make connections with wider national and global struggles and movements.

Notes

1 This revised text of a talk presented at the annual conference of the Women's Studies Network (UK) in July 1990 was revised during September 1990, so that any reference to the Gulf situation is applicable only to the events as they had unfolded by the end of that month.
2 The concept of class fraction is the subject of considerable debate in the literature on 'race' and ethnic relations. See, for instance, Phizacklea and Miles (1980); Miles (1982); Siranandan, A. (1982); Rex and Mason (1986).

References

ADAMS, M.L. (1989) 'There's No Place Like Home: On the Place of Identity in Feminist Politics', in *Feminist Review*, 31, Spring.
BRAH, A. (1987) 'Women of South Asian Origin in Britain', in *South Asia Research*, 7, 2.
BRAH, A. (forthcoming) 'Difference, Diversity and Differentiation, in DONALD, J. and RATTANSI, A. (Eds) *Identity and Difference in Postmodern Culture.*
BROWN, C. (1984) *Black and White Britain*, Heinemann.
BRUEGEL, I. (1989) 'Sex and Race in the Labour Market', in *Feminist Review*, 32, Summer.
ENLOE, C. (1990) *Bananas, Beaches and Bases: Malcing Feminist Sense of International Politics*, London, Pandora Press.
MAMA, A. (1986) 'Black Women and the Economic Crisis', in FEMINIST REVIEW (Ed.) *Waged Work: A Reader*, Virago.
MILES, R. (1982) *Racism and Migrant Labour*, Routledge and Kegan Paul.
MINH-HA, T. (1989). *Woman, Native, Other Writing Post Coloniality and Feminism*, Indiana University Press.
MITTER, S. (1986) *Common Fate, Common Bond: Women in the Global Economy*, Pluto.
MOHANTY, C.T. (1988) 'Under Western Eyes: Feminist Scholarship and Colonial Discourses', in *Feminist Review* 30, Autumn.
PARMAR, P. (1989) 'Other Kinds of Dreams', in *Feminist Review*, 31, Spring.
PHIZACKLEA, A. and MILES, R. (1980) *Labour and Racism*, Routledge and Kegan Paul.
REX, J. and MASON, D. (Eds) (1986) *Theories of Race and Ethnic Relations*, Cambridge University Press.
SIRANANDAN, A. (1982) *A Different Hunger*, Pluto.

Section IV

Making a Difference

Introduction

What impact has Women's Studies had on the mainstream/malestream academic disciplines? In what ways does feminist knowledge differ from orthodox systems of thought within the academy, and how has it been received? All four of the papers included in this final section illustrate that the tacking of feminist perspectives on to any discipline as a marginalized alternative viewpoint, in the form of an optional undergraduate course, or a brief chapter on women added at the close of an otherwise gender-blind book, is ultimately unsustainable. A feminist perspective, with its roots in the politics of everyday experience, questions the criteria by which orthodox knowledge is constructed, disclosing as problematic such categories as the 'scientific' or the 'objective'. It calls for the reconceptualization of each discipline, and breaks down the boundaries dividing traditional subject areas.

The first two chapters describe the differing responses to feminism in two representative disciplines. Pamela Abbott's paper details the current situation with regard to sociology, a discipline which has acknowledged the impact of feminism to a limited extent, but persists in an attempt to marginalize it, even though in so doing it leaves unanswered basic questions within its own field. A similar account could be given of many of those subject areas within the humanities and social sciences upon which feminism has succeeded in making some imprint. Sue Wilkinson's paper deals with feminism's relation to psychology, which, through its insistence on the 'scientific', resists feminist interventions with particular ferocity: the situation she describes can be seen as an indicator of feminism's difficult relation to scientific disciplines generally. In her concluding paragraphs, Wilkinson refers to the difficulties for academic feminists generally in breaking through their 'socialization' within the value-systems and characteristic discourses of the various orthodox subject areas in which they were initially trained. Routes out of such intellectual fetters are illustrated in the final two papers of this section, in which a sociologist, Liz Stanley, and an 'English' specialist, Tess Cosslett, cut across the boundaries of their respective disciplines to disclose the ways in which a feminist perspective reveals all knowledge as arising out of subjective positions located in particular social contexts. Their work provides examples of how the traditional discourses and boundaries of academic disciplines are radically altered by feminist knowledge, and point towards future developments in the relation of Women's Studies to higher education.

Chapter 14

Feminist Perspectives in Sociology: The Challenge to 'Mainstream' Orthodoxy

Pamela Abbott

In writing this paper I am very aware of myself as a middle-class white academic sociologist concerned to analyze the impact that feminist thought and research has had on and in the discipline of sociology. I would argue that sociology is a discipline dominated by males — while the majority of students are female, the majority of lecturers are male — and that this has far-reaching implications for its theories and its methods. Despite at least twenty years' criticism of this 'malestream' orientation, little appears to have changed. Women are rare in the senior posts, and women are taught 'malestream' sociology; they are inducted into a knowledge which is itself influential in justifying the inferior social position of the majority of British women.

> Male orientation may so colour the organisation of sociology as a discipline that the invisibility of women is a structured male view, rather than a superficial flaw. The male focus, incorporated into the definitions of subject areas, reduces women to a side issue. (Oakley, 1974, p. 4)

There has indeed been some change since the mid-1970s. Sociologists can no longer afford to ignore women and gender divisions entirely, and the discussion of 'malestream' bias is now a permitted exercise. Books have been published by women sociologists, writing from feminist perspectives, and indeed this has become a fashionable 'line' with publishers. However, most sociological research still has a strong tendency to generalize from male samples to the whole population. Textbooks add 'women' on as a chapter, rather than taking seriously the now substantial body of feminist work in all the traditional areas of sociology. While 'malestream' sociology may now feel that it cannot avoid the gender issue and still look plausible, it tends to deal with it as an addendum — a criticism of received wisdom, or an additional sub-area worth a lecture or two, or something for the women to teach as a third-year option. What I intend to argue here is that what is required is *not* integrating women into sociology, but the reconceptualization of sociology itself. This task, I shall suggest, has barely begun to be tackled.

The need to transform sociology so that the problems of the oppressed can at least be formulated as questions needing answers, rather than 'defined out' as non-sociological, is by no means confined to the area of gender. For example, many of the criticisms that I and other white feminists have made of sociology (e.g. in Abbott and Wallace, 1990) have left us open to the charge of ignoring racism. While we have criticised knowledge as man-made, including much sociological understanding, we have tended to ignore the fact that the men who made that knowledge were white — that the knowledge is not only patriarchal but also racist.

In previous work (e.g. Abbott and Wallace, 1990) I have attempted to demonstrate the centrality of feminist analysis to sociology and the contribution that feminist scholarship has made to sociological reasoning and understanding. Mary Maynard, in a 'trend report' in *Sociology* (1990), has also demonstrated the impact that feminism has had on sociology. She suggests that it has influenced three developments in the discipline:

1 the importance of the interrelationship of the public and the private,

2 the reconceptualization of sociological phenomena — for example, the realization that 'work' applies to domestic labour and unpaid caring just as much as to paid employment, and

3 the recognition that gender and gender relationships are central.

She also points out that the impact of feminism has not been uniform throughout sociology, being more influential in some areas than others. She cites social class and theory as areas where feminism has had less impact. While I would agree that there has indeed been an impact on sociology, I want also to argue that this is often superficial and that feminist sociology is still marginalized and has not become central.

In the 1990 book which I co-authored with Claire Wallace we suggested a tripartite framework for classifying feminist attempts to reform sociological theory and research:

Integration: the main problem being the sexist bias of 'malestream' sociology, the main task is to remove the bias by reforming existing ideas and practices, to bring women in and thereby fill the gap in our existing knowledge. The way forward is to carry out research incorporating women, and reform of existing theories to remove sexism. (The main problem with this approach is that women are likely to continue to be marginalized. They will be added to the syllabus, and lip service will be paid to incorporating them into research samples, but the basis of the discipline is left untouched and no account is taken of feminist criteria of what is to count as knowledge. For example, this approach fails to challenge assumptions about the division of the social world into public and private, the primacy of paid work, that social class is *the* fundamental social division, and so on.)

Separatism: a position arguing that what is needed is a sociology for women by women. It is concerned not with changing existing sociology but with developing a sociological knowledge seen from women's perspectives and intended to change women's lives. Gender is seen as the primary division in society, with all women sharing a common position of being exploited and dominated by men. (The problem is that this may perpetuate the marginality of women; 'malestream' sociology can continue with 'the real analysis' and safely leave the question of women to women. Further, by ignoring men and 'malestream' sociology such a new discipline would not only lose many of the valuable insights of the old one but potentially fail to theorize the *relationship* between men and women and the importance of relational analysis for understanding women's subordination.)

Reconceptualization: This position recognises the need to locate women within social structures and social relationships as a whole, and therefore to carry out research on boys and men as well as girls and women. However, at the level of theory it demands a recasting of sociology to make it compatible with the concerns, interests and experiences of women — something which will help explain women's position to women (and men's to men) rather than concealing it by a set of discourses which deny women the very terms in which the debate might be held. (The major problem is resistance on the part of male sociologists, many of whom would deny that such a revolution is needed. Nonetheless this was and is my own position in the debate.)

I feel that the feminist criticisms of 'malestream' sociology have still not had a sufficient impact on the discipline, because 'malestream' orthodoxy has not recognized their full implications. I accept that most textbooks now have a chapter on gender divisions and that much research now includes women in its samples. Sexist language is now nearly eradicated in published research, and most authors, editors and publishers follow the sort of non–sexist guidelines detailed in Margaret Eichler's 1988 book. However, this goes very little beyond 'adding women in' — the perspective of 'integration' outlined above. The chapters on gender divisions in textbooks are mainly about women and summarize relevant research mainly about women. In other chapters on substantive areas of sociology in the books women are rarely mentioned and feminist research findings are even less frequently cited. This is in part a consequence of the history of sociology — much of the sociology to which it is seen as necessary to refer was published before the growth of feminism — but it also relates to a failure to recognize what the implications of the feminist critiques of 'malestream' sociology are for the discipline itself. That is, 'malestream' sociology fails to recognize that feminists are making a fundamental criticism of existing sociological theorizing. Similarly, research tends to be carried out either on women in isolation or, where men *and* women are sampled, the results tend to be analyzed separately by gender; women are often seen as the deviants where they differ from men. The areas where women have had the most impact tend to be the sub-areas of sociology that have almost become seen as a female preserve and not the concern of men. Also, much of the research that has genuinely taken account of the need to reformulate sociological theory has been undertaken by women. Most of the examples that Mary Maynard (1990) quotes, of research that has taken seriously the importance of the interaction of the public and the private and has reconceptualized some of the old sociological concepts, was undertaken by women. Perhaps more important still as an indicator of how things stand are the reactions of our third-year Gender Divisions students during the first few weeks of the course. They tell us that many members of the teaching staff not only do not recognize the centrality of gender divisions but also rarely refer to feminist theory or research. Perhaps my colleagues are an exception to a general trend but, talking to colleagues from other institutions and reading the scripts from centres for which I am external examiner, I suspect not. Even when our students are aware of feminist ideas, these have rarely been incorporated in a gender framework, but have been seen as an addendum — something extra, on the 'woman question'.

In other words, women have been added on to 'malestream' sociology as it has become increasingly difficult for it to ignore completely the work of feminist sociologists. There have been some important changes in sociology as a result of the feminist challenge, but there is also a long way to go. Many of those working in 'malestream' sociology continue to ignore the feminist critiques, and many others continue to resist them. This is crucial because many of those regarded as authoritative within the discipline who take this stance are also in key institutional positions. Their intellectual stance on the feminist critique reduces the chance that it will be taken seriously, and this is reinforced by their ability to use institutional positions to underpin their attitudes. Sara Delamont (1989) has pointed to the importance of women's work being taken seriously if women are ever to be recognized as authoritative academics, while Caroline Ramazanoglu has illustrated the ways in which men have used institutional power to marginalize women. This intellectual resistance and marginalization is of key importance, as it is most notable, as Mary Maynard points out, in three central areas of sociology — theory, social class, and political sociology. These are high-status, male-dominated areas of sociology; the accepted key figures in these areas are men, and notable among them are men most resistant to the feminist challenge (see e.g. Goldthorpe, 1983, 1984; Goldthorpe and Payne, 1986; Lockwood, 1986). This is true not only of scholarship and research, but also of teaching. In my own institution, for example, the most vocal criticisms made by our female students concern the absence of feminist theory from Sociological Theory courses and of feminist analysis of ideology from Political Ideology courses. However, even adding on a lecture or lectures in feminist theories and feminist ideologies — which has happened in recent years as a response to student pressure — does not mean that feminist scholarship has been incorporated into the courses. Indeed, I am concerned that in my own teaching I myself frequently 'add women on' rather than reformulating what I teach to take account of the criticisms I make of 'malestream' sociology. A key question is why this should be the case. The answer is that sociologists (including me!) have not reformulated their sociology to take full account of feminist criticisms. This is partly because sociology has resisted the fundamental challenge which feminism raises for the discipline, and partly because the task is a difficult one and will take time. This difficult task of reformulation which those of us face who are trying to undertake it is made all the more difficult by the resistance of 'malestream' sociology.

I will illustrate the argument with reference to class theory. Class has been central to sociological analysis since the foundation of the discipline. Incorporating the feminist criticisms of 'malestream' sociology requires the reformulation of our understanding of class and class processes, not just incorporating gender, age and race as further fundamental variables. (I accept that they *are* fundamental variables, but just to incorporate them in the analysis in an additive sort of way is not sufficient.) I will not re-rehearse here the full range of criticisms that feminists have made of conventional social class theorization and conceptualization (see for example Acker, 1973; Stanworth, 1984; Arber *et al.*, 1986; Abbott and Sapsford, 1987; Payne and Abbott, 1990). Two key interrelated concerns have emerged, however. First, it has been demonstrated that the class scales generally used within sociology are inadequate for classifying women's social class. Secondly, it has been shown that women's social mobility has not been incorporated adequately into mobility studies (see e.g. Payne and Abbott, 1990).

The criticism that the class scales are inadequate is so central an issue that is seems to me of considerable concern that in practice little has been done to remedy this. Sociologists see social class as fundamental, and in most empirical research it is seen as a key variable. Yet the conventional instruments for measuring it are inadequate for classifying over half the population. The attempts made by feminists to develop more appropriate scales have been inadequately funded and have not as yet resulted in the production of adequate scales. Some have been devised which are for use on female samples only — e.g. the City Scale (Roberts, 1985, 1986) — and are useful for research on women but not for research that wants to incorporate gender relations. Others have been attempts to revise existing scales — e.g. the Surrey Scale (Dale *et al.*, 1983). However, these attempts have left many of the key questions and issues raised by feminists unanswered. Do women form a social class in opposition to men, and if so then in what senses? How does household class relate to market class? Two central points need to be made here. First, these are *not* questions that relate only to women; once we realize that they need to be asked we realize that they are just as important for men. They are not just feminist but also sociological questions. Secondly, the reason why we cannot answer them is that they have not been researched; they become evident as central questions only when we start to take women seriously. 'Malestream' sociology, however, has on the whole remained blind (or perhaps deaf) to the need to answer them. As far as I am aware, no large-scale research has been funded by research councils or other agencies to look into these very central sociological issues.

Similar points can be made if we look at social mobility research. A crucial problem here, of course, is that allocating individuals to a class position based on their market situation is the starting point for such studies. Given what was said above, this is not possible; that is, the enterprise cannot logically be undertaken because we cannot adequately reflect women's class position using the existing ('malestream') class scales. The best one can do is to make a first approximation to such a study, by using currently available data and class schemas to include women in the analysis of mobility — or at least, those women who are in paid employment. This is what has been done by those who have started to consider the social mobility of women (e.g. Abbott and Sapsford, 1987; Marshall *et al.*, 1988; Payne and Abbott, 1990). Even this limited research has been able to demonstrate that gender — not studying women *per se* — is what is crucial about reformulating sociology. The study of female patterns of social mobility demonstrates that they are markedly different from those of men, that women's experiences are not the same as men's, in terms of both intergenerational and intragenerational mobility. Crucially, Britain is not as open a society for women as for men, and even where women are in the same occupational class as men they tend to be at the bottom and men at the top. (This of course relates as much to the evaluation of skill and expertise as it does to the actual abilities needed to do a particular job — see Abbott and Wallace, 1990.)

The response by the dominant 'malestream' theorists to the feminist challenge to their orthodoxy was initially to reject the need to incorporate women, and subsequently to argue that incorporating women made no difference to the major conclusions from research on male-only samples (e.g. Goldthorpe, 1983; Goldthorpe and Payne, 1986). Thus in the 1986 article John Goldthorpe and Clive Payne suggest that if women had the same labour-market occupational distribution as men, then the patterns of intergenerational mobility for men and women would be broadly the same. In other words, studying female intergenerational occupational mobility adds nothing to what is learned from studying male-only samples. This of course ignores the main theoretical concern of 'malestream' mobility studies — assessing the increase in 'openness' brought about by structural changes to occupational distributions — and it ignores the fact that studying women results in a challenge to the main theoretical conclusions of such research (Abbott and Sapsford, 1987; Abbott, 1990). Goldthorpe *et al.* (1980) conclude from analysis of the Oxford Mobility Study's all-male sample that there is no evidence of social closure — those in the highest social class do not necessarily have a father in the same class — but very few women finish up in the highest class, whatever their father's class. The Oxford Mobility Study fails to show any part of the class scale acting as a 'buffer zone' to limit the extent of male mobility, but routine non-manual work quite clearly acts as such a zone for women (both upward and downward intergenerational mobility tends to lead to this class). The massive presence of women in this class tends to limit the downward mobility of men with middle-class fathers, while facilitating upward mobility of working-class men into middle-class regions beyond the area of routine non-manual work. Finally, the Oxford study failed to find evidence that increased mobility via educational achievement is counterbalanced by a decline in working-life mobility, for men, but there is considerable evidence that women are very rarely upwardly mobile as a result of workplace promotion and that the class of their first job is often the highest that they achieve. Thus there is social closure — against women —

Table 2   *Changes in Labour Market Structure, 1921–71*

Socio-economic group	Males		Females		Ratio		Ratio of rates of
	1921 %	1971 %	1921 %	1971 %	1971/1921 M	F	increase: F/M
Self employed and higher-grade salaried professional workers	1.6	6.1	0.9	1.4	3.8	1.6	0.4
Employers and proprietors	7.7	5.2	4.7	2.9	0.7	0.6	0.9
Administrators and managers	4.3	9.9	2.1	3.3	2.1	1.6	0.7
Lower-grade salaried professionals and technicians	1.8	5.5	6.3	10.8	3.1	1.7	0.5
Inspectors, supervisors and foremen	1.9	4.5	0.3	1.2	2.4	4.0	1.7
Clerical workers and secretaries	5.1	6.1	9.8	28.0	1.2	2.9	2.4
Sales and shop personnel	4.1	3.9	7.5	9.4	1.0	1.3	1.3
Skilled manual workers	32.3	29.4	20.3	9.3	0.9	0.5	0.5
Semi-skilled manual workers	24.5	21.2	40.0	27.3	0.9	0.7	0.8
Unskilled manual workers	16.7	8.2	8.1	6.4	0.5	0.8	1.6

Note: the 1971/1921 ratios indicate the degree of increase, separately for males and females: a ratio of 1.0 indicates no change, one smaller than that a decrease, and one larger an increase. The ratio in the final column compares the two rates of increase: a ratio of 1.0 indicates no difference between males and females, one smaller than that a larger increase for males than females, and one larger than that a larger increase for females than males.

Source: adapted from Abbott and Sapsford (1987), Table 70 on p. 180.

there is a buffer zone — women form it — and there is no counter-mobility for women.

More fundamentally, the line adopted by Goldthorpe and Payne ignores the gendered division of labour and the fact that the social mobility of men is crucially dependent on the slots in the labour market that women occupy. The changes in the occupational structure in this century, and consequently in the structure of opportunity, are not gender-neutral. There has been a dramatic expansion of white-collar occupations, in the proportion of jobs done by women, and in the percentage of women engaged in waged work. Men and women could in principle have benefited equally from the mobility opportunities generated by the changes in demand for labour, but women have exhibited a different pattern of mobility from men, and women's participation in the labour force has changed mobility opportunities for men. Abbott and Sapsford (1987) demonstrate that studies of intergenerational mobility give a false impression even of male mobility unless women are included in them. Women's participation in the labour market adds to the effect of structural changes, because certain classes of job become 'women's work' and men become excluded from them. Table 2, for example, shows that between 1921 and 1971 men's employment increased substantially, and substantially more than women's, in particular categories of work: as salaried or self-employed professional workers, lower-grade salaried professionals and technicians, and skilled manual workers. Conversely, women increased their employment (at the expense of men) as unskilled manual workers, as supervisors of manual workers, and above all as clerical workers and secretaries. Women come in at the bottom of a class — unskilled manual work, routine non-manual work — and thereby 'drive' men further up the occupational scale. Thus some of the increased social mobility of men in the twentieth century generally attributed to structural factors (changes in the overall distribution of jobs in the occupational structure) is in fact a result of women replacing men. The practice in 'malestream' research of only comparing fathers with sons cannot reveal this and therefore wrongly attributes the whole difference to structural changes in the class distribution of jobs in the labour market.

The point I am making is that gender needs to be taken seriously, *both* as a structuring variable in its own right *and* in its interaction with other structuring variables. In the example above, for example, it has been shown that we cannot adequately understand social mobility nor build an adequate theory of social class unless we take gender into account. I have done so at a purely structural level, without even drawing on the vast amount of reconceptualization which is required if one is to provide an adequate account of women's relationship to paid employment — research which casts doubt, for example, on the concepts 'unemployment' and 'employment' as currently formulated, for men as well as women. What we need most crucially is the ability to realize that when our existing theories and concepts do not enable us to explain our findings adequately, for men and for women, then it is *necessary* to rethink them. Further, we need to realize that the questions which research on women may throw up, questions which research on men did not suggest, may be equally applicable to men and may force us to build new theoretical concepts if our existing conceptual framework is not adequate to deal with them.

Gender is fundamental and central to the sociological enterprise. I have chosen to illustrate my central point by reference to social class, but there are many other areas of sociology which I could equally well have chosen. In some the feminist challenge has had more impact already — theories and concepts have been reformulated and, to some extent at least, replaced 'old' malestream ones. In others the feminist challenge has not yet even been taken as seriously as it has in the area of social class. At least the dominant 'malestream' class theorists have entered into debate with feminists who have challenged them, and some — for example Geoff Payne, Tony Heath, Gordon Marshall, David Rose — have tried to incorporate the feminist contributions into their own research designs and analyses. However, given the continued centrality of social class to sociology, one must say that feminist contributions in this area have not yet been taken seriousl enough to lead to any attempt at re-theorizing it so that it adequately exp.esses the experience of both men and women.

Sociological theory is also, of course, central both to the way the discipline conceptualizes the social world and to its empirical research, yet this has probably been even less influenced by feminist work than has social class theory. Without going into detail, I would argue that this is an area where feminist theory has clearly been 'added on'. 'Malestream' theories, whether they be Marxist, Weberian, functionalist or whatever, continue relatively untroubled by the feminist critiques — although it is important to recognize that there have been feminist critiques by, for example, Heidi Hartmann (1978), Michele Barrett (1980), Dorothy Smith (1987) and Rosalind Sydie (1987). Feminist theories are seen as, at best, relevant to women and to theorizing research on women, but nothing more. However, if gender is to be taken seriously then theories need to be developed that encompass the position(s) of women as well as of men and the relationships between them at both an individual and a structural level.

What I have tried to argue here is that, despite the quantity and quality of the feminist contribution to sociology, it remains marginal within the discipline. It is not ignored, but the contribution of feminists tends to be lumped under the 'gender' label and given a couple of lectures or a chapter in a book; 'malestream' sociology can then carry on as normal. However, feminists' contribution to sociology has done more than provide knowledge about women to incorporate with the existing knowledge on men; it fundamentally challenges the theories and concepts of 'malestream' sociology, and in so doing it generates new questions and areas of research. In some areas this has had some impact, especially in areas where there are a significant number of women sociologists — areas which indeed in some cases are almost becoming identified as 'female areas' (for example, 'family' and 'health') — but in many areas, especially the high-status male-dominated ones, feminism has made little or no impact. The resistance to feminism and feminist ideas in sociology is both intellectual (see e.g. Smith, 1987; Abbott and Wallace, 1990) and institutional — men still hold a disproportionate number of permanent lecturing and professorial posts in universities and polytechnics. They are able to use their intellectual power to ensure the continued marginalization of feminist scholarship (see Delamont, 1989) and their institutional power to subordinate women (see Ramazanoglu, 1987).

Acknowledgments

This paper continues joint work begun with Claire Wallace of the University of Lancaster, and most of the ideas have been discussed with her and bear her imprint. My thanks are also due to Roger Sapsford (Open University) for his help in preparing the manuscript and commenting on it.

References

ABBOTT, PAMELA (1990) 'Three Theses Re-Examined: Class Mobility in Britain', in PAYNE, GEOFF and ABBOTT, PAMELA (Eds) *The Social Mobility of Women*, Basing-
ABBOTT, PAMELA and SAPSFORD, ROGER (1987) *Women and Social Class*, London, Tavistock.
stoke, Falmer.

Pamela Abbott

ABBOTT, PAMELA and WALLACE, CLAIRE (1990) *An Introduction to Sociology: Feminist Perspectives*, London, Routledge.

ACKER, JOAN (1973) 'Women and Social Stratification', in *American Journal of Sociology*, 78, pp. 2–48.

ARBER, SARA, DALE, ANGELA and GILBERT, NIGEL (1986) 'The Limitations of Existing Social Class Classifications of Women', in JACOBY, A. (Ed.) *The Measurement of Social Class: Proceedings of a Conference*, Guildford, Social Research Association.

BARRETT, MICHELE (1980) *Women's Oppression Today*, London, Verso.

DALE, ANGELA, GILBERT, NIGEL and ARBER, SARA (1983) *Alternative Approaches to the Measurement of Social Class for Women and Families*, Report to the Equal Opportunities Commission.

DELAMONT, SARA (1989) *Knowledgeable Women*, London, Routledge.

EICHLER, MARGARET (1988) *Non-Sexist Research Methods*, London, Allen and Unwin.

GOLDTHORPE, JOHN (1983) 'Women and Class Analysis: In Defence of the Conventional View', in *Sociology*, 17, pp. 465–488.

GOLDTHORPE, JOHN (1984) 'Women and Class Analysis: A Reply to the Replies', in *Sociology*, 18, pp. 491–499.

GOLDTHORPE, JOHN and PAYNE, CLIVE (1986) 'On the Class Mobility of Women: Results from Different Approaches to the Analysis of Recent British Data', in *Sociology*, 20, pp. 531–555.

GOLDTHORPE, JOHN, LLEWELYN, CATRIONA and PAYNE, CLIVE (1980) *Social Mobility and Class Structure in Modern Britain*, Oxford, Oxford University Press.

HARTMANN, HEIDI (1978) 'The Unhappy Marriage of Marxism and Feminism: Towards a More Progressive Union', in *Capital and Class*, 8, pp. 1–33.

LOCKWOOD, DAVID (1986) 'Class, Status and Gender', in CROMPTON, R. and MANN, M. (Eds) *Gender and Stratification*, Cambridge, Polity.

MARSHALL, GORDON, ROSE, DAVID, NEWBY, HOWARD and VOGLER, CAROLYN (1988) *Social Class in Modern Britain*, London, Hutchinson.

MAYNARD, MARY (1990) 'The Re-Shaping of Sociology? Trends in the Study of Gender', in *Sociology* 24, 2, pp. 269–290.

OAKLEY, ANN (1974) *The Sociology of Housework*, London, Martin Robertson.

PAYNE, GEOFF and ABBOTT, PAMELA (Eds) (1990) *The Social Mobility of Women*, Basingstoke, Falmer.

RAMAZANOGLU, CAROLINE (1987) 'Sex and Violence in Academic Life, Or You Can Keep a Good Woman Down', in HANMER, J. and MAYNARD, M. (Eds) *Women, Violence and Social Control*, London, Macmillan.

ROBERTS, HELEN (1985) 'Women and social class', in *Survey Methods Newsletter*, Spring, pp. 3–4.

ROBERTS, HELEN (1986) *The Social Classification of Women*, paper presented to a British Sociological Association conference at Loughborough.

SMITH, DOROTHY (1987) *The Everyday World as Problematic: a Feminist Sociology*, Milton Keynes, Open University Press.

STANWORTH, MICHELE (1984) 'Women and Social Class Analysis: A Reply to Goldthorpe', in *Sociology*, 18, pp. 159–170.

SYDIE, ROSALIND (1987) *Natural Woman, Cultured Man*, Milton Keynes, Open University Press.

Chapter 15

Why Psychology (Badly) Needs Feminism

Sue Wilkinson

Psychology is now the fourth most popular subject of study in British higher education, and particularly attracts women students: a recent survey of six university psychology departments found that 79 per cent of first-year students were female (Morris *et al.*, 1990a). However, psychology rarely features on the British Women's Studies curriculum, and, as a discipline, has resisted feminist influence more concertedly than most. Women are largely excluded from positions of power within the institutions of psychology; we are still often invisible in psychological research, or our experience is distorted by assimilation to male norms and by the consideration of women as a unitary category; and prevailing research traditions de-emphasize social/structural factors and effectively depoliticize the majority of psychological research and practice.

In attempting to demonstrate why psychology badly needs feminism, I will first sketch in some details of the current status of the discipline, in terms of where women are in psychology and in terms of what we generally find there. I will then look at some of the recent feminist interventions in psychology, together with the discipline's resistance to them, and consider some of the means by which the institutional and intellectual status quo is vigorously defended. Finally, I will raise some issues relating to the kind of impact feminism is having — or might expect to have — upon psychology. These issues will include: the asymmetry of the relationship between feminism and psychology; limits on the potential for change; and the possibility that feminism and psychology might ultimately prove incompatible.

Women and Psychology

Across academic and professional psychology, women are under-represented in senior posts. Kagan and Lewis (1989) report that in British university and polytechnic psychology departments, only 22.2 per cent of academic staff, and 15.9 per cent of senior academic staff, are women (in stark contrast to the number of women undergraduates); while Humphrey and Haward (1981) and

Lamb *et al.* (1987) present a similar picture for clinical psychology and occupational psychology respectively. Within the British Psychological Society (the main academic and professional organization for psychologists in this country), only 38 per cent of Associate Fellows (sic) and 12 per cent of Fellows (regarded as the two most 'senior' membership grades) are women, again strikingly different from our majority position in the two most 'junior' membership grades; also, women constitute only 26 per cent of the membership of the major Society committees (Morris *et al.*, 1990b).

The intellectual traditions of psychology do not provide a fertile ground for feminist research. The individual person is the favoured locus of explanation, with a preference for identifying biological — or more recently cognitive (information-processing) — factors in causation. There is a concomitant failure to address subjectivity/ies (except in a limited way in the sub-discipline of psychoanalysis), or intersubjectivity, together with profound neglect of the social and political domain: it is rare to find acknowledgment, let alone analysis, of structural inequalities. There is an insistence on the generalizability (and preferably 'universality') of knowledge, as opposed to recognition of any social, cultural or historical specificity; this entails, of course, the ascription of the white, Western, male world view to the unitary category 'people' (or more typically — and accurately! — 'man'). To the extent that psychology considers gender, it is as 'difference' between the sexes (Hare-Mustin and Marecek, 1990): a 'specialism' which has been pursued with extraordinary tenacity, in the attempt to justify social inequality while denying its existence (Shields, 1982). Women's experience (when addressed) is understood only in comparison with men's experience: i.e. in terms of male norms or man-made stereotypes; differences among women (or men) and the interactions between gender and other inequalities are not addressed at all. Finally, there is an emphasis on 'scientific method' (narrowly conceived and favouring positivist empiricism), which proclaims psychological enquiry to be value-free and concerned with establishing objective facts. Arguments from the philosophy and sociology of science which posit neutrality and objectivity as male values and present alternative epistemologies focusing on the relationship between knower and known (e.g. Sampson, 1978) are largely unknown or disregarded.

Psychology, then, is not woman-friendly. The expectant undergraduate, taught a gender-blind (if not actively misogynist) psychology by a largely male staff, is likely to become disillusioned very rapidly: Sue Sharpe and Jane Jefferson (1990) provide graphic accounts of this experience. It is scarcely surprising that so many leave the discipline, under the impression it is not for them. Women who remain in psychology, and particularly those of us who seek to make feminist interventions, may well also come to feel this, for we generally encounter considerable resistance to our efforts.

Feminist Interventions and Psychology's Resistance

Feminist intervention in psychology appears only to be acceptable insofar as it can be accommodated within the discipline's traditional empirical framework: for example, insofar as a feminist research orientation focuses attention on sex/gender bias, such bias can be removed, producing 'better science'; in this context feminism has also been welcomed as 'revitalizing' psychology by directing attention to new research questions and new types of analysis (Shaver and Hendrick, 1987). However, as soon as feminism begins to challenge traditional epistemologies and modes of enquiry, and directs attention to hierarchies of power and status (and the institutional practices that maintain them), it is no longer welcome. Then we see a 'closing of the ranks', and strenuous efforts being made to defend the status quo.

I have argued elsewhere (Wilkinson, 1988), using a sociology of science analysis, that one manifestation of this defence is a formidable three-step process. First, if possible, control is exercised by means of definition (feminist work is defined as inappropriate or illegitimate); second, it is maintained by means of tactics designed to ensure exclusion or continued marginalization (e.g. withholding information, denial of platforms on which to speak); and third, it is justified by means of apparently plausible rhetoric (e.g. democracy, meritocracy). I will go on to exemplify this process in operation in relation to a number of specific feminist interventions in psychology.

Feminists within psychology have indeed raised the possibility of a transformation of psychological enquiry, and are working to produce resistances to and reconstructions of the discipline. This includes the utilization of different models of knowledge (as socially and temporally specific; as acknowledging subjectivity and values; in which the knower not only shapes but is an integral part of what is known); and the development of different theories and methods (grounded in the complexities of women's lives; more sensitive to diversity, variability and inconsistency; more reflexive). It also entails explicit analyses of power relations (with respect to the research relationship itself; the institutional structures and practices that systematically disadvantage women; and the socio-political conditions that govern the development and legitimation of new knowledges). Such work is reflected not only in our research (see Wilkinson, 1986 for a range of examples), but in our teaching, professional activities, and psychological practice (see Burman, 1990 for diverse examples). We are also becoming more visible in the wider context of feminist scholarship and publishing, via contributions to multidisciplinary feminist journals and books (such as this one!), as well as an increasing number of discipline-specific publications. However, in all this work, we are encountering considerable resistance from mainstream psychology.

Getting Published

One index of this resistance is the difficulty many of us have encountered in getting feminist research published in peer-reviewed psychology journals. Celia Kitzinger's work on the social construction of lesbianism (e.g. Kitzinger, 1987) is a good example. Her research project involved the collection of accounts of lesbianism from lesbians, and the exploration of the multiple meanings of these accounts in relation to their ideological and political contexts. She identified five main discourses of lesbianism (as a source of self-fulfilment; as a consequence of 'falling in love' with a woman; as a private sexual preference; as a self-defined political position; and as a personal failing) and examined the utility of each for lesbians and for the dominant culture. In particular, she noted the way in which the liberal humanistic discourses of 'personal growth' and 'choice' may be used to depoliticize lesbianism and legitimate status quo ideologies.

The work was well received within the feminist community and the feminist psychological community (indeed, it received the (USA's) Association of Women in Psychology's Distinguished Publication Award in 1990); however, it was rejected by a number of psychology journals (as have been a number of her other papers reporting research on human rights and injustice in schools). Her account of these rejections (Kitzinger, 1990) provides a good illustration of the processes of institutional control in operation, while numerous conversations with feminists working in psychology in Britain and the USA (and, indeed, my own experience) suggest it is by no means an isolated example.

First, we can see the attempt at control by definition:

> when I write as a feminist, I am defined out of the category of 'psychologist'. When I speak of social structure, of power and politics, when I use language and concepts rooted in my understanding of oppression, I am told what I say does not qualify as 'psychology'. (1990, p. 124)

Then, the prevailing definition of psychology is maintained, by excluding feminist work from its main journals, or marginalizing it in less 'prestigious' publications:

> Because those who control the definition of 'psychology' act as gate-keepers for the professional refereed journals, I cannot be published in them. Although I am constantly asked to contribute chapters to edited books and articles for the radical press ... my work is generally rejected by the editors of refereed journals.... (1990, pp. 124–5)

Finally, the rejections are justified with reference to the prevailing rhetorics of 'science' (objectivity, neutrality, detachment), falsely polarized against 'politics' (polemic, ideology):

> Central to these rejections, then, is the sense that my work is not 'balanced' or 'objective', that it is an attempt to 'persuade' the reader of a particular point of view ... and that it is politically biased — 'polemical' or 'ideological'.... Suggestions about my writing style are frequent: that it should be 'moderated' or 'toned down' — that it

should be less 'journalistic' or 'emotion-laden' . . . 'The text is replete with value-laden words' commented one anonymous reviewer; 'a more scientific presentation is needed', wrote another. (1990, p. 127)

The insistence that psychology is 'science', that feminism is 'politics', and that politics has no place in science, is an argument that is repeatedly used, as will be seen in the examples that follow. It is, of course, extremely powerful, for it provides mainstream psychologists with grounds for dismissing feminist research as illegitimate, and protects them from any need to address the political dimension of their research and practice.

The 'Psychology of Women' Section

My second example of a feminist intervention in psychology which has met with considerable resistance is the formation of a 'Psychology of Women' Section within the British Psychological Society (BPS). The name of the Section is a story in its own right (see Burns and Wilkinson, 1989), and the early history of the Section has been documented at greater length elsewhere (Wilkinson and Burns, 1990). It is also instructive to look at the remarkable similarities between the British experience and that of women organizing in psychology in other English-speaking countries (Wilkinson, 1990).

Women began to seek more adequate representation for our work and concerns within mainstream psychology in the mid-1970s, at the height of second-wave feminism; however, it was the mid-1980s before the first formal attempt to establish a BPS Section was made. This initiative, largely conducted by a group of postgraduate students (and including a very successful one-day conference organized by two members of the group — Jan Burns and Mathilde Idema — in Cardiff), culminated in the rejection of the proposal by the BPS Council in October 1985: a move unprecedented in the history of BPS Sections. This was followed by the formation of an independent organization, Women in Psychology (WIP), which ran thriving local groups in London and the north-west and held a second successful conference (co-ordinated by Sheila Rossan at Brunel University).

However, a number of us within WIP felt that the lack of a forum within the national psychological organization was ensuring the continued marginalization of our concerns, and in 1987 we began to prepare a second proposal for a Section. This was successful, and the 'Psychology of Women' Section was inaugurated in December that year. In its first years, the Section has been both popular and active, but it has come under constant scrutiny from the Society (in ways that other Sections have not), and there have been continuing attempts both to limit the range of its activities and to undermine their success. I will turn now to some of the specific arguments and practices deployed in opposition to the move to establish a Section, and during its early days. Again, I will refer to the three-step process of control by definition; maintenance of low status and limited influence by marginalization; and justification by means of rhetoric.

In the early stages of the first attempt to establish a Section, concerted attempts were made to circumscribe its nature by means of definition. For example, there was a protracted debate over whether the proposal was closer to a 'Section' (which is 'concerned with special branches or aspects of psychology': BPS, 1988) or a 'Special Group' (which is 'concerned with [a] principal area in which psychologists provide advice, tuition or services': BPS, 1988), and indeed, whether it fitted the definition (in the Society's Charter) of either. There were also attempts to impose definitions which do not appear in any formal document:

> [Council members] questioned whether there is a theoretical or methodological basis to the study of the psychology of women, as pertains to other areas of our discipline. . . . [The conclusion was] the psychology of women as an area of the discipline lacks the necessary cohesion to be the basis of a scientific Section of the Society in the same way we would not expect to have a psychology of animals Section. The focus is on the subject of the investigation rather than on the theoretical or methodological approach. (BPS, 1985b)

The requirements of 'cohesion' or a distinctive 'theoretical or methodological basis' were not applied to other recently-established Sections (e.g. History and Philosophy; Health Psychology), and it is doubtful whether they could be met by many of the long-established Sections (e.g. Social Psychology; Occupational Psychology) — yet the argument is advanced that without them the psychology of women is an inappropriate area of activity for a Section.

Similarly, attempts were made to define the purpose of the proposed Section as illegitimate (note the science-politics dichotomy here again):

> . . . some of the things you have in mind for the Section are sufficiently loaded politically for the whole proposal to fail. I am sure that by rephrasing the difficulties can be overcome, as long as you also share the conceptual distinction between the scientific duty (sic) of the psychology of womanhood . . . and a feminist pressure group seeking to promote causes on the basis of moral conviction alone. (BPS, 1985a)

Such attempts at delimiting the Section's scope by definition were reinforced by a range of control strategies, both during the time it was being set up and in its early days. Collectively, these operated such that it was very difficult for the Section to become established, and that its activities — and their impact — were substantially limited: in other words, the Section's continued marginalization was ensured. So, for example, despite a clear statement in the Section proposal that membership would be open to all interested Society members, the arguments against it continued to assert that it had separatist aims. More dramatically, the Section's inaugural symposium — on feminist work in clinical psychology — was rejected by the Standing

Conference Committee; its draft rules (carefully modelled on those of other sections) were referred back to the committee by Council, with the request that they be rewritten to limit the Section's remit to 'scientific' activities related to the psychology of women; and the press releases for its first conference were edited — without consultation — by the Society's Press Office to remove all reference to feminism. These examples are far from exhaustive.

Such activities were justified with reference to a range of powerful rhetorics. These include 'meritocracy', 'rights and duties', 'freedom to challenge the system', 'democracy', 'non-discrimination', and 'equal opportunities'. Thus, for example, it was argued (by the discussant in a symposium I convened on issues of legitimacy in psychological research):

Is the BPS really like one of Goffman's asylums? There are dangers here. BPS members have rights. The Society has elections, newsletters, correspondence columns, conferences, workshops, meetings — all contexts where established views can be challenged. And of course, unlike an institution, you are free to come and go as you please. Of course things go wrong. Witness the difficulties experienced in setting up the Psychology of Women's (sic) Section. But things do change. Time does reshape our attitudes. And they surely change because, unlike institutions, people can buck at the system? (Gale, 1988)

Above all, however, we see the continuing insistence on the dichotomy between 'science' (defined as 'objective knowledge') and 'politics' (defined as supporting a particular point of view). Thus the grounds for rejecting the Psychology of Women Section's inaugural symposium were that it was 'unscientific and political'; and its rules had to ensure that 'only' scientific activity was permissible. The strength and tenor of such arguments (and their prevalence within the wider community of psychologists) is well illustrated by the following extract from a letter in the Bulletin of the Australian Psychological Society (which, incidentally, was a branch of the BPS until 1965!). This letter appeared in the context of a debate about the formation of Interest Groups within the Australian Psychological Society, and, in particular, in response to the proposal for a Women and Psychology Interest Group:

... the Society rests on the claim that its members are scientists and thus capable of the objectivity and detachment that characterize science. The promotion of interest groups could represent a conflict with this position: it is the taking of a position which is of necessity partisan and thus in conflict with a basic objective of the Society, i.e. of objectivity.... if 'psychological knowledge' is not objective, we may then become like any other Community group. What is our distinction if the professional body is identifiably partisan and is not maintaining integrity through objectivity? ... if we are seen by the public and governments as partisan, as supporting particular points of view, our credibility is lost. (Little, 1985)

The Gender Representation Working Party

Another activity in which I have recently been involved is an attempt to improve the position of women within the British Psychological Society (see above), as convener of a working party on gender representation. The working party presented a report containing thirty-eight specific recommendations to the BPS Council in October 1989. The fate of this report is a good example of the extent and depth of resistance to attempted feminist interventions in psychology.

Again, I will begin with examples of control by definition. A number of arguments were deployed in an attempt to discredit the report: it was defined as 'not scholarly', because it failed to back every assertion with research evidence (despite citing more references than most working party reports), and because it had been completed quickly (in fact the working party was also congratulated by the Chair of Council for being the first of several to report — and, indeed, it was the only one of these that was on time!). It was also defined as 'not legitimate', on the (unjustified) grounds of lack of consultation (in fact, the working party consulted much more widely than is usual).

A range of tactics was used to neutralize the impact of the report. A lengthy consultation exercise was embarked upon (manifestly a 'defusing' tactic, as, once the responses had been collated, there was no discussion of them). Publicity was minimized and/or distorted: for example, I co-convened a workshop at the Society's annual conference to publicize the report, but the title of the workshop was omitted from the conference programme, my name did not appear in the programme, and the workshop was credited to the (male) co-convener, under the title of his paper. The initiative has now been absorbed into a new 'task force' on equal opportunities — without, as yet, implementation of any of the major recommendations of the working party. No member of the gender representation working party was originally asked to join the new task force.

The main justification for such actions and, particularly, for the failure to implement the recommendations of the working party has been largely in terms of 'equal opportunities' rhetoric; I will look at just a couple of instances of this in operation. Take, for example, the finding that only 12 per cent of BPS Fellows are women (for which the working party offered a number of explanations and suggested remedies). This has been rendered unproblematic for the Society by means of equal opportunities rhetoric (Morris *et al.*, 1990b). Peter Morris analyzed the acceptance/rejection rates for Fellowships and showed that they were not significantly different for male and female applicants. His conclusion is that the Society does not discriminate: men and women have equal opportunities to become Fellows. Now not only does this argument completely occlude institutional discrimination (cf. the working party's suggestion that the criteria for Fellowship may be harder for women to fulfil), it has the invidious effect of throwing the problem back onto women: why don't more of us apply for Fellowship? (and the clear implication is that it is our individual responsibility to do so).

The working party also recommended the commissioning — and resourcing — of a comprehensive database on the position of women in academic and professional psychology. The Board responsible for considering this responded as follows:

> This recommendation . . . was supported in principle by the Board provided the focus for the data base is on the characteristic (sic) of the membership and the gender distribution of both men and women in psychology. The Board took the view that it is just as important to find out why fewer men are now entering psychology as to obtain data about the career pattern of women psychologists. (BPS, 1989)

More worrying still, this equal opportunities rhetoric was translated very rapidly into action: a student enterprise project was commissioned looking at the reasons applicants give for choosing to study psychology at university, with particular reference to gender differences; and funding was requested for a study of why so few men are going into psychology.

Feminism's Impact on Psychology

Given this degree of resistance, it is hardly surprising that the impact of feminism on mainstream psychology has not been substantial. There have been a number of recent attempts to assess this impact, in particular by means of content analyses comparing different types of academic journal, or by monitoring change within particular journals over time (e.g. Lykes and Stewart, 1986; Fine and Gordon, 1989). Even when the criteria for change are extremely conservative, the picture presented is uniformly gloomy: the traditional experimental paradigm maintains an apparent stranglehold, and the central tenets of feminism are diluted and assimilated. As Michelle Fine and Susan Gordon wryly comment: 'When feminism and psychology mate, feminism seems to bear only recessive genes' (1989, p. 150).

More worrying still is the difficulty that 'feminist psychology' appears to have in developing thoroughgoing, radical analyses: on many occasions it still shows a tendency to reflect and reproduce the values and conventions of the mainstream discipline. Thus, in the USA, feminist empiricism is rife — and developing ever more sophisticated variants on traditional research methods. A good example of this is Alice Eagly's meta-analysis of sex differences research (e.g. Eagly, 1987), which aggregates and interprets data from a large number of studies. While this work is evidently feminist in intent (in showing the exaggeration of sex differences — as feminists in psychology have been doing since 1910), it does not question the validity of the sex differences paradigm, or the framework of values within which it developed. The work still rests firmly on the empiricist argument that scientific methods, properly applied, are value-neutral and capable of discovering objective facts about reality.

Similarly, Carol Gilligan's much-lauded work on moral reasoning (e.g. Gilligan, 1982), and that of Mary Belenky and colleagues on 'ways of knowing' (e.g. Belenky *et al.*, 1986), is trapped in an essentialist, individualist, sex differences paradigm. Its implications, too, are played out in terms of special (different) treatment for women (e.g. educational programmes, therapy or counselling that recognizes our 'different needs'), failing both to recognize the powerful structural determinants of psychological life (e.g. 'race', class, age, sexual identity), and to challenge the socio-political framework within which they operate.

What, then, are the prospects for the future? It is not surprising that in recent years a number of feminists have given up on psychology (some of those who have not left academic life have found more congenial 'homes' in Cultural Studies or, indeed, Women's Studies); while those of us who remain (and those who join us) cannot but be aware of the costs and compromises of our position, as we struggle to reconcile conflicting goals and modes of operation. I want to argue here that, as our energies are absorbed by the daily exigencies of this struggle, we should not lose sight of its broader parameters. In particular, I will raise three key issues which I believe should frame our efforts.

The first of these is the asymmetry of the present relationship between feminism and psychology. I hope it is clear from the examples above how badly psychology needs feminism if it is properly to address women's experience in its research endeavours and professional practice, and properly to represent women and our concerns in its institutions. However, it is not at all clear how far feminism needs psychology, or indeed, what the discipline — as presently constructed — has to offer. Nor should we forget that historically psychology has provided many 'theories' and research 'findings' that have been used systematically to oppress women, from Freudian notions of 'penis envy' to Bowlby's promulgation of a link between 'maternal deprivation' and 'juvenile delinquency', and the subsequent use of this to justify nursery closure. One partial answer regarding what we, as psychologists, can offer feminism is a deconstruction of such processes; we can shift the focus from individual pathology and woman-blaming to the socio-political arena — where we can then address these processes as feminists.

The second issue concerns the limits on the potential for change; I would argue that we need to develop our awareness of what these might be. It is easy to underestimate the power of mainstream psychology in maintaining the status quo. The examples of institutional practices given above illustrate this, but intellectual practices are equally powerful. It is also easy to underestimate the power of our own 'socialization' into the discipline (Unger, 1982), and the consequent difficulty of transcending it (cf. the feminist research examples given above). Mary Parlee (1991) comments on the ways in which the writing and reporting conventions of psychology shape what is seen as possible as well as what is achieved; Celia Kitzinger (1991) goes further in demonstrating how the modes of intellectual engagement (claims and counter-claims of more careful methods or more sophisticated analyses) deflect attention from the questions that are being asked — and seriously constrain the agendas we are able to set.

Such analyses can readily be extended beyond psychology (e.g. see Dorothy Smith, 1991, for a more general consideration of the conventions of social science), and indeed they recall Adrienne Rich's identification of one of the main dangers of continuing to engage on 'the playing fields of male discourse':

> In the common world of men, the struggle to make female experience visible at all ... assume[s] the status of an intellectual problem, and the real intellectual problems may not be probed at all. (Rich, 1980, p. 208)

There are other dangers, too, of our immersion in a mainstream discipline and its institutions: there are rewards to be gained from conformity (and we have been 'socialized' to value such rewards) — thus the dangers of co-option are ever-present. Such co-option may be particularly difficult for British feminists working in psychology to resist because our psychology has rarely developed out of feminist activism, nor do many of us have extensive contact with either grass-roots feminism or academic feminism in the shape of Women's Studies.

The third and final issue I want to address is the possibility that the value-orientations and objectives of feminism and psychology are so disparate that, ultimately, the two must be regarded as incompatible. A serious and creative engagement between feminism and psychology will require large-scale change. If feminism is to have an appreciable impact upon psychology, the discipline will need to become politicized to an extent that would probably render it unrecognizable to most of its present practitioners. The threat of this degree of change is so substantial, and the power asymmetry between psychology and feminism so marked, it seems inevitable that psychology will continue in its efforts (and with some success) to depoliticize feminism by incorporating it within its mainstream practices and traditions. As feminists, we will have to work hard to resist this process — and there may yet come a point at which we will choose to separate from the mainstream of psychology, rather than continue to engage with it.

In sum, psychology badly needs feminism, yet is desperately resistant to it. As feminists in psychology, trying to sustain a dual allegiance, we are caught up in a complex web of conflicts, costs and — inevitably — compromises. There is a growing feeling that psychology's intransigence is forcing us to choose to give priority either to feminism or to psychology. It is to be hoped that opting for feminism will not also have to mean opting against psychology: the discipline would be immeasurably the poorer for it.

References

BELENKY, M.F., CLINCHY, B.M., GOLDBERGER, N.R. and TARULE, J.M. (1986) *Women's Ways of Knowing: The Development of Self, Voice and Mind*, New York, Basic Books.

BRITISH PSYCHOLOGICAL SOCIETY (1985a) Letter to proposers of Psychology of Women Section.

BRITISH PSYCHOLOGICAL SOCIETY (1985b) Letter to proposers of Psychology of Women Section, circulated to Section supporters.

BRITISH PSYCHOLOGICAL SOCIETY (1988) *The Royal Charter, The Statutes, The Rules*, Leicester, BPS.

BRITISH PSYCHOLOGICAL SOCIETY (1989) Response from Scientific Affairs Board to Gender Representation report.

BURMAN, E. (Ed.) (1990) *Feminists and Psychological Practice*, London, Sage.

BURNS, J. and WILKINSON, S.J. (1989) 'What's in a Name?', in *Psychology of Women Section Newsletter*, 3, Spring, pp. 35–38.

EAGLY, A.H. (1987) *Sex Differences in Social Behaviour: A Social Role Interpretation*, Hillsdale, NJ, Erlbaum.

FINE, M. and GORDON, S.M. (1989) 'Feminist Transformations of/despite Psychology', in CRAWFORD, M. and GENTRY, M. (Eds) *Gender and Thought: Psychological Perspectives*, New York, Springer-Verlag.

GALE, A. (1988) Discussion of symposium 'Issues of legitimacy in psychological research', British Psychological Society Annual Conference, University of Leeds, April.

GILLIGAN, C. (1982) *In a Different Voice: Psychological Theory and Women's Development*, Cambridge, MA, Harvard University Press.

HARE-MUSTIN, R.T. and MARECEK, J. (Eds) (1990) *Making a Difference: Psychology and the Construction of Gender*, New Haven, Yale University Press.

HUMPHREY, M. and HAWARD, L. (1981) 'Sex Differences in Clinical Psychology Recruitment', in *Bulletin of the British Psychological Society*, 34, pp. 413–414.

KAGAN, C. and LEWIS, S. (1989) 'Transforming Psychological Practice', paper presented in symposium 'Psychology Constructing Women; Women Reconstructing Psychology', British Psychological Society Annual Conference, University of St Andrews, April.

KITZINGER, C. (1987) *The Social Construction of Lesbianism*, London, Sage.

KITZINGER, C. (1990) 'Resisting the Discipline', in BURMAN, E. (Ed.) *Feminists and Psychological Practice*, London, Sage, pp. 119–136.

KITZINGER, C. (1991) 'Politicising Psychology', in *Feminism and Psychology: An International Journal*, 1, 1.

LAMB, P., BUTLER, F. and HARTNETT, O. (1987) 'Gender and Domestic Responsibilities as Barriers to Career Progression in Occupational Psychology', in *The Occupational Psychologist*, 3, December, pp. 51–54.

LITTLE, R.B. (1985) Letter in the *Bulletin of the Australian Psychological Society*, November, p. 25.

LYKES, M.B. and STEWART, A.J. (1986) 'Evaluating the Feminist Challenge to Research in Personality and Social Psychology: 1963–1983', in *Psychology of Women Quarterly*, 10, pp. 393–412.

MORRIS, P.E., CHENG, D. and SMITH, H. (1990a) 'How and Why Applicants Choose to Study Psychology at University', unpublished preliminary report, University of Lancaster.

MORRIS, P.E., HOLLOWAY, J. and NOBLE, J. (1990b) 'Gender Representation Within the British Psychological Society', in *The Psychologist*, 3, 9, September, pp. 408–411.

PARLEE, M.B. (1991) 'Happy Birth-day to Feminism and Psychology!', in *Feminism and Psychology: An International Journal*, 1, 1.

RICH, A. (1980) 'Conditions for Work: The Common World of Women', in *On Lies, Secrets and Silence: Selected Prose 1966–1978*, London, Virago, pp. 203–214.

SAMPSON, E.E. (1978) 'Scientific Paradigms and Social Values: Wanted — a Scientific Revolution', in *Journal of Personality and Social Psychology*, 36, 11, pp. 1332–1343.

SHARPE, S. and JEFFERSON, J. (1990) 'Moving Out of Psychology: Two Accounts', in BURMAN, E. (Ed.), *Feminists and Psychological Practice*, London, Sage, pp. 33–46.

SHAVER, P. and HENDRICK, C. (Eds) (1987) *Review of Social and Personality Psychology 7: Sex and Gender*, Newbury Park, CA, Sage.

SHIELDS, S.A. (1982) 'The Variability Hypothesis: The History of a Biological Model of Sex Difference in Intelligence', in *Signs: Journal of Women in Culture and Society*, 11, pp. 321–324.

SMITH, D.E. (1991) 'Writing Women's Experience Into Social Science', *Feminism and Psychology: An International Journal*, 1, 1.

UNGER, R.K. (1982) 'Advocacy Versus Scholarship Revisited: Issues in the Psychology of Women', in *Psychology of Women Quarterly*, 7, 1, pp. 5–17.

WILKINSON, S.J. (Ed.) (1986) *Feminist Social Psychology: Developing Theory and Practice*, Milton Keynes, Open University Press.

WILKINSON, S.J. (1989) 'Barriers to Feminist Social Psychology', in OLIVER, S.M. (Ed.), *Proceedings of an International Research Conference on Women and Work*, Brighton, P-SET Centre.

WILKINSON, S.J. (1990) 'Women's Organisations in Psychology: Institutional Constraints on Disciplinary Change', in *Australian Psychologist*, 25, pp. 18–31.

WILKINSON, S.J. and BURNS, J. (1990) 'Women Organizing Within Psychology: Two accounts', in BURMAN, E. (Ed.) *Feminists and Psychological Practice*, London, Sage, pp. 140–162.

Chapter 16

Feminist Auto/Biography and Feminist Epistemology

Liz Stanley

Introduction

Recent feminist discussions of a 'feminist methodology' have variously criticized this as essentialist, individualist and subjectivist, and also matter-of-factly described it as a set of epistemological assumptions already fully embedded in the working practices of most feminist researchers (and these debates are reviewed in detail in Stanley and Wise, 1990). Such a lively disagreement indicates not only a semantic confusion concerning 'epistemology' and its relationship to 'methodology' (or perspective) and 'method' (or techniques), but also the existence of feminismS, feminism as a plural phenomenon. This chapter is concerned with locating ideas about a 'feminist auto/biography' in the context of these debates concerning feminist epistemology and feminist methodology.

An interest in the auto/biographical enables — indeed almost constrains — a multidisciplinary focus; and my own work, discussed later, in particular unites elements of sociology, history and literary theory. Such a multidisciplinary approach has become a hallmark of academic feminism which indicates its difference from conventional, discipline-specific, academic work and provides common ground with cultural politics and Cultural Studies. My academic interest in the auto/biographical springs from my longstanding reader's interest in and voracious consumption of auto/biographical writing of all kinds. I am not alone here, of course. Biographies and autobiographies are now big business for feminist and conventional publishing houses alike. There is clearly a large and buoyant interest in reading auto/biography. Also the last few years has seen the growth of more analytic feminist discussions of auto/biography (Jelinek, 1980; Spender, 1987; Stanton, 1987; Benstock, 1988; Brodzki and Schenck, 1988; Graham *et al.*, 1989; Stanley, forthcoming). However, the links between feminist auto/biography and questions of feminist epistemology remain under-discussed. There is a tendency to seal auto/biography within the concerns of, in particular, history and literary criticism; while I shall propose that there is much to be gained by tracing its points of interconnection with social science and philosophy debates within feminism concerned with epistemology and methodology.

This is the topic of this chapter. It begins by discussing whether auto/ biography can take a distinctly feminist form, and examines the components of a 'feminist epistemology'. It then proposes that the link between these is formed by the notion of 'intellectual autobiography'; and then key elements in a feminist auto/biographical method are outlined. Around this, a number of objections to a feminist concern with auto/biography are discussed, including those of feminist varieties of deconstructionism and postmodernism.

What's in a Name? Some Issues Concerning Feminist Auto/Biography

Feminist publishing houses and imprints, in Britain at least, have increasingly published auto/biography in their lists. However, the relationship between 'feminism' and these biographies about and autobiographies of a mixed bag of women is a complex and interesting one; and it raises questions concerning whether such a thing as a distinctly feminist auto/biography exists. Certainly there are biographies and autobiographies written by feminists — biographies by Ruth First and Ann Scott (1980) of Olive Schreiner, by Cathy Porter (1980) of Alexandra Kollontai, by Judith Okely (1986) of Simone de Beauvoir, and autobiographies by Elizabeth Wilson (1982), Ann Oakley (1984), and Carolyn Steedman (1986), spring to mind here. But is the fact that a text is *feminist authored* sufficient to define it as feminist auto/ biography? are there actually differences *in kind* as well as degree between biographies written by feminists and by non-feminists? and are there differences *in kind* as well as degree between autobiographies written by feminist and by non-feminist women? The point I am raising here concerns whether the *form* or structure of what is written as feminist auto/biography, and not just the subject who forms the bones of its *content*, is actually different from any other auto/biography; and I now consider this point in relation to the above six examples of feminist auto/biographical writing.

The first thing that strikes me about these is that the biographies are considerably more conventional in form than the autobiographies. With the partial exception of Judith Okely's de Beauvoir, the biographies could have been written by *any* competent biographer. The feminism of these biographers has very little influenced the form, whatever impact it has had on their interpretation of the content. Judith Okely's approach is different to the extent that she examines the interweavings in her own autobiography of the impact of de Beauvoir's (1953) *The Second Sex*. Its difference, then, turns on the explicit recognition that biography as a genre is by no means separate from the autobiography of those who produce it. This recognition is dealt with descriptively and not analytically; however, it is there, unlike in the others.

The autobiographies are very different, more immediately exciting in their self-conscious and self-confident mixing of genres and conventions.

Here the boundaries of self and other, biography and autobiography, fact and fiction, fantasy and reality, are traversed and shown to be by no means as distinct as is conventionally supposed; and these 'opposites' not only coexist but intermingle in ways that encourage, not merely permit, active readership. Feminist autobiography pushes hard at the boundaries of conventional autobiographical form and plays with some of its conventions such as the 'autobiographical pact' (Eakin, 1985) of truth-telling, a narrative that moves unidirectionally from birth/beginning to maturity/end, and an insistence on a unitary self; and it does so by interweavings of writing genres which stretch our readerly involvement with the text.

Virginia Woolf, it has been variously claimed, wrote no autobiography; wrote autobiography in various works of fiction; wrote autobiography as the highly crafted memoirs published in *Moments of Being* (1978); produced her true autobiography in *A Room of One's Own* (1929) and *Three Guineas* (1938). Howsoever 'autobiography' is defined, it is clear that claims can be made for an autobiographical corpus in Woolf's writings which exists largely outside of the conventional form of autobiography and which haunts much of her 'other' writing. Her claims as a biographer are more definite. There is, resoundingly, the magical and revolutionary *Orlando* (1928), the longest and clearest-eyed love letter in English literature and which completely subverts the biographical form and its conventions of person, time and much else. There is *Flush* (1933), a fictional biography of Elizabeth Barrett Browning's spaniel that contains much illuminating factual biography of the poet herself — a truly lese-majesty approach, biography from below. And then there is *Roger Fry: A Biography* (1940). Reading Woolf's *Letters* (1975, 1976, 1977, 1978, 1979, 1980) and *Diary* (1977, 1978, 1980, 1982, 1984) over the period of the writing and publication of this last necessarily more conventional biography, it is clear that she experienced boundaries here in a way that she did with no others of her books. At points exasperatedly she curses 'the letters' and 'the facts', which constrained her to work within limits set by 'the evidence' and 'the proprieties', rather than craft new limits which would take her closer to the truth as she experienced it, but which could be objected to as unsupported by 'the evidence' and also as a view of Fry that defied social propriety.

Thus biography poses problems for the construction of a distinctly feminist form in a way that autobiography does not, and these problems centre on the boundaries set by 'the facts', the external collectable readable challengeable facts. Here an overt mixture of genres — fact and fiction, biography and autobiography — is less readily acceptable. I find Woolf's *Orlando* and *Flush* far superior to *Roger Fry*; I find Fay Weldon's (1985) fictional depiction of Rebecca West more convincing than the highly factual accounts that exist; and I also find Virginia Woolf's (1985; see Stanley, 1987a) fictional creation of the feminist historian Rosamund Merridew, who discovers and reads the equally fictional diary of Mistress Joan Martyn, considerably more illuminating than factual histories of the period in question. However, in general there is an unwillingness to stretch biographical convention thus far, a conviction that when 'fiction' and 'fantasy' enter openly then biography as 'the truth about a self' necessarily departs. At first sight, then, it appears that biographical form is much less easy for feminism to subvert, to extend, to play with. However, doing so using literary means is not the only possibility.

'Biography' is already a site for multidisciplinary activity from professional biographers, historians and literature specialists. There are also social scientists who produce biographies; but, ironically, an awareness of the epistemological possibilities and limits of the genre, and the reverberations of these ontologically, is entirely absent from these (and see for example Lukes, 1973; McLellan, 1973; Bendix, 1960). Nonetheless, in the following section I shall argue that there are suitable alternative means of constructing a subversive feminist biographical form, and these are found in social science and philosophical discussions of a specifically feminist epistemology: feminist knowledge.

'Feminist Methodology'

There have been a number of criticisms of the idea of a distinct 'feminist methodology' by some academic feminists, the nub of which is the claim that this idea is essentialist, individualist and subjectivist. In these critics' view, because 'feminist methodology' is concerned with an analytic exploration of 'women's experience' it must lay claim to the existence of an essential 'woman', and this claimed essentialism is seen as naive and politically dubious as well as relying on biologisms. In addition, because some discussions of feminist methodology have argued for the incorporation of the research labour process (how the feminist researcher comes to know what she knows, rather than only the what) it has also been characterized as individualistic, as providing information about the researcher only and not those others who form her research objects. Also the concern with locating feminist analysis on the same critical plane as the understandings of 'subjects' is depicted as thereby atheoretical, for here 'theory' is defined as transcendent, and theorists as analyzing and theorizing in ways that 'people' are incapable of. My response to such criticisms is as follows.

Firstly, I find it strange to observe *feminists* decrying use of the word 'women' as necessarily implying essentialism in either biological or psychological terms. Whilst I whole-heartedly recognize 'difference' within the category 'women' (Stanley, 1990) on grounds of sexuality, age and able-bodiedness as well as class and race, I remain convinced that there is a common external material reality that all women face characterized by inequality, exploitation and oppression; and it exists precisely because we are indeed women and not men. This is *not* to say that all women are oppressed in the same ways, but rather to recognize that while oppression is common the forms it takes are conditioned precisely by race/ethnicity, age, sexuality and so forth, to produce a *common structure* of oppression which is internally *fractured in content* and so containing difference *as well as* sameness between women. No supposed 'essentialism' is needed to argue this, merely the recognition that 'common' need not be read as 'the same'. Would the same critics feel that the black movement is based on an essentialism of race? Surely it is rather based on the understanding that the oppressions which cohere around 'race' form a common external reality which all black people face — whilst also encapsulating fractures within the category 'black' on grounds of gender, sexuality, age, able-bodiedness, age and class. And thus with analytic uses of the category 'women': there is no necessity to treat it as essentialist and unitary, every reason to insist on its social construction and internal differentiation. And this is precisely what proponents of 'feminist epistemology' do, rather than what the critics claim in what sometimes seems like a wilful misrepresentation.

Secondly, *all* research and theorizing is 'individualistic', in the sense that its 'findings' are always those derived from a research/theorizing labour process engaged in by a researcher/theorist. And although mainstream social science has well-established and discipline-legitimated means of removing 'self' from the written products of the research process, most readers prefer open texts which explain how conclusions are arrived at, views are formulated, for they can then *engage* with the text rather than having to take a piece of writing and the 'reality' it supposedly incorporates on trust.

Thirdly, people theorize their own experience — unlike, presumably, quasars and amino acids; and so researchers of the social are faced with an already 'first order' theorized material social reality. Thus the criticism that 'feminist methodology' is atheoretical *because* it is concerned with experience derives from a complete misunderstanding of what is meant by the term 'experience'. This is not — for anyone — a morass of unformed inchoate sensation: people observe, categorize, analyze, reach conclusions — which is exactly what 'theory' is. Theorizing is certainly no prerogative of a self-proclaimed theoretical vanguard within feminism.

In some contrast to the criticisms outlined and responded to above, some discussions of 'feminist methodology' (also reviewed in Stanley and Wise, 1990) conclude that a distinct feminist methodology not only exists but is shared by most feminist researchers and indeed is a defining feature of 'feminist' in academic terms. Here 'feminist methodology' is defined as a longstanding set of research practices in which: feminist theory is derived from experience; the feminist researcher locates herself as on the same critical plane as the experiencing, researching and theorizing people she deals with; and in which feminist academics reject the subjective/objective dichotomy, recognizing instead that 'objectivity' is a set of practices designed to deny the actual 'subjective' location of all intellectual work.

What these premises signify is actually better described as a feminist *epistemology* than a methodology. Indeed, some critics of 'feminist methodology' conflate 'method' in the sense of technique, 'methodology' as a perspective or framework, and 'epistemology' as the specification of 'knowledge' in feminist terms. That is, much of the criticism appears based on the misunderstanding that what is being proposed is a different *method* or technique rather than a specifically feminist theory of *knowledge*.

My interest is in questions of epistemology and thus with what is defined as 'knowledge', under what circumstances, what distinguishes it from 'opinion', who is seen as a legitimate 'knower', and how competing knowledge-claims are adjudicated. These are crucial matters for academic feminism. For feminist sociologists such as myself, a concern with such issues takes us onto the high ground of the discipline, the sociology of knowledge. Feminist sociology must now make an impact at the level of epistemology, not only at the level of substantive findings and arguments (which is not to say that this latter is not important, only that it is not enough).

What Jürgen Habermas (1972) calls 'Scientism' produces alienated knowledge: knowledge alienated from the conditions and circumstances of its production. Scientistic knowledge hides, through a series of textual means, its labour process: objective knowledge rises, triumphant, from a sea of subjectivity — or so it is claimed. What is 'science' in social science terms certainly brings professional approbation. However, it is indeed *alienated* knowledge, which determinedly strips from it everything which makes knowledge production interesting and powerful; that is, it removes its details, its context, its reasoning procedures, and it ought not to be emulated by feminists. An unalienated knowledge, in feminist terms, at least in outline can be specified and would adhere to the components of feminist epistemology identified earlier.

Firstly, feminist theory would be directly derived from 'experience', whether this is experience of a survey or interview or an ethnographic research project, or whether it is experience of reading and analyzing historical or contemporary documents. Thus its analysis would centre on an explication of the 'intellectual autobiography' (Stanley, 1984b) of the feminist researcher/theoretician: it would produce *accountable* knowledge, in which the reader would have access to details of the contextually-located reasoning processes which give rise to 'the findings', the outcomes. Secondly, feminist unalienated knowledge would locate its practitioners firmly and irrevocably on the same critical plane as other people. It would reject any special or privileged vanguardist role for researchers/theoreticians, and instead recognize that everybody works from detailed knowledge of specific instances of social life to construct frameworks for understanding this; that is, we all competently theorize. And thirdly, as well as rejecting Scientistic separations between 'researchers' and 'mere people', a feminist epistemology would reject the dichotomy 'objectivity v. subjectivity', for it is this which underpins Scientism's claims to scientific status by emphasizing the distinctiveness of its working practices from those which characterize 'ordinary understanding'.

An unalienated feminist epistemology also requires specifications for other fundamentals, such as: how do we recognize what indeed is 'feminist knowledge' and distinguish it from 'just opinion'? Basic to this is how we define *who* is a 'knower' in feminist terms. My response here is unequivocal: knowers are, first, women; second, women who identify publicly and in their work as feminists (of whatever 'type' or 'kind'); and third, women who attempt to put into practice the three epistemological basics sketched out above. Equally fundamental is how competing knowledge-claims are to be adjudicated; I would suggest that the basic means of adjudication are that the adherence of claimants to these three epistemological basics should be scrutinized. And if two competing knowledges adhere to all of these basics, then we have precisely competing knowledges: different but equally (in feminist terms) valid viewpoints on an aspect of social reality. And this ought not to present feminists with any problems at all: we simply opt for our own preference, for that which best fits our own experience and understanding; *and* we respect the rights of the other to valid existence.

At this point I want to begin to trace the links between the argument so far and the notion of 'feminist auto/biography'.

'Feminist Methodology' and 'Feminist Auto/Biography'

The prime link between feminist auto/biography and feminist epistemology is provided by the idea of 'intellectual autobiography'. This term describes both the 'indexicality' of knowledge (that is, it is context-dependent) and its 'reflexivity' (that is, our descriptions or glosses of events and behaviours and the original events and behaviours are mutually constitutive; indeed, after the event such descriptive glosses *are* the social reality the talk about them is constitutive of). In other words, this approach is fundamentally concerned with *method*: with *how* people come to understand *what* they understand; and in this it refuses to falsely separate questions of methods from answers of theory, recognizing that all good theory is both indexical and reflexive, and insisting that abstract generalized theoretical knowledge is actually contextually-dependent knowledge which has been stripped, by semantic and textual means, of its context.

In these terms, then, all knowledge is *autobiographically-located* in a particular social context of experiencing and knowing. What Scientistic approaches do is to work as a kind of asset-stripper, removing through usually textual means the persons and the specifics of time, place and understanding, to produce supposedly generalized knowledge.

When we conversationally relate our autobiographies to other people we are, at least in a formal sense, faced with two choices concerning what this autobiography will be like. We can descriptively go about the business of presenting 'I' by beginning at the beginning and working forwards — 'I was born in ... I am now ...'. However, it is more usual to present what is in effect a model of 'I', a 'theory of my self': 'I am this kind of person, doing this kind of work, living in this kind of place, having these kinds of principles, likes and dislikes'. It is important to recognize that *both* choices involve theoretical presentations and so summations or models of the self, not just the second. Autobiographical experience is such that even the most apparently elaborate of descriptions actually and necessarily gloss 'what happened', for even one day's events cannot be fully described in words and on paper.

All autobiographies are theoretical formulations through and through, firstly because nothing else is possible, and secondly because people self-consciously produce multiple accounts of themselves. To one person I present myself as articulate and clever, to another reserved and sensitive; and both of these are *true* versions of my self, although neither are the *whole* truth. Moreover, we also produce similarly structured biographies of other people: 'oh Professor V is this kind of person, writes these kinds of things, behaves like this, is this kind of administrator, take last Wednesday when she....'. Succinctly, autobiography and biography in their everyday forms share the same defining characteristics of indexicality and reflexivity, and their apparent descriptions contain highly glossed and actually theoretical formulations of selves.

If 'biographical experience' (like all other experience) is never direct experience, is always at least first-order theorized, then what of 'intellectual autobiography'? The term indicates a concern with 'mind', in the form of analytically examining the reasoning procedures, located in a material research context (whether a library, a study, or 'the field' in one of its many forms), whereby researchers sift through a mass of detailed evidence, to come up with the glossed description called a 'research report' or 'research monograph' and also its formally presented 'theory' (formal theory should be seen as a third-order theory of the researcher's second-order theory-cum-description of the everyday first-order theorizing she and others have already engaged in making everyday events comprehensible). Intellectual autobiography, then, is the careful analytic explication of the reasoning procedures used in interpreting and theorizing whatever 'research data' the researcher is concerned with.

The links with 'feminist epistemology' should be apparent. Feminist epistemology locates the feminist researcher and other people on the same critical plane as equally theorizing subjects and does not treat the latter as the objects of the former. It recognizes that the formal theory of researchers is not produced out of 'direct experience' (whether the researcher's or anyone else's), for experience is already first-order theorized. It emphasizes that experience-as-analyzed can be of *anything*: critics who say that this approach is limited to what the researcher can directly experience have failed to grasp the point that 'the researcher's experience' can encompass anything her mind deals with and howsoever it enters that mind, including through books, journal articles, television, as well as from 'the field' in which substantive research projects are located. Because the analytic focus here is on reasoning procedures, mind, intellect and the process of comprehension and interpretation, it is of course centrally concerned with 'intellectual autobiography', here a specifically feminist intellectual autobiography.

As a feminist sociologist, my prime concern has been with the analytic features of how different kinds of 'knowledge' are produced, by what people, and against what competing knowledge-claims. In doing so I have followed the precepts for the analysis of ideology specified by Karl Marx and Friedrich Engels (1968) in *The German Ideology*, examining ideology as a material reality embedded in sets of concrete practices by the activities of specific groups and individuals.

All knowledge is 'ideological' in the sense that it embodies the beliefs, assumptions and views of some, particular, people but not others. Like Marx and Engels, I can see no good reason (though plenty of bad) for treating as ideology only those knowledges I happen to disagree with. Therefore by 'ideology' I mean, not 'false knowledge' or 'mystification', but all knowledge-claims and howsoever and by whosoever made (this chapter, for instance, is a textually-located ideological construct: it makes specific knowledge-claims, and it explicitly seeks to persuade readers that these are preferential claims to those made by other accounts of feminist epistemology or feminist auto/biography).

In addition, knowledge is *political*: competing knowledge-claims are adjudicated, most are labelled as mere opinion and usually only one is treated as knowledge itself (for, conventionally, knowledge is treated as unitary and mutually exclusive: two views of the same thing cannot both be true!). Here one superordinate 'Knowledge' is the product of a political process in which competing knowledges are rendered subordinate. Sociological knowledge is a good example of this (as indeed is that of other academic disciplines), in which the fetish with that three-headed beast known as 'Marx-Weber-Durkheim' both acts as a tribal totem and is a marker of a political process in which many theoreticians and researchers — and plenty of feminist sociologists among them over the last 150 years — have been relegated to a tribal wasteland.

It was because of my feminist concern with knowledge-making as a political process through and through that I became interested in diaries, biographies and autobiographies. The first step was through reading the diaries of Arthur Munby (Hudson, 1972), in which small selections from the diaries of Hannah Cullwick appear in editorial passages, as do many more mentions of Hannah in Munby's diaries. I was immediately intrigued, in part because the tale of upper-class Munby and decidedly lower-class Hannah echoed a similar cross-class relationship in my own family history, but more importantly because, in reading these three 'voices' of Hudson, Munby and Hannah, a clash of 'knowledges' was half-revealed. I wanted to know more, and ended by spending some four years of my life transcribing and typing the voluminous diaries of Hannah Cullwick, and also in responding to these not as repositories of alternative *truths* to those advanced by Munby and by Derek Hudson but rather as alternative *constructions* designed for a (changing over time) purpose (Stanley, 1987a).

I wanted to ensure that the Cullwick diaries appeared in print, for then and now these seem to me almost unique: within them a thoroughly working-class woman of the 1850s, 1860s and 1870s speaks, writes, in her own voice. I was also concerned to recognise the intertextuality of the Cullwick and Munby diaries and to emphasize that both used their diaries to promote a highly particular view of the relevances of the — very different — social realities each engaged in. That is, working on the two diaries brought home to me in a very direct way that the diary form, although apparently descriptive and written in the immediacy of the moment, is in fact as selective and as highly glossed a theoretical formulation as any autobiography, biography or piece of formal academic theorizing.

While editing the Cullwick diaries for publication, I was serendipitously asked to write an essay on Olive Schreiner (Stanley, 1983). In doing so I became interested in the role of Olive Schreiner's estranged husband, 'Cron' Cronwright-Schreiner (he took her name on marriage), in establishing a particular view of Schreiner through his widower's biography (Cronwright-Schreiner, 1924a) and his edited (to the extent sometimes of fabrication and sometimes of eradication) collection of her letters (Cronwright-Schreiner, 1924b). His view, in particular because of the apparent paucity of other sources, has formed an important pivot of a feminist biography of Schreiner (First and Scott, 1980), which has largely uncritically repeated what is actually a ruthlessly negative construction of Schreiner known to her friends as 'Cronwright's novel'.

Initially I provided an alternative reading of the life and work of Olive Schreiner to that contained in First and Scott's in my view problematic treatment. Then through textual analytic means I examined in detail the Cronwright-Schreiner biography (see Stanley, 1986b) to unpick and analyze its material ideological practices. In the terms introduced earlier, Cronwright-Schreiner strips from small snippets of behaviour and highlights of character the contextual specifics (which can be pieced back together from other sources) which establishes these as reasonable responses to particular moments; however, he presents them as instead generalized and context-transferable permanent traits indicative of the 'inner' and 'real' character of Olive Schreiner. And this character or personality is of an irredeemably flawed genius, 'difficult', indeed almost impossible to engage with at an interpersonal level.

Biographies are by their nature oddities. In Victoria Glendinning's (1983) phrase, they place under the spotlight one individual alone, casting everyone else into the shadows. This is singularly unlike life, where the lives of even the famous and infamous are densely peopled by peers. Only on paper does one person occupy the limelight. And only on paper is that limelighted person seen through the views of one commentator alone, who selects the evidence to be presented, decides what to include and what to exclude, which of the friends and lovers and acquaintances are significant and which not, what is meaningful and what trivial. Cronwright-Schreiner took a good deal of trouble to permit only one sharply clear 'Olive' to enter his pages. The Olive Schreiner that other people experienced as magnetic, fun, bewildering, infuriating, of unshakable feminism, pacifism and socialism, and surrounded by dearly loved and loving feminist friends, is completely excluded. The means he utilizes are discernible once trust in the biographer is suspended and his goodwill not accepted, trumpeted though it is.

However, in saying this I am not suggesting that Cronwright-Schreiner's method was in any *essential* different from the legitimate tools of all biographers. What separates him from the general run of biographers is his lack of goodwill towards his subject and his activity in changing and modifying the content of original documents such as letters. Otherwise the textual means he uses are the standard practices of selecting and summarizing to produce a particular view of 'the life of' any biographical subject. And of course autobiographers can be as complicit here as biographers, indeed are usually more so, in producing 'a life' as an unseamed, uncontradictory whole in which there is a clear linear progress of development from beginning to, if not an end, then at least a plateau. But lives are only like this in the telling; living them is a much messier and considerably more interesting business.

Olive Schreiner was a woman whose life was deeply embedded in a context of feminist friendship. One of the trajectories of my interest became centred on feminist social networks or 'webs of friendship' (Stanley, 1986a). I chose six feminist women that Olive Schreiner met and became friendly with (to a lesser or greater degree) — Eleanor Marx, Emma Cons, Edith Lees, Constance Lytton, Dora Montefiore and Virginia Woolf — and traced each of these women's feminist involvements and connections. In doing so, I compared the formal separations of different feminist organizations with the complexities of interconnections between feminist women, who in their interpersonal involvements multiply traversed such divisions by being actively involved with each other across formal lines of division.

Feminist Auto/Biographical Method

What I have provided above around some of my biographical work are the elements of my construction of a feminist auto/biographical method. In summary, these are:

1 a textual recognition of the importance of the labour process of the researcher/theoretician in reaching the interpretations and conclusions she does;

2 an insistence that works of auto/biography should be treated as textually-located ideological practices (and this of course includes any auto/biography produced by the feminist researcher/theoretician herself) and analytically engaged with as such;

3 a requirement that due recognition be given not only to the fact that a feminist biography should eschew the 'spotlight' approach to a single individual, but also and relatedly that it should emphasize that the informal organization of feminists through friendship can be as important as formal organization;

4 an insistence that biography cannot be treated as sealed from autobiography, for its production has many autobiographical reverberations which in turn impact on biography itself.

These features highlight the epistemological aspects of a 'form' or structure for feminist auto/biography. Each of these features structures the work I did with Ann Morley in looking at the role of Emily Wilding Davison and her 'militant' friends within the Women's Social Political Union (WSPU), the so-called 'suffragettes' (Stanley, 1988). This book encapsulates my approach to feminist auto/biography, for it was written as, among other things, an account of the labour process involved in producing it and thus of my 'intellectual autobiography' in doing so. Relatedly, it provides detailed commentary on the various histories of Edwardian feminism and the ways in which these treat the WSPU as a 'deviant' mainstream national political organization rather than exploring its myriad of local informal activities and involvements that coexisted with the formal organization. And connectedly, the patterns of comradeship and friendship of Emily Davison's closest colleagues are traced out; and in doing so a very different view of 'the WSPU' and its dealings with other contemporary feminist organizations is provided than is found in even feminist histories.

So far I have stressed the positive and desirable aspects of feminist auto/biography and located these within a feminist epistemological framework. I now want to discuss some of the objections that have been made to a feminist concern with auto/biography.

It has been suggested that auto/biography is by definition about an individual self, and that if feminist auto/biography departs from this then it is no longer auto/biography but something different in kind. It is certainly usual to see auto/biography as about single selves, and the general run of auto/biographies do indeed have the 'spotlight' approach noted earlier. However, it is equally true that there are already many auto/biographies that depart to one degree or another from this convention. Margaret Mead's (1972) *Blackberry Winter*, for example, although written in a conventional narrative form actually locates its author primarily in a female descent group that includes her grandmother, mother, herself and her own daughter, as well as Ruth Benedict and other close women friends and colleagues; and then among a group of male mentors and colleagues that includes her father, Franz Boas and ex-husbands Luther Cressman, Reo Fortune and Gregory Bateson. And Colette's (1922 and 1929/1968) *'My Mother's House' and 'Sido'* is on one level an autobiography within a single time-span in her childhood, but on another it is a mythologized biography of her mother, the magical Sido, and the no less magical world she created for her children in her garden, her house and neighbourhood.

These are both well-known autobiographies that do not fixate on the authorial self to the exclusion of others; indeed, their concern is with a self refracted through others. There are also biographies that look at networks of interconnections: for instance, Gillian Hanscombe and Virginia Smyers (1987) discuss a network of women writers influenced by modernism; Barbara Caine (1986) the lives, work and feminism of the Potter sisters; and Philippa Levine (1990) networks of friendship and political connections between feminist women from the 1850s to 1900.

It has also been suggested that it isn't possible to be concerned with an auto/biographical self without trading on essentialist and/or reductionist ideas about a 'real self'; and it is certainly true that one of the main forms that autobiographies have taken is the tracing out of the unfettering of an 'essential' inner self. However, this is by no means a *necessary* emphasis, and equally illustrious alternative constructions of self can be found. Virginia Woolf (1978), for example, uses the notion of 'moments of being' to describe those seemingly crystal-clear collections of memories that act as rafts for 'self' to stand on and thus to exist as the collection of such apparently past moments. This is an entirely social self, one that is both ontologically shaky and continually renewed by self-conscious present-time acts of memory and writing. And Rosemary Manning (1971) has written an apparently conventional autobiography which is actually the record and proof of how, after an almost successful suicide attempt, she goes about the business of constructing a self who is capable of living. Then in a subsequent text (1987) she uses a 'corridor of mirrors' metaphor to describe the assemblage of selves that we present to others, and also the artfulness of autobiography in enabling a seemingly 'factual' yet artfully constructed self to be publicly shown in 'an autobiography'.

Biographers, typically, are much less ready openly to deal with such complexities about their subject, but again there are exceptions to be found. For instance, Gertrude Stein (1933) writes what is apparently a biography of Alice Toklas but actually an autobiography of herself, and what is apparently an autobiography in *Everybody's Autobiography* (1938) but which is actually a biography of the human condition.

Lastly here, it has been suggested that proposing that feminist auto/ biography should be reflexively concerned with its own production, its own labour process, is merely narcissistic. I find it paradoxical that a concern with opening up the research process for scrutiny should be so labelled by *feminists*. After all, the effect is to democratize by enabling many more people to analytically engage with the written account of that process. For instance, Caroline Steedman's (1986) *Landscape for a Good Woman* points up the severe limitations of most feminist work for those of us who are not middle-class (or white, or heterosexual) and emphasizes how interwoven her own autobiography is with her construction of her mother's biography; and also it illuminatingly shows the reader that understanding these links involves an intellectual process which is contextually located. It is difficult to understand how objection can be made to work such as this, which seems to me immensely open, concerned to reject a narrow version of 'self' and to argue instead for its social construction within a network of others.

Conclusion

Discussions of feminist auto/biography and feminist epistemology are two particularly fruitful areas of current academic feminist debate and writing, and both do indeed 'make a difference' to academic convention. However, although both are concerned with the same fundamental questions concerning what 'feminism' should look like in textual terms, how to understand the relationship between feminist research and its subjects, and what the relationship between experience and feminist theory should be, these discussions have been conducted in parallel. Questions concerning the researcher's 'self' have only hesitantly been considered in discussions of feminist research; while the epistemological issues of research have been largely ignored in discussions of feminist auto/biography. There is much to be gained by bringing these two important academic feminist debates closer together.

Autobiography, feminist autobiography in particular, has produced interesting and innovative approaches to 'self', to 'narrative' and to points of interconnection between biography and autobiography, fiction and fact and reality and fantasy. However, by and large these innovations have had little impact on feminist biography. I have argued that the conventions of 'fact' and the so-called 'autobiographical pact' are stronger here; and I think that innovations in form for feminist biography will come from another source. That is, from discussions of the parameters and concerns of feminist epistemology located largely within feminist philosophy and social science.

The link between these two debates is provided by the notion of 'intellectual autobiography' as a detailed analytic account of the labour process involved in producing research outcomes, including auto/biographical ones. One additional element of a feminist auto/biographical approach involves focusing on biographies and autobiographies as sites of complexly constructed ideological practices, to develop textual analytic means of engaging with them in such terms. Another is the recognition that a 'spotlight' approach to a single individual is inappropriate given the feminist insistence on the social character of knowledge and action, thus insisting upon the importance of examining informal feminist organization based on ties of friendship and political commitment. And yet another is the insistence that 'the self' is no biological or psychological or any other essentialism — not even of language as in Lacanian views — but is rather a social production which can be, and often is, deconstructed and reconstructed. Ironically in view of the feminist criticisms of an auto/biographical approach, this can embed deconstructionist and postmodernist ideas more readily than the more conventional work of the critics, for only by confronting in appreciative detail an apparently unitary self can its fractures and discontinuities be fully and sensitively recognized and analytically explored.

Biographies and autobiographies are as popular as they are because they tell an interesting story and usually tell it very accessibly; because apparently they let us into lives very different from our own; and because they can provide feminist heroes to stand alongside the more traditional subjects of auto/biography. These sources of popularity need to be recognized and accepted as legitimate by academic feminists, not treated as a supposedly naive essentialist and individualist response to auto/biography. However, we also certainly need to develop the means of a more active readerly engagement with such writings, so that they are not taken on trust as sources of indisputible fact, but rather their ideological role in the construction of particular views of the 'self' is fully and analytically recognized and unpacked in feminist terms.

The question of how feminists should *read* auto/biographies is important; equally important is the question of whether and in what ways there are distinctly feminist ways of *writing* them. I have suggested that a distinct feminist autobiography is in the process of construction, characterized by a self-conscious and increasingly self-confident traversing of the conventional boundaries between different genres of writing. However, a feminist biography is less well-developed because innovations in the form of biography are less easily accomplished, and I have argued that innovations in form here will derive from a feminist social science concern with questions of epistemology, outlining what I see as key elements of a feminist biographical approach. And overarching all of this is my abiding respect for the power of auto/biographical writing to engage readers, myself included, on multiple levels.

References

BEAUVOIR, SIMONE DE (1953) *The Second Sex*, Harmondsworth, Penguin.

BENDIX, REINHARD (1960) *Max Weber: An Intellectual Portrait*, London, Heinemann.

BENSTOCK, SHARI (Ed.) (1988) *The Private Self: Theory and Practice of Women's Autobiographical Writings*, London, Routledge.

BRODZKI, BELLA and SCHENCK, CELESTE (Eds) (1988) *Life/Lines: Theorising Women's Autobiography*, Cornell University Press.

CAINE, BARBARA (1986) *Destined To Be Wives: The Sisters of Beatrice Webb*, Oxford, Clarendon Press.

COLETTE (1922 and 1929/1968) *'My Mother's House' and 'Sido'*, Harmondsworth, Penguin.

CRONWRIGHT-SCHREINER, SAMUEL (1924a) *The Life of Olive Schreiner*, New York, Haskell House.

CRONWRIGHT-SCHREINER, SAMUEL (Ed.) (1924b) *The Letters of Olive Schreiner*, London, Fisher Unwin.

EAKIN, PAUL (1985) *Fictions in Autobiography*, Princeton University Press.

FIRST, RUTH and SCOTT, ANN (1980) *Olive Schreiner*, London, Andre Deutsch.

GLENDINNING, VICTORIA (1983) *Vita: Life of Vita Sackville-West*, Harmondsworth, Penguin.

GRAHAM, ELSPETH, HINDS, HILARY and WILCOX, HELEN (Eds) (1989) *Her Own Life: Autobiographical Writings by Seventeenth Century Englishwomen*, London, Routledge.

HABERMAS, JÜRGEN (1972) *Knowledge and Human Interest*, London, Heinemann.

HANSCOMBE, GILLIAN and SMYERS, VIRGINIA (1987) *Writing For Their Lives: The Modernist Women 1910–1940*, London, The Women's Press.

HUDSON, DEREK (Ed.) (1972) *Munby: Man of Two Worlds*, London, John Murray.

JELINEK, ESTELLE (Ed.) (1980) *Women's Autobiography: Essays in Criticism*, Indiana University Press.

LEVINE, PHILIPPA (1990) 'Love, friendship and feminism in later nineteenth century England', in *Women's Studies International Forum*, 13, pp. 63–78.

LUKES, STEVEN (1973) *Emile Durkheim: His Life and Work*, Harmondsworth, Penguin.

McLELLAN, DAVID (1973) *Karl Marx: His Life and Thought*, London, Paladin.

MANNING, ROSEMARY (1971) *A Time And A Time*, London, Marion Boyars (originally published under the pseudonym of Sarah Davys).

MANNING, ROSEMARY (1987) *A Corridor of Mirrors*, London, The Women's Press.

MARX, KARL and ENGELS, FRIEDRICH (1968) *The German Ideology*, Moscow, Progress Publishers.

MEAD, MARGARET (1972) *Blackberry Winter*, London, Angus and Robertson.

OAKLEY, ANN (1984) *Taking It Like A Woman*, London, Flamingo Books.

OKELY, JUDITH (1986) *Simone de Beauvoir*, London, Virago Press.

PORTER, CATHY (1980) *Alexandra Kollontai*, London, Virago Press.

SPENDER, DALE (Ed.) (1987) 'Personal Chronicles: Women's Autobiographical Writings', special issue of *Women's Studies International Forum*, 10:1.

STANLEY, LIZ (1983) 'Olive Schreiner: New Women, Free Women, All Women', in SPENDER, DALE (Ed.) *Feminist Theorists*, London, The Women's Press, pp. 229–243.

STANLEY, LIZ (Ed.) (1984a) *The Diaries of Hannah Cullwick*, London, Virago Press; Rutgers University Press.

STANLEY, LIZ (1984b) 'How the Social Science Research Process Discriminates Against Women', in ACKER, SANDRA and PIPER, DAVID WARREN (Eds) *Is Higher Education Fair To Women?*, London, Nelson, pp. 189–209.

STANLEY, LIZ (1986a) 'Feminism and Friendship in England from 1825 to 1938', in *Feminism and Friendship: Two Essays on Olive Schreiner*, Studies in Sexual Politics no. 8, University of Manchester, pp. 10–46.

STANLEY, LIZ (1986b) 'How Olive Schreiner Vanished, Leaving Behind Only her Asthmatic Personality', in *Feminism and Friendship: Two Essays on Olive Schreiner*, Studies in Sexual Politics no. 8, University of Manchester, pp. 47–79.

STANLEY, LIZ (1987a) 'Biography as Microscope or Kaleidoscope? The Case of 'Power' in Hannah Cullwick's Relationship with Arthur Munby', in *Women's Studies International Forum*, 10, 1, pp. 19–31.

STANLEY, LIZ (1987b) 'Editing Hannah Cullwick's Diaries', in FEMINIST RESEARCH SEMINAR, Feminist Research Processes, *Studies in Sexual Politics* no. 16, University of Manchester, pp. 88–99.

STANLEY, LIZ (1988) *The Life and Death of Emily Wilding Davison*, London, The Women's Press.

STANLEY, LIZ (forthcoming) *The Auto/Biographical I: Theroy and Practice of Feminist Auto/Biography*, Manchester University Press.

STANLEY, LIZ (1990) 'Rescuing 'women' in history from feminist deconstructionism', in *Women's Studies International Forum*, 13, pp. 151–157.

STANLEY, LIZ and WISE SUE (1990) 'Method, Methodology and Epistemology in Feminist Research Processes', in STANLEY, LIZ (Ed.) *Feminist Praxis: Research, Theory and Epistemology in Feminist Sociology*, London, Routledge, pp. 20–60.

STANTON, DOMNA (Ed.) (1987) *The Female Autograph*, University of Chicago Press.

STEEDMAN, CAROLYN (1986) *Landscape For A Good Woman*, London, Virago Press.

STEIN, GERTRUDE (1933) *The Autobiography of Alice B. Toklas*, Harmondsworth, Penguin.

STEIN, GERTRUDE (1938/1985) *Everybody's Autobiography*, London, Virago Press.

WELDON, FAY (1985) *Rebecca West*, Harmondsworth, Penguin.

WILSON, ELIZABETH (1982) *Mirror Writing*, London, Virago Press.

WOOLF, VIRGINIA (1928) *Orlando*, Harmondsworth, Penguin.

WOOLF, VIRGINIA (1929) *A Room of One's Own*, London, Granada.

WOOLF, VIRGINIA (1933) *Flush: A Biography*, Harmondsworth, Penguin.

WOOLF, VIRGINIA (1938) *Three Guineas*, Harmondsworth, Penguin.

WOOLF, VIRGINIA (1940) *Roger Fry: A Biography*, Harmondsworth, Penguin.

WOOLF, VIRGINIA (1975, 1976, 1977, 1978, 1979, 1980) *Letters, Vols 1 to 6* (Ed. Nigel Nicholson), London, Chatto and Windus.

WOOLF, VIRGINIA (1977, 1978, 1980, 1982, 1984) *Diary, Vols 1 to 5*, London, Chatto and Windus.

WOOLF, VIRGINIA (1978) *Moments of Being* (Ed. Jeanne Schulkind), London, Granada.

WOOLF, VIRGINIA (1985) 'The Journal of Mistress Joan Martyn', in *The Complete Shorter Fiction of Virginia Woolf* (Ed. Susan Dick), London, The Hogarth Press, pp. 33–62.

Chapter 17

Questioning the Definition of 'Literature': Fictional and Non-Fictional Accounts of Childbirth

Tess Cosslett

Despite its title, this paper is mostly about non-fictional accounts of child-birth. It arises, however, directly out of some work I have been doing on fictional accounts, which I have written about elsewhere (Cosslett, 1989; Cosslett, forthcoming), and throughout the paper I draw comparisons between fictional and non-fictional accounts. For me, as someone who re-searches in English Literature, this paper represents a new departure. In my previous work on female friendships in Victorian Literature, I was very concerned to stress the *difference* between literary representations of female friendships, and what social historians have discovered about them from other sources. The literary representations seemed to be governed by particu-lar narrative conventions that had nothing to do with what friendship was 'really' like. But this difference could also be seen as not between literature and 'reality' but between different *genres*: the social historians' evidence most-ly comes from private *letters*, which have a different set of conventions (Cosslett, 1988, pp. 1–3, 10–11). Feminist literary criticism, with its challenge to the conventional 'canon' of literature, also challenges generic boundaries that have excluded much writing by women. Women have often been prevented, or discouraged, from writing in 'high' literary forms such as poetry (Homans, 1980); feminist critics have instead drawn attention to the female creativity diverted into forms such as letters, journals, or religious writings (Hobby, 1988). Non-fictional genres can also be studied from a feminist literary critical point of view. This approach is still valid and useful even when there are no longer any obstacles to women writing 'high' literature: feminist approaches challenge the *hierarchies* that assert that one genre is inherently 'higher' or more 'literary' than another. Now we have seen how useful techniques of literary analysis can be to the understanding of non-fictional materials, a vast field of contemporary women's writing opens up for investigation.

In my new research on the representation of childbirth by women writers, another consideration has also pushed me towards non-literary material: childbirth is a relatively *new* subject in literature, especially when narrated from the woman's point of view, but it has been much spoken about and written about elsewhere, particularly in two traditional genres, the expert's advice book, and the female oral tradition — I shall discuss these two genres later in this paper. The non-fictional accounts of childbirth on which the paper mainly concentrates interest me especially because they do not precisely belong to either of these genres, though they have complex relationships with both — like the fictional accounts, they are innovative and to some extent transgressive.

In my research on fictional accounts of childbirth I have been very struck by the way descriptions of this so-called 'natural' process are structured by cultural beliefs and practices. I was therefore very interested to come across two collections of non-fictional birth accounts by women, one entitled *Giving Birth: How it Really Feels*, edited by Sheila Kitzinger (1987), and the other, Ann Oakley's *From Here to Maternity* (1981), whose blurb claimed that the book answered the question 'What is it *really* like having a baby?'. Though there are some similarities between the two sets of accounts, the many differences between them, as well as the different uses to which they are put by their editors, immediately undermined the claim of either to be showing us the 'real' version of birth, though both use different strategies to claim authenticity.

Ann Oakley's book consists of transcriptions of interviews with a group of women, who were questioned at intervals, both before and after the births of their first children, about their experiences of pregnancy, childbirth, and early motherhood. The material thus belongs to the genre of the sociological study — but Oakley has written up her sociological conclusions in another, separate book (1980). In *From Here to Maternity*, she reverses the usual priorities between interviewee's words and interviewer's comments, relegating the latter to italics, and making the women's words the subject of the book (p. 5). The accounts she has selected, the way she has arranged them, and her own interspersed comments, are all nevertheless in the service of a particular thesis, which she clearly points out: 'the picture is deliberately black. What many of the women who were interviewed said was that they were misled into thinking childbirth is a piece of cake and motherhood a bed of roses.... I have constructed the book around this conclusion' (p. 6). Reading her women's accounts of childbirth, I was struck with how often their narratives are constructed in *opposition* to other narratives of birth — either the 'story' of the medical experts, or the 'story' of the exponents of natural childbirth — and sometimes in opposition to both these stories at once.

By contrast, the stories in Sheila Kitzinger's book are all confirmations and examples of the editor's natural childbirth approach — though the blurb stresses that there is 'no one right way to give birth', nevertheless none of the stories essentially questions Kitzinger's philosophy of birth. Kitzinger is a bit vague about the exact provenance of her stories — some are from letters written to her, some are from various research projects she is engaged in. One important difference from Oakley's accounts is that Kitzinger's are all written, not transcripts of oral material. This seems to have given them greater shape and coherence — though this may also result from the writers' single-minded espousal of Kitzinger's philosophy. The accounts in Oakley, on the other hand, are much more rambling and self-contradictory.

The only precedent for these two collections of women's accounts of childbirth is Margaret Llewellyn Davies's 1915 collection, *Maternity: Letters from Working Women*, which is much more narrowly focused on the campaign for Maternity Benefit — the women's letters provide a mass of evidence of low income and poor health in pregnancy, but hardly ever describe childbirth itself. Childbirth from the woman's point of view is also a relatively recent subject in fiction — in nineteenth-century novels it usually occurs off stage, or is seen through the eyes of husband and attendants (Poston, 1978; Kreppel, 1984). The traditional genres for the representation of childbirth were on the one hand the female oral tradition — the 'old wives' tale' — and on the other hand the textbook by the medical 'expert'. The medical expert is usually hostile to the female oral tradition — for instance, Gordon Bourne in his authoritative book on *Pregnancy* claims that 'the majority of old wives' tales are essentially destructive or demoralising.... Probably more is done by wicked women with their malicious lying tongues to harm the confidence and happiness of pregnant women than by any other single factor' (1975, pp. 6, 7). It is interesting that women's *fictional* accounts of birth are sometimes concerned to distance themselves not only from the experts' books, but from the bad reputation of the female oral tradition. Thus in Margaret Drabble's *The Millstone*, the heroine tells us with distaste of the birth stories told in the ante-natal clinic: 'I hated most of all the chat about birth that went on so continually around me in the queue: everyone recounted their own past experiences, and those of their sisters and mothers and friends and grand-mothers ...' (1968, p. 60).

Oakley's book is much more favourable to the female oral tradition as a source of both truth and support. The book itself is relying on oral testimony, and the stories told by women to each other are set against the 'official' versions adhered to by doctors and natural childbirth educators. Several women recount their mothers' stories of their own births, which often have the ring of folk-tales, celebrating powerful women and extra-ordinary events. For instance:

> My mother had eleven; she nearly had me in a drill of potatoes ...
> she was digging potatoes and she felt all wet down one of her legs —
> that was the water breaking. She had her little case packed, my
> mother always had her little case packed.... She used to take her
> little case and run down the lane about half a mile and thumb a lift
> from anything that was going along the road to take her to hospital;
> it was 22 miles away. (p. 78)

Oakley does however include one woman who takes the official line on the female oral tradition: 'I'm not going to listen to my mother or my mother-in-law because they do go on.... They just describe how awful it was for them.... They rather *enjoy* telling you about it' (p. 79). But it is interesting that Oakley later makes a point of telling us that this particular informant, 'who when pregnant refused to listen to her mother's tales about birth, is now beginning to wonder whether her mother might not be right after all' (p. 193). The high value placed on mothers' verbal accounts contrasts with the continual repudiation of books and experts throughout the book. Oakley seems to be claiming the authenticity of the female oral tradition for her accounts. As responses to interviewers' questions they do not really qualify as mothers' birth stories, which are traditionally occasioned as advice to other pregnant women, but a high degree of woman-to-woman intimacy seems to have been generated in the interviews, and one of the informants confesses that 'I could never speak to my own doctor about it. You see I feel like this, but I can talk to you about it and I can talk to my sister about it' (p. 282).

The accounts in Kitzinger's book also exist in a context of inter-female intimacy — Kitzinger's pupils are reporting back to their female mentor. It is interesting that mothers very rarely feature in these accounts — Kitzinger has to some extent taken on the function of the mother for these women: several accounts tell of a phone call to her to seek advice and support at crucial moments of decision. The traditional function of the oral birth story is thus reversed in these accounts: instead of the mother giving her story as advice to the daughter, the daughter tells her story as a tribute to the mother. Kitzinger's motherly advice, and her own story, appear in the introduction, where she displays an interestingly ambiguous attitude to the female oral tradition, and its relation to the purposes of her book. She derides the insulting dictionary definition of 'old wives' tales', and insists that it is the medical care system, and not other women, 'who instil and fuel anxiety in most pregnant women' (p. 16), and seems to be aligning her book with the female oral tradition as a useful way for women to share their experiences. But at the same time she deplores both women's *reticence* in telling each other about childbirth, and certain 'other women who describe with apparent relish each ache and pain and who flaunt obstetric difficulties as if they were rosettes, prizes for having suffered in labour, to be exhibited proudly in front of those who have not yet been put on trial' (p. 15).

In emphasizing women's reticence, and in reviving the stereotype of the horrific old wives' tale, Kitzinger creates a place for her book — if women were communicating usefully, there would be no need for it. Moreover, as a self-appointed 'expert' herself, she must necessarily be suspicious of folk-wisdom — when she does appeal to it, it is in the reassuringly remote context of the 'Third World', where women still have access to a culture of 'emotional support and sharing between women' (p. 10) during childbirth. Her contradictory attitude to the female oral tradition reflects the contradictory nature of her book itself — women's first-hand accounts of birth, carefully contained within several introductory and concluding chapters that expand Kitzinger's beliefs about birth. Thus the women's words are being used in the service of an expert's advice book. While, as I have said, Oakley's accounts and her comments indicate a continuing suspicion of books, in Kitzinger's accounts books and writing turn out to be surprisingly potent allies for her women in their fight against hospital authorities.

Having sketched out the relationship of the two books to the female oral tradition and the expert's advice book, I now want to look in a little more detail at some of the distinguishing features of the two books, which I have already touched upon. In the case of Oakley, I want to show the way her accounts are constructed in opposition to other types of story, and also the way they often contain strands of contradictory versions of events. In Kitzinger's book, I want to consider further the way the accounts function as testimonies to Kitzinger's beliefs, and I also want to investigate the paradoxical importance of books, writing and medical terminology in accounts dedicated to a belief in what we still refer to as 'natural' childbirth — though interestingly Kitzinger in her Introduction repudiates the word in favour of some other, rather problematic definitions. After considering the two books separately like this, I want to raise an interesting and complicated problem that involves both of them: that is, the question of narrative perspective or point-of-view in women's accounts of childbirth.

Hilary Graham, in her article on 'Images of Pregnancy in Antenatal Literature' (1977), points out that these images fall into two contradictory groups: there are the romantic photographs of pregnant women in natural settings, and there are the down-to-earth drawings of pregnant women consulting their doctors or being shown how to do their exercises. These opposing images, she argues, reflect a contradiction in the attitude of the official literature to pregnancy: on the one hand it is a 'natural' and healthy state, in which the woman has control over her own body; on the other, it is an illness, for which she needs medical advice and control. Graham associates the 'romantic' image of pregnancy with the natural childbirth movement, and Oakley's accounts can be seen to be negotiating with and between these two types of 'official' story, 'natural' and 'medical'. Typically, the account in Oakley's book by 'Alison Mountjoy' (the names are all fictitious) is a narrative of decisions and actions taken by medical authorities — it begins with the words 'The doctor had said at the hospital . . .' — with occasional protesting or triumphant interventions by the mother. So, although threatened with an induction, 'there I was starting off by myself: I felt so proud of myself, and I didn't tell anybody for about an hour.' The not telling is interesting — the woman keeps control and knowledge of the story to herself for a while here. But 'they' soon take over again: 'So when they did take me upstairs, they didn't do anything. Until about twelve when they decided they wanted to monitor the baby which apparently they do *routinely* there. And the bag [membranes] hadn't broken by then so they had to do it — I said why, what for? But of course they didn't listen.' While this woman questions and tries to oppose medical interventions like the induction, she is not doing so from a convinced natural childbirth point of view, and also disputes the natural childbirth version of events: 'By then these pains were coming quite fast and they were pretty painful. You're not allowed to call them pains, are you? They're contractions. It always makes me laugh when I read that because I *knew* they bloody well hurt.... Also the breathing wasn't working — it's a load of old codswallop, that breathing' (p. 87). The 'pains'/'contractions' opposition here emphasizes the importance of terminology in constructing or opposing different versions of childbirth.

The whole story is told like this in opposition to other versions — even the mother's description of first holding the baby is implicitly in terms of having heard or read about this allegedly marvellous moment: 'It felt very strange. I mean yes: it was *my* baby, and I loved her, but I think I was just so shattered by then that whatever I was feeling I couldn't feel much of' (p. 91). It is this sense of deviation from standard versions of the story that gives Oakley's accounts their air of authenticity. While these mothers mostly attack 'official' images from films and books, in order to oppose these they sometimes have to use other stereotyped images. Thus 'Kate Prince' explains her disillusion like this: 'somebody had said well it's not like it is in the films or something. And I thought well it's exactly like 'Gone With the Wind' — it's *exactly* like those old movies when they're all writhing about in agony: that's *exactly* what I was doing' (p. 109). 'Pauline Diggory' uses the same analogy: 'I think women ought to be told that it's painful. I suppose if I recall all those films of women in labour ... holding onto the bedstead and all this sort of thing — I suppose if I'd recalled that ...' (p. 97). The old films provide an image of struggle and agony to set against both modern accounts, the 'medical' and the 'natural'.

Other women rather opportunistically set one version against the other, in an attempt to rationalize their experience. So one woman who had an epidural and 'felt guilty', the expected response in a natural childbirth story, turns on a representative of natural childbirth in the next bed: 'There was this woman in the bed next to me and she was an intelligent woman and she said if you do the breathing exercises you can cope. I said well, why should I bloody have to cope? She was all for having it naturally. I think that's disgraceful, you know' (p. 95), and then becomes a self-righteous convert to the medical version: 'I just said I think it's a disgrace, no other operation in the world does one have to go through so much pain!' (p. 96). Conversely, a woman who had an epidural which didn't work becomes an equally self-righteous convert to natural childbirth rhetoric: 'Now I am glad the epidural didn't work, at the time I wished it had done.... I took the full brunt of it, whereas these people who had had it said that they couldn't feel a thing. Well to me that isn't having a baby. What's the point? I said it was awful. But it's not awful really' (pp. 93–4). There is an interesting tension here between feelings at the time and later rationalizations. Nearly all the accounts are full of this sort of ambivalence — the mothers do not go in for a simple self-consistent version of events: their accounts are taken over at different times by different and often contradictory discourses.

As you might expect, the accounts in Kitzinger's book are much more self-consistent, both because they are written, and because they share a central belief in Kitzinger's philosophy. Kitzinger's first introductory chapter is uncompromisingly headed 'Birth: A Personal Statement of Belief', and it ends with 'the atmosphere of a room where birth takes place' according to

Kitzinger's teaching, being compared to 'the silence of a Quaker meeting' (p. 12). This invocation of Nonconformist religion seems especially appropriate to the form of the personal accounts which follow. Each recounts a battle with the establishment on behalf of unorthodox ideas, to which the women continuously testify in the face of opposition. They are persecuted and tempted by the medical establishment, but they triumph with renewed faith and often end with an encouraging moral for the believer. There are occasional telling uses of religious terminology in the accounts: for instance, one woman writes of how she 'was sorely tempted to accept Bridget's [the midwife's] offer of pethedine' (p. 72). By making this religious analogy, I do not actually want to undermine the credibility or the power of these testaments. Nonconformist Christianity has often given women the opportunity to voice their beliefs and to believe in their own voices (Hobby, 1988, pp. 26–75). These accounts have an impressive sense of purpose and self-assurance. Unlike Oakley's confused and sometimes self-contradictory women, these women have a clear sense of who and where they are in the experience of birth. On the other hand, religious certainty also generates guilt and self-blame in those who cannot live up to its prescriptions — so in an account of a Caesarian birth a woman writes of how 'The experience shattered me and my confidence in myself as a woman and gave me a feeling of failure at not being able to perform the function for which I was intended.... It hurts terribly to read glowing accounts in magazines about wonderful births' (p. 113). These feelings are validated by Kitzinger in her introductory note, and not questioned as perhaps *produced* by her system of beliefs and the 'glowing accounts' it inspires, rather than being the 'natural' feelings to have in this situation. Here I rather longed for one of Oakley's informants to explode the 'glowing accounts' of the magazines.

In her Introduction, Kitzinger is cautious about using the term 'natural childbirth' to describe what she advocates: instead, she uses a new metaphor: childbirth is an *art*, whose techniques have been so well learnt and practised that when put into action it *seems* 'natural' (p. 26). The metaphor of 'art' does not quite hold together all that she is demanding of her followers. On the one hand, they are to let go of their minds, and experience their bodily sensations with complete acceptance — here another analogy is brought in, birth as orgasm, a profound sexual experience. On the other hand, they are to master and make use of a full knowledge of not only medical terminology, but of 'the way the medical system works' *and* 'some understanding of the medical system in social and political terms'. As she rightly says, 'information is power' (p. 29). The metaphor of art does not quite unify all these goals — how can one have an orgasm whilst also remaining aware of the medical technicalities and the social and political context? It is interesting that in her introductory chapters Kitzinger gives two quite different parallel but separate accounts of birth — one is a lyrical 'fantasy' describing her own experience of childbirth 'in terms of imagery of water and its movement' (pp. 23–4); the other is a standard medical description of 'the usual pattern of labour', in terms of first stage, transition, second stage, and what the cervix and the uterus are doing at each stage (pp. 53–4).

In the accounts of birth by the other women in her book, I found instead, surprisingly, that it was the medical account that predominated — there was much use of medical terminology, of books, and especially of written birth plans, as weapons of power. Rather than letting go and experiencing childbirth 'naturally', these women were using all the resources of culture to gain control over their own experiences. When they did describe bodily sensations or emotions, it was either in medical terminology — 'contractions', 'transition' — or in the most general or clichéd language: for instance, 'It was such a beautiful and emotional experience' (p. 90). So, despite the book's title, I did not get any sense of 'how it really feels' — which, incidentally, is something that women writing *fictional* accounts are often very concerned to convey, especially through the use of metaphor. It is interesting that there is a very close parallel to Kitzinger's 'fantasy' about birth in terms of water imagery in Enid Bagnold's 1938 novel *The Squire* (pp. 101, 145). This sort of account has to be clearly labelled 'fantasy' to be admitted into a non-fiction book like Kitzinger's — while in the fictional accounts, metaphor is used as part of a painstaking attempt to describe 'realistically' what birth is like, and medical terminology is usually banished, in order to create an effect of immediacy and authenticity. An interesting exception to this banishing of medical terminology is Fay Weldon's *Puffball* (1980), where extremely technical, scientific language is used at intervals to describe the development of the heroine Liffey's pregnancy — but these descriptions are carefully isolated in chapters called 'Inside Liffey', and the rest of the text deals with the pregnancy in emotional and psychic terms, even suggesting a parallel psychic cause (another woman's curse) for the physical problems Liffey experiences. Liffey herself has no awareness of the physical processes going on 'inside'.

Conversely, the Kitzinger accounts show women fully aware of the medical version of what is going on in their bodies, *and* of what the medical authorities are up to, and how to combat them. As I have said, books and writing are important in this contest. It is interesting that *fictional* heroines either show no signs of having read, or even ostentatiously ignore ante-natal advice books (Drabble, 1968, p. 92; Byatt, 1986, p. 8) — in the fictional accounts we are being given an illusion of 'pure' experience, uncontaminated by 'culture'. With technical know-how on their side, Kitzinger's women are able to carry on informed arguments with their medical attendants. My favourite example of this is from the account of a woman determined to have twins with as little intervention as possible: 'between contractions I continued the forceps discussion' (p. 80). Her account is full of an easy and informed use of medical terminology (p. 78). This woman had also written to her consultant in advance detailing her wishes. By using medical terminology for their own purposes, and especially by the power of written 'plans', these women are able to challenge the authority of the medical establishment's version of events more creatively than could Oakley's informants, one of whom describes the power of writing being used against her: 'When they examine you they write in the file ... and I asked her what it was and she said I can't tell you.... She said what is written in the file is strictly confidential' (p. 92). Instead of just helplessly objecting, Kitzinger's women, armed with their own written plans, cause their own versions of events to come into being, and impose their own point of view on the narrative.

The question of point of view, or narrative perspective, in accounts of childbirth is of especial interest to feminist critics. As Carol Poston points out, in her article on 'Childbirth in Literature', descriptions of 'birth from the audience rather than the participant point of view is nearly universal' (1978, pp. 20–1; see also Kreppel, 1984, p. 2). In the twentieth century, several women novelists have pioneered the description of childbirth from the woman's point of view — the ones I have read are Enid Bagnold in *The Squire* (1938), A.S. Byatt in *Still Life* (1986), Margaret Drabble in *The Millstone* (1968), and Doris Lessing in *A Proper Marriage* (1956). All these writers stick scrupulously to their heroines' points of view — that is, they tell us only what she could have felt and known at the time. As I have said, they also further protect the authenticity of their accounts by making them seem uncontaminated by either the female oral tradition or the medical expert tradition. But when we turn to the 'real-life' accounts in Oakley's and Kitzinger's books, we find the point of view is not nearly so consistent. The women bring in all sorts of details they could not have seen or known at the time. Very often, they tell us how their attendants or companions have to give them information about what is happening, when they themselves are unaware. At other times, they just incorporate something into their accounts that they must have been told by an outside observer, but without explaining this.

There are of course obvious physical limitations to a woman's 'view' of the event of birth. Not only may she be occasionally semi-conscious, but also, as one of Oakley's informants puts it, 'you've got your legs on the table and you have a foot on each nurse's shoulder, so you have to rick your neck to look down and you can't do it, because you are trying to breathe at the same time. Alan see it.... He saw the head ... and then he said they cut you and I said to him, how did you know, and he said, well I see it didn't I?' (p. 93) This reliance on the husband to report back on what is happening 'at the other end' recurs in the accounts: 'he kept running down the other end and looking and coming back and telling me what was happening' (p. 207). This disabling division of the woman into two 'ends' is partly bridged in some of Kitzinger's accounts, when the women ask for *mirrors* so they can have a view of the head emerging, or of their stitches. Clearly all the women feel that what is happening 'down there' *is* part of their experience, even if they are unaware of it, and they incorporate it in various ways. Kitzinger's women are, as you might expect, more aware that there is an 'objective' version of what is going on: for instance, 'At 1.45 the baby's head was visible. I didn't take in the fact that crowning had occurred' (p. 73). Here the woman is giving us both the 'objective', technical account of what was happening, and her own subjective unawareness of it. Oakley's accounts are less technical, and more reliant on the attendants' reports, but these are also incorporated as part of the story: for instance, 'He was stuck in the neck of the womb, he got stuck coming round the corner. They told me that' (p. 98). Kitzinger's women do also need help from attendants to reconstruct their stories: 'I didn't remember the sequence of things so I asked her [the midwife] to review what had happened' (p. 147).

Most of the 'first-hand' accounts are fairly clear about what the woman was aware of at the time, and what she was told by onlookers, then or later. But some of them incorporate outside points of view with no acknowledgment of where they come from. Here is an example from one of Oakley's accounts: 'I always thought you could push when you wanted to push, but you don't: you have to wait for their command. They feel your tummy and your face is all crinkled up with agony and they say oh you've got a pain, you can push now . . .' (p. 93). Here, the woman has moved over into 'their' point of view, observing her own face 'crinkled up with agony', and deducing from this that she must be having a pain. The context of this slippage in the perspective — 'their' control of 'your' pushing — suggests that this woman's own version of events is being taken over by the powerful official one of the hospital staff, so much so that she takes on their point of view, and allows herself to be constructed by their narrative perspective. A very different effect is produced by a similar slippage in one of Kitzinger's accounts. This is an idyllic story of a home birth, which begins with bread-making and ends with milking the goat. But the actual moment of birth is described like this: 'One more push and my son slid out, with an Apgar level of nine, into the sunshine' (p. 108). The glossary informs us that the 'Apgar level' is 'a quick and simple way of estimating a baby's health and responsiveness to the challenges of living based on the observation of the baby's reflexes, muscle tone and breathing. It is carried out at one and five minutes after birth. Ten is full marks' (p. 211). Obviously, this woman cannot have known what her son's Apgar level was as he actually emerged from the womb: she must have been told this later by the midwife. But clearly in retrospect his high score has become part of the whole triumph of his successful birth, and the way the outside technical information is incorporated into her account suggests an effortless appropriation of the official medical description of her son.

What, then, can we conclude from these various accounts? They all seem to show women resisting, appropriating, or being constructed by two dominant, powerful discourses about childbirth, and ultimately about the nature of women. The discourse of the medical experts constructs women as passive patients, assemblages of bodily functions (Graham, 1977; Martin, 1987; Rich, 1977, pp. 128–85), while the discourse of natural childbirth constructs them as primitive vehicles of instinctive bodily wisdom (Graham, 1977; Rich, 1977, pp. 128–85; Wertz and Wertz, 1979, pp. 178–200). Those of Oakley's accounts which resist *both* these discourses could be seen as following Julia Kristeva's strategy for women caught in the definitions of patriarchal language: 'It follows that a feminist practice can only be negative, at odds with what already exists so that we may say "that's not it" and "that's still not it"' (1981, p. 137). Kitzinger's women, on the other hand, enthusiastically take over both discourses, using the language of medical expertise in the service of an ideal of natural womanhood. Though successful in most cases, in giving the women a powerful and central role in their stories, this strategy of appropriation leads to feelings of failure and abnormality in women who do not succeed in combating the medical establishment with its own weapons: they are not able to say 'that's not it', but must accept the definition of themselves as having failed the supreme test of womanhood. In allowing their identities to be constructed by the discourse of natural childbirth, these women resemble those in Oakley's accounts who are completely taken over by the discourse and the narrative point of view of the medical experts. Between these three extremes of resistance, appropriation and assimilation are those women in Oakley's accounts who opportunistically make use of whatever discourse is at hand to define and justify themselves. The fictional accounts which present themselves as 'uncontaminated' by either of these dominant discourses are nevertheless often structured by an implicit natural childbirth model, and in opposition to the medical-institutional model, and also of course by literary codes and conventions (Cosslett, 1989). By comparing the fictional and non-fictional, we can see how the fiction engages with the discourses of the 'real' world; and, perhaps more importantly, how the 'real-life' stories are also literary constructs, in a different genre, but not of a different species altogether. There is no simple test by which we can say any of these accounts, fictional or non-fictional, are more 'authentic' or more 'real'. Instead, they alert us to the cultural element in what we may have assumed to be a natural process, and they suggest different strategies that women can adopt in order to gain control over the 'story' of their own bodies.

References

BAGNOLD, E. (1938) *The Squire*, reissued 1987, London, Virago.

BOURNE, G. (1975) *Pregnancy*, London, Pan.

BYATT, A.S. (1986) *Still Life*, Harmondsworth, Penguin.

COSSLETT, T. (1988) *Woman to Woman: Female Friendship in Victorian Fiction*, Brighton, Harvester.

COSSLETT, T. (1989) 'Childbirth from the Woman's Point of View in British Women's Fiction: Enid Bagnold's *The Squire* and A.S. Byatt's *Still Life*', in *Tulsa Studies in Women's Literature*, 8, 2, pp. 263–86.

COSSLETT, T. (forthcoming) 'Childbirth on the National Health: Issues of Class and Gender Identity in Two Post-War British Novels', in *Women's Studies*.

DAVIS, M. LLEWELLYN (1915) *Letters from Working Women*, reissued 1978, London, Virago.

DRABBLE, M. (1968) *The Millstone*, Harmondsworth, Penguin.

GRAHAM, H. (1977) 'Images of Pregnancy in Antenatal Literature', in DINGWALL, R. *et al.* (Eds) *Health Care and Health Knowledge*, London, Croom Helm, pp. 15–37.

HOBBY, E. (1988) *Virtue of Necessity: English Women's Writing 1649–88*, London, Virago.

HOMANS, M. (1980) *Women Writers and Poetic Identity*, Princeton, Princeton University Press.

KITZINGER, S. (Ed.) (1987) *Giving Birth: How it Really Feels*, London, Victor Gollancz.

KREPPEL, M. (1984): 'Books I've Read: Crosscurrents in Obstetrics and Literary Childbirth', in *Atlantis*, 10, pp. 1–11.

KRISTEVA, J. (1981) 'Woman Can Never Be Defined', in MARKS, E. and DE COURTIV-
RON, I. (Eds) *New French Feminisms*, Brighton, Harvester, pp. 137–41.
LESSING, D. (1956) *A Proper Marriage*, reissued 1977, London, Granada.
MARTIN, E. (1987) *The Woman in the Body: a Cultural Analysis of Reproduction*, Boston,
Beacon Press.
OAKLEY, A. (1980) *Women Confined: Towards a Sociology of Childbirth*, Oxford, Martin
Robertson.
OAKLEY, A. (1981) *From Here to Maternity*, Harmondsworth, Pelican.
POSTON, C. (1978) 'Childbirth in Literature', in *Feminist Studies*, 4, pp. 18–31.
RICH, A. (1977) *Of Woman Born: Motherhood as Experience and Institution*, London,
Virago.
WELDON, F. (1980) *Puffball*, London, Hodder and Stoughton.
WERTZ, D. and WERTZ, R. (1979) *Lying-In: A History of Childbirth in America*, New
York, Schocken.

Notes on Contributors

Jane Aaron is a Lecturer in English at the University College of Wales, Aberystwyth, where she teaches courses on Romanticism, women's writing, and psychoanalytic and feminist criticism. She is the author of *A Double Singleness: Gender and the Writings of Charles and Mary Lamb* (Oxford University Press, 1991), and is currently working on a more general study of gender and Romanticism for Open University Press.

Pamela Abbott is Principal Lecturer in Sociology and Social Policy at Polytechnic South West, Plymouth. She has contributed to Open University units, and has written *Women and Social Class* (with Roger Sapsford, Tavistock, 1987) and *Introducing Sociology: a Feminist Perspective* (with Claire Wallace, Routledge, 1990). She has also edited several books on health, the caring professions, and gender.

Avtar Brah is a Lecturer in Birkbeck College at the University of London. Her research and publications cover such areas as ethnicity, gender and work; 'race' and education; and ethnicity, culture and identity.

Lyndie Brimstone lives in London with her 'pretended' family and is currently completing a full length study of Twentieth Century Lesbian Writers. She has contributed to a number of anthologies including *Lesbian and Gay Writing* by Mark Lilly (Ed.) (Macmillan, 1990) and *What Lesbians Do in Books* by Elaine Hobby and Chris White (Eds) (The Women's Press, forthcoming 1991).

Juliet Cook is about to take up an appointment in the Continuing Education Department of the Open University. She has worked in a variety of university/higher education settings in Britain and abroad. Her current teaching and research include issues of 'race' and gender, youth and community work, anti-racist education, and developing and implementing equal opportunities policies with particular reference to employment and professional practice.

Tess Cosslett is a Lecturer in the Department of English, University of Lancaster, where she teaches mainly nineteenth-century and women writers courses, and hopes to contribute to an interdisciplinary Women's Studies Part One course next year. She took her undergraduate and graduate degrees at Oxford. Her previous publications are: *The 'Scientific Movement' and Victorian Literature* (Harvester and St Martins, 1982); (Ed.) *Science and Religion in the Nineteenth Century* (Cambridge, 1984); *Woman to Woman: Female Friendship in Victorian Fiction* (Harvester and Humanities Press, 1988). She is now working on the representation of childbirth by twentieth-century women writers, about which she has several articles in print or forthcoming, which may form the basis of another book.

Claire Duchen is a Lecturer in French at the University of Bath. She is the author of *Feminism in France from May '68 to Mitterand* (RKP, 1986) and *French Connections: Voices from the Women's Movement in France* (Hutchinson, 1987). She is currently working on a history of women in France from the Liberation to May 1968.

Mary Evans was educated at the London School of Economics and the University of Sussex. She teaches sociology and Women's Studies at the University of Kent at Canterbury and is the author of various books and editions, including *Jane Austen and the State* and *Simone de Beauvoir: A Feminist Mandarin*.

Jalna Hanmer is a Senior Lecturer and Coordinator of the MA in Women's Studies at the University of Bradford. She is co-author of *Well-Founded Fear: A Community Study of Violence to Women* and co-editor of *Women, Violence and Social Control* and *Women, Policing and Male Violence: International Perspectives*. She is also co-author of *Women and Social Work: Towards a Woman-Centred Practice* and *Man-made Women: How New Reproductive Technologies Affect Women*. She is managing editor of *Reproductive and Genetic Engineering: Journal of International Feminist Analysis*.

Gillian Hanscombe and Suniti Namjoshi live in Devon. GH was born in Melbourne, Australia, in 1945. She completed a DPhil at St Hugh's College, Oxford, in 1979, and worked variously as a teacher, office worker, and journalist before moving to the country in 1986 to write full time. SN was born in India in 1941. She has worked as an Officer in the Indian Administrative Service and in academic posts in India and Canada. From 1972 to 1987 she taught in the Department of English at the University of Toronto and now writes full time.

Maggie Humm is Coordinator of Women's Studies at the Polytechnic of East London, which instituted Britain's first full degree in Women's Studies. Her publications include *Feminist Criticism, An Annotated Bibliography of Feminist Criticism* and *The Dictionary of Feminist Theory* (Harvester Press) and chapters in *Women's Writing* (Harvester Press), *Prespectives on Pornography* and

Twentieth Century Suspense (Macmillan Press), *Teaching Women* (Manchester University Press) and *Infertility* (Pandora Press). Her articles on education and feminism have appeared in *Women's Studies International Forum, Feminist Teacher, Canadian Women's Studies*, and other writing in *Fiction International*. She has just completed *Border Traffic: Strategies of Contemporary Women Writers* (Manchester University Press) and become a Section Editor of *The International Encyclopedia of Women's Studies*, ed. C. Kramerae and D. Spender (Pergamon Press).

Mary Kennedy has taught in LEAs and the WEA, and is currently the Lecturer in Women's Studies in the Centre for Extra-Mural Studies at Birkbeck College, University of London.

Renate Klein is widely published in Women's Studies and biotechnology. Her books include *Theories of Women's Studies* (with Gloria Bowles, 1983); *Test-Tube Women* (with Rita Arditti and Shelley Minden, 1984); *Infertility* (1989) and *The Exploitation of a Desire: Women's Experiences with IVF* (1989). She is a co-founder of the Feminist International Network of Resistance to Reproductive and Genetic Engineering and an editor of *Issues in Reproductive and Genetic Engineering, Women's Studies International Forum* and the Athene Series. She is currently researching hormone replacement therapy and the politics and medical reality of RU 486 and is a Research Associate and Lecturer in Women's Studies at Deakin University, Australia.

Sue Lees is coordinator of the Women's Studies Unit at the Polytechnic of North London and joint chair of the Women's Studies Network (UK). She has published in the areas of the construction of sexuality, equal opportunities, feminism and race, violence against women, and women and technology. She is author of *Losing Out: Sexuality and Adolescent Girls* (Unwin, 1986), and is writing a book, *Sexual Reputation: From Adolescence to the Criminal Justice System*. She lives with her son and daughter.

Cathy Lubelska is a Senior Lecturer in Social History and Women's Studies, and course leader of Women's Studies at Lancashire Polytechnic. Her current research explores experiential and interdisciplinary approaches within feminist methodology and women's history.

Paulina Palmer teaches an undergraduate course in 'Feminist Approaches to Literature' in the English Department at the University of Warwick, and contributes to the teaching of the Women's Studies MA. Her publications include *Contemporary Women's Fiction: Narrative Practice and Feminist Theory* (Harvester Wheatsheaf, 1989); a study of the fiction of Angela Carter, in Sue Roe, ed., *Women Reading Women's Writing* (Harvester, 1987); and an essay on 'Contemporary Lesbian Fiction', in Linda Anderson, ed., *Plotting Change: Contemporary Women's Fiction* (Arnold, 1990). She has a story in Jan Bradshaw and Mary Hemming, eds, *Girls Next Door* (Women's Press, 1985). Her essay 'Antonia White's *Frost in May*: a lesbian feminist reading' will appear in

Susan Sellers, ed., *Feminist Criticism: Theory and Practice* (Harvester Wheat-sheaf, forthcoming). She is currently working on a book on *Contemporary Lesbian Writing* for the Open University Press.

Brec'hed Piette is Senior Lecturer in Communication Studies at Sheffield City Polytechnic. She has taught Women's Studies on pre-degree, under-graduate and postgraduate courses.

Liz Stanley is working-class and Romany by birth, a lesbian by luck and a northerner in England by choice. She has taught in the Sociology Depart-ment at Manchester University since 1977. Most recently her research in-terests have focused on historical topics and feminist autobiography, although her abiding sociological and feminist concern is with the processes by which 'knowledge' is produced and contested. Publications include *The Diaries of Hannah Cullwick* (Rutgers UP, 1984); *The Life and Death of Emily Wilding Davison* (The Women's Press, 1988); *Feminist Praxis: Research, Theory and Epistemology in Feminist Sociology* (Routledge, 1990) and *The Auto/Biographical I: The Theory and Practice of Feminist Auto/Biography* (Manchester University Press, in press).

Sylvia Walby was the first Chair of the Women's Studies Network (UK), 1988–90, and Director of the Women's Studies Research Centre and Women's Studies teaching programmes at Lancaster University during the 1980s. She is now Lecturer in Sociology at the London School of Economics. She is author of *Patriarchy at Work* (Polity, 1986) and *Theorizing Patriarchy* (Blackwell, 1990); joint author of *Localities, Class and Gender* (Pion, 1985), *Restructuring: Place, Class and Gender* (Sage, 1990), *Contemporary British Society* (Polity, 1988) and *Sex Crime in the News* (Routledge, 1991); and editor of *Gender Segregation at Work* (Open University Press, 1988).

Shantu Watt worked as a generic and specialist social worker for a number of years before becoming a staff development officer. Since then she has been a Senior Lecturer on a social work course and is currently teaching at the University of Warwick on the MA/CQSW course. She also acts as a consul-tant to a number of agencies.

Sue Wilkinson is Principal Lecturer in Psychology at Coventry Polytechnic, and has been responsible — together with two colleagues — for introducing Women's Studies courses there. She edits the journal *Feminism and Psychology* and the book series 'Gender and Psychology', both published by Sage. She has been active in the British Psychological Society for a number of years as a feminist, and — more recently — as a lesbian.

Christine Zmroczek is Managing Editor of *Women's Studies International Forum* and a freelance researcher, teacher and consultant. A former Research Fellow of the University of Sussex, where she published widely on women and technology, she is currently finishing a PhD on women's experiences of household technologies, preparing a book about working class women's lives, and teaching on the MA in Women's Studies in Education at the Institute of Education, University of London.

Index

Aaron, Jane 1, 233
Abbott, Pamela 179, 181, 233
academia
  challenge to status quo in 96–102
  intervention in 2–3
academy, politics of 49
Access courses 5, 9, 30, 31, 34–8
  assessment in 36
  content of 35
  expansion of 96
  future of 37–8
  issues and problems 36–7
actors, social 72, 73
adult education 9, 30, 31–4, 38
  relationship with grass roots feminism 9
  women's education in 31
andocentricity 78, 79, 111
Ardener, Shirley 53
Asian women 169–70, 171
assertiveness training 31
assessment
  authority of 57
  procedures 51
Australian Psychological Society 197
auto/biography 204, 210–11
  feminist 204, 206, 210–18
    and feminist methodology 210–14
    method of 214–16
  intellectual 205, 209, 210, 211, 214, 217
autonomy, female 145

Bagnold, Enid 227, 228
Bakhtin, M. 55, 56
Barry, Kathleen 84
Beauvoir, Simone de 205
Bezucha, Robert 59
Bhavnavi, Kum-Kum 132

biography, see auto/biography
biotechnology 81
bisexuality 151, 154
black women 46, 54, 55, 75, 131–41
  empowering of 137
  experiences of racism 171, 172–3
  impact of racism on lives of 133
  marginalization of 110, 117
  opportunities for 36, 38, 137, 138
  shared experiences of 137
  and Social Services Departments 132, 136
  visibility of 133–4, 140
  working strategies for 138–40
Black Women's Studies 16, 123
Bocock, Jean 96
body languages 58
Bourne, Gordon 222
Bradford, University of 105, 106, 110, 112, 113
Brah, Avtar 118, 168, 233
Brimstone, Lindie 117, 119, 233
British Psychological Society (BPS) 192, 195, 196, 197, 198
  gender representation working party 198–9
  'Psychology of Women' Section 195, 196, 197
Brodribb, Somer 83
Bunch, Charlotte 146, 147
Burford, Barbara 153
Byatt, A.S. 228
Byrne, Eileen 50

Caine, Barbara 215
centre/margins theory 117, 124–5
Chang, Pilwha 81